Date Due

APR. 20	MAR. 10 1992	
JAN 3	AUG 27 1992	
FEB 11	DEC 1 6 1995	
Dungannon APR 1	DEC 2 8	
Ap 8	JAN 1 5	
Ap 22	JAN 2 8	
Bayfield	FEB 2 6 1	
FEB 10	A	
Ap 9 74'		
Ap 19 74'		
De 27 74'		
NOV 2 7		
JA		

1066		20062
1657	APR 20	
11410	JAN 3	NOV 27 1975
	211	3267
6090	JAN 7 1977	
9549	12199	
9549	Ap 9 70	FEB 10
3497	Ap 1974'	
	My 2 74'	

The Howling Arctic

The Howling Arctic

The Remarkable People who made Canada Sovereign in the Farthest North

Ray Price

Peter Martin Associates Limited

Special thanks are due to the Governor and Committee of the Hudson's Bay Company for much of the information found in chapters 1 and 2: and to *Eskimo Quarterly*, published by the Oblate Fathers of the Hudson Bay Vicariate, for material in chapters 19, 26 and 27.

First printing July 1970
Second printing October, 1970

Printed in Canada by The Alger Press Limited

Library of Congress Catalog Card Number 73-131391
ISBN 0-88778-045-8

Peter Martin Associates Limited
17 Inkerman Street, Toronto 5, Ontario

Contents

Preface

It is a pity that most Canadians have no chance to see for themselves the vast expanses of our northland, nor to meet some of the remarkable people who live there.

Those of us who have been fortunate enough to travel in the Territories have sensed something of the special attitude towards their own country and towards the rest of the world which seems to bind together the people of the north.

Of many memorable experiences in the Territories, I particularly remember sharing breakfast one Sunday morning with the students of Akaitcho Hall in Yellowknife. We talked about Sir John Franklin and about Akaitcho, the Chief of the Coppermines. I remember the warmth of the students' response and their pride in the history and the future of their land.

I hope that the Northwest Territories Centennial will encourage Canadians in all parts of the country to increase their knowledge and their understanding of our northland and its people.

Pierre Trudeau
January 1, 1970

Acknowledgements

Research for a book like this is lengthy, difficult and costly and without the strong financial support of the Government of the Northwest Territories it could never have been done. To all the men in the government service, therefore, who were responsible for the decision to commission me to write this book I say a heartfelt thanks. It has been a thrilling task.

Although it is not easy to select particular individuals who have helped there are two men who deserve special mention. They are Mr. S.M. Hodgson, Commissioner of the Northwest Territories and James Whelly, General Manager of the Northwest Territories Centennial. Mr. Hodgson has given me his support from the outset. It was he who suggested I write about the Eastern Arctic and it was he who was responsible for making the project possible. Without Mr. Hodgson's efforts the book would never have been written. In a somewhat similar fashion Mr. Whelly has undergirded my efforts. He read the manuscript and criticized it. He suggested avenues of investigation and helped me along them. Within the organization of the Northwest Territories Centennial I have been directly responsible to James Whelly. He has been easy to work with.

There are many others to whom I want to express my thanks; policeman, missionaries, traders, prospectors, whalers and adventurers. All of those whom I have interviewed have been patient and have shared with me their experiences in Canada's Eastern Arctic. Many of them appear in the book. Some do not. Whether they are written about or not, however, I found their company both stimulating and entertaining.

Finally a word of appreciation to Ethel Major, my secretary, who has worked patiently and persistently. She has been much more than a typist. She has been a research assistant. Her help has been invaluable.

It has been a privilege to write this book. I hope it will make you as excited about Canada's north as it has made me.

Ray Price
June 9, 1970

For Michelle Joyce
and
in memory of Lisa June

1
The Duke
of Richmond

It was cold. For days on end the wind had been sweeping in over the frozen sea. Ground drifts softened outlines and destroyed distance. The curtain of snow obscured the sea and the forest. It was the time of the Arctic twilight. Everything was shadowed grey and inhospitably dark. The countryside offered little to cheer its inhabitants.

At the foot of Hudson Bay, on the south-east coast, the Hudson's Bay Company had built a tiny outpost at Little Whale River. It was here that four men and a boy huddled for warmth. They were not happy. Conversation was desultory. They longed to get outside. They wanted to hunt. The food they had to eat was monotonous. The cabin seemed to be getting smaller and smaller and their dislike of confinement greater and greater. They stayed in the cabin because they had been ordered not to stray from it by Mr. J. Potts, the factor at Richmond Gulf, some thirty miles to the north-east. He was directly responsible for all that went on at Little Whale River. The outpost was simply an extension of the major operation at Richmond Gulf. The orders to stay near the cabin had been given because recently there had been an unusual number of encounters with the Eskimos. Mr. Potts was afraid of the Eskimos. He did not know them, so he feared them.

"If no Eskimos come today I'm going hunting tomorrow," said Henry Pollexsen.

"Do you think you should?" asked Hugh Corston.

"I do. It's ridiculous living off salt pork when there's partridge to be had and bigger game, too."

"I agree," said George Clark. "Tomorrow, let's hunt."

Matthew Warden said nothing. He was only a fourteen-year-old boy and had no voice in the affairs of men. He was just a cook and everyone's servant. Orders were given for him to obey—even though he was the Duke of Richmond. Ever since the day in England when he had joined the Hudson's Bay Company he had been a company servant and he was now in the process of learning the fur trade from the bottom up. Matthew, like the others, felt the discomfort of the cramped quarters but, young boy that he was, he knew fear and had been infected by the fears of Mr. Potts. The fears they shared were well founded.

There were many tales told by the local Indians of the Eskimos and their ferocity. It was a sobering fact of history too that white men had not remained unscathed. The crew of mutineers who sent Henry Hudson and his son adrift in the bay that now bears his name had a violent encounter with the Eskimos as they passed through the strait into the open sea. The Eskimos were not proving easy to woo. They seemed to flit across the ice, settling occasionally, but rarely seen. They were proudly independent and able to survive in this country where white men more often died.

It was, in fact, this small group at Little Whale River who had been the first to come face to face with the Eskimos of that area. In previous years the Eskimos had been seen but not encountered. They had been watched through telescopes as they passed over the ice to the west but they had never approached the Company posts. They kept to their highway on the ocean, avoiding the woods and the Indians.

On the 21st of November, 1754, Mr. John Stephenson, Mr. George Humble, James Inkster and Matthew Warden were sent to Little Whale River by Mr. Potts to hunt partridge. They stayed there until the end of January, 1755, and then returned to the fort at Richmond Gulf. Just two days before they set out for what they fondly referred to as home, a lone Eskimo turned up near the outpost. Matthew Warden was out with some Indians at the time and it was he who reported it to Mr. Stephenson. This disturbed Stephenson. Everyone was apprehensive about the Eskimos, and the Indians hated them. The appearance of this Eskimo was important enough for Mr. Stephenson to tell the factor at Richmond Gulf as soon as they arrived there and

Mr. Potts took immediate action. He sent Henry Pollexsen, a carpenter and his mate, and Matthew Warden back to Little Whale River. Four other men travelled with them on this occasion to help haul their equipment. It was the 28th of January when this small group reached Little Whale. It is clear from the journals that Mr. Potts had intended sending a carpenter and small crew to Little Whale anyway. He just hurried up the matter because of the proximity of Eskimos. Pollexsen and his crew were under instructions to build another house for use during the summer whaling season. On the 29th of January the four men who had helped carry the supplies to Little Whale were supposed to return to Fort Richmond but the weather closed in and they stayed behind. By next morning the weather had cleared and these four men set off for Fort Richmond. They left behind Henry Pollexsen, the carpenter, his helper, and Matthew Warden.

"Weather's good. Let's see if we can get some fresh meat," suggested Henry. The other three welcomed the suggestion.

They grabbed their guns and followed him outside. It was not their intention to be gone long so they made no elaborate preparations. Some hours later they returned to the outpost. Henry Pollexsen was with George Clark, the carpenter. As they came in sight of the spot they were astonished to see four Eskimos not more than 100 yards from the building.

They called out to them, "Chimo! Chimo! . . . Hello! Hello!"

The Eskimos heard them. They stopped, turned and waited. As Henry and George approached, the four men who had left earlier that day for Richmond Fort, came out of the house. They learned later from the four that they had been making their way over the sea ice when they met the Eskimos. They managed to assure the Eskimos of their friendly intentions and finally persuaded them to return to the post. When Henry Pollexsen and George Clark arrived the Eskimos were just leaving.

"I'd say they've been here about three hours," one of the men told Mr. Pollexsen. "We wanted them to stay longer because we thought you would like to meet them."

"Good. I'm glad I arrived on time. Have you given them any gifts?"

"No."

"Fetch me an iron hoop. They'll find some use for that.

They can have the partridges we just shot, too."

Henry Pollexsen approached the strangers with his gifts and signed to them that the things he had were for them. Smilingly they received the hoop and partridges but they resisted Henry's pressing invitation to come back to the post and stay longer. They turned and, pointing to the sun, indicated that it was getting late. The short winter day was almost over and everywhere the stunted spruce trees were squatting at the foot of their own enormous shadows. With gesticulations and head nodding the Eskimos made it clear they would return the next day with a great many more of their countrymen. This message given, they turned and headed north-west, out towards the silent sea and their own mysterious hamlet hidden among the hillocks of ice.

No sooner had they left than Henry Pollexsen ordered the four men, who had brought the Eskimos back to the post, to leave at once for Richmond Gulf.

"I want you to tell Mr. Potts exactly what has happened here today and I want him to send trading stores to me immediately. If those Eskimos return tomorrow with a large following of countrymen, I'm just not going to be able to give them anything." The urgency of the moment comes out clearly in the letter Henry Pollexsen wrote on February 4th, 1755. The four men who had already walked the better part of 30 miles that day were given no more time to rest. Contact with the Eskimos had been made. The contact had been free of bloodshed. Everyone was on friendly terms. This might well mark the beginning of a new direction for the fur trade. If things went well, then it could be that the Eskimos would become prime suppliers of the very best in fur. The event presented an opportunity that could not be missed.

Discussion at Little Whale was excited that night. These three men and the boy had by chance become the spearhead in the Company's contact with the Eskimos. Certainly it was not the first contact that had been made with these hardy people but it was friendly and these were days of fear and suspicion.

It was late—very late—by the time the three men and the boy settled down to sleep. They were tired and, in spite of the excitement, soon slept. Next morning they kept a sharp lookout for the approach of the Eskimos. Shortly after the new light of dawn had crept upon them, Eskimos appeared. It seemed as if hundreds of them had suddenly materialized out of the sea. They came in far greater numbers than Henry had expected.

"There are hundreds of them," said Matthew excitedly.

"Actually I can count fifty," Mr. Pollexsen stated a little stiffly.

"Sure looks like a hundred."

And it did.

The dogs, drawing huge sledges, advanced slowly in on the post.

"Like an army," observed the carpenter, a trace of fear in his voice.

"Come on," urged Henry Pollexsen, "we've got to get busy. We must make this house as secure as we can. It must be turned into a fort."

With as much dispatch as possible the men set about strengthening the house. Bars were placed on the windows. Barricades were prepared and all the ammunition and weapons they possessed laid in readiness.

The boy kept his eye on the approaching Eskimos.

"They've stopped," he called out. "They're about five hundred yards away."

When all was as secure as possible, Henry Pollexsen and the carpenter prepared to go out to meet the Eskimos.

"We'll take our swords and our guns," Henry said to the carpenter. "I want you two to cover us as well as you can and should anything untoward happen you are to do everything in your power to defend the Company's property."

Matthew Warden and the carpenter's helper understood their roles and took up vantage points inside the house as Henry Pollexsen and the carpenter went out to meet the strangers.

They advanced cautiously. This was a moment of drama. The Eskimos saw them and became quiet. Far out at sea the low-slung sun shot gold onto the hillocked ice. The sky lifted clear and blue. With outward authority and inward uncertainty the two men stepped across the snow. When they were about a hundred yards from the Eskimos, Henry said to the carpenter, "Do as I do."

He then held aloft his gun and placed it on the ice. The carpenter followed suit. It was meant as a gesture of peace and it was interpreted as such. Pollexsen writes, "They came to us jumping and capering, calling out 'chimo' all the time." With unexpected exuberance the Eskimos went wild with demonstrations of friendliness. "They hugged us and showed us all signs of friendship imaginable."

Henry persuaded them to accompany him to the house where he entertained them in as kindly a way as he could. He wished fervently that he had on hand some trading goods but, being without them, he gave away some personal possessions—clothes, stockings and the like. These seemed to delight his guests. He then tried to tell them about the big house at Richmond Gulf where they could trade for things like the clothes he wore and all manner of other things too. By signs, he tried to explain that the man at the store would like to give merchandise in exchange for the things the Eskimos had. Things like the boots they had on and the heavy deerskins they were wearing. It was exhausting work, trying to talk without an interpreter to a people of whom he was a little suspicious and a trifle afraid. He was not sorry when they indicated it was getting late and that it was time for them to return. All but two went away. The two who remained stayed for a meal and did not leave for another hour and a half. As they were leaving they made it clear that they would be back the next day.

It was, therefore, no surprise to the three men and the boy when they awoke next morning to find several Eskimos camped nearby. According to a letter written by Henry Pollexsen, "There came five or six and tented, some of which had not been there the day before." Their presence posed a serious problem to Mr. Pollexsen. He had no trade goods. Nothing had arrived from Richmond Gulf. What few things he had had been disposed of the previous day. "Having nothing to give them," he writes, "I was apprehensive they would come no more."

The men talked it over.

"I think what I'll do," said Henry, "is try to persuade them to come with me to the fort. It's just possible those two who stayed longest last night will come. I see that they're here again."

This plan seemed reasonable and Pollexsen acted on it. He

went out to greet the Eskimos and to invite them to come with him and the boy, Matthew Warden, to Richmond Gulf. Gradually the message got across and by noon Henry, the boy Matthew, and the two Eskimos who had made themselves noticed, were ready to set out for the fort. They travelled over the sea ice because the Eskimos had no snowshoes. The distance was greater but travel in the forest without snowshoes was next to impossible. Late that night they reached the fort. Mr. Potts was delighted to see them. Only that day he had despatched a quantity of trade goods to Little Whale River.

"If you'd travelled the overland route you'd have met the porters with the merchandise you requested," explained Potts to Pollexsen.

"We had no choice," replied Pollexsen, pointing to the Eskimos' feet.

"Well, come on in," invited Potts, who was outside the fort where he had gone to meet them.

"We want you to see the inside of the fort," he said, beckoning to the Eskimos who followed him into the house.

The first thing he did was feed them. He offered them some bread and water which they wolfed down with gusto. Mr. Potts then gave them a couple of fresh-killed partridges. Rapidly the Eskimos picked the feathers. Without more ado they proceeded to tear the birds apart and eat them completely raw. They left nothing. Heart, liver, guts and all went the same way. Pollexsen and Potts watched, fascinated. In view of the fact that they had eaten so voraciously, Mr. Potts gave them two more partridges. This time he offered them a kettle in which to boil the birds. He could not stomach watching them eat in quite the same way again. After they had boiled and eaten the birds and washed the lot down with more water, Mr. Potts began to press a few gifts on them.

He writes, "I then gave them each a laced hat, a hatchet, two knives and several things of all which they was extremely pleased." Having done this, Mr. Potts began to get down to business.

"Come with me," he said as he motioned to them.

"See this." He showed them a fox skin.

"See this." He showed them a wolf skin.

"See this." He showed them a bear skin.

"Now see these," and he motioned them into another area. And it was there that the Eskimos stood wide-eyed. They had never seen so many trading goods. Cloth was there by the roll and guns by the rack.

As they stood staring at it all an Indian hunter came in. He paused when he saw the Eskimos. For generations the Indians had learned to hate the Eskimos and now here they were, right in Indian territory. Why had they come? What were they doing? Uneasily his eyes flickered around the room as if it suggested a trap.

"Here," said Potts peremptorily, "shake hands." They shook hands. Then, according to Potts, the Eskimos made a great deal of the Indian, so much in fact that Potts wrote in his journal, "The reception accorded the Indians by the Eskimos gave us great hopes of making peace between the Indians and them." Seeing this moment as an advantageous one and wanting to press home the dètente that was apparently being reached between the Indians and Eskimos, Mr. Potts gave the Indian two knives and told him to present these to the Eskimos. This the Indian did.

It was with pleasure and the feeling of a day well spent that Pollexsen and Potts eventually turned in.

The next morning before Pollexsen and the two Eskimos left the fort (Matthew Warden was to be left behind this time) Mr. Potts thought it as well to give the Eskimos a demonstration of white man's power. There were at the fort a number of cannon so he gave the order for one of these to be prepared for firing. While some of the men positioned, primed and loaded the gun, two others set up a post some distance away. When all was ready Mr. Potts gave the order, "Fire!"

The noise rolled out across the frozen sea. North and west it went, carried by the wind to the mysterious unvisited islands of the bay. What a noise! What a surprise for the wide-eyed, startled Eskimos! No sooner had the noise engulfed them than the target post was split from top to bottom by the single, well aimed shot. This was great magic. Rarely had there been such excited and astonished Eskimos as these two. Full of the wonders of the fort they set out towards the north.

When Mr. Potts had that gun fired he was in dead earnest. Although he was more than keen to start trade with the Eskimos, he believed it to be dangerous. Not long after the gun was fired and the Eskimos, together with Mr. Pollexsen and another man had left, he wrote in his journal, "They seemed well pleased when they went away and shake hands with us and made signs they would come back and bring some more of their people with them, which I hope they will for a trade with them I will have should my life be the consequence of it."

Even at this stage of proceedings Mr. Potts shows considerable unease. No tragedy has yet befallen, and yet there was fear. Fear of an unknown people. He closed the entry of his journal for this day, "Sent some of our people that's at home to the partridge tents to order all hands home for the defence of the fort if the Eskimos should become troublesome. Three men came home from the lakes this evening. This day five partridges was killed near the fort. Later part of this day blowing drifting weather and very cold."

Owing to Mr. Potts' distrust of the Eskimos the three men now staying at Little Whale River were huddled together like prisoners. Mr. Potts had given Henry Pollexsen strict instructions not to leave the post untended. He did not want them straying in the forest for wood or game. Only the greatest necessity was to take them from the house and even then they were to leave at least one person to guard the Company possessions.

While these three remained in semi-isolation at Little Whale River, Mr. Potts stirred everybody into activity at Richmond Fort. The day after the men left was Sunday, but this did not halt preparations for defence. Potts writes, "Those people that was at home was employed all day as follows: viz. We drawed and reloaded all the small arms we had and got two cannon placed in the South West and North West flanks to clear the sloop should the Esquimaux offer to do her any damage." Frozen in the harbour was the sloop, *Eddystone*,—an item of considerable value to the Company and an item rather difficult to defend. Mr. Potts did not overlook this and did his utmost to prepare for every eventuality.

That same day, as defensive preparations continued apace, a few more Eskimos were seen coming towards the fort. The lookout spotted them when they were a mile and a half away.

"Several Eskimos approaching from the west," he sang out.

Mr. Potts peered through his spyglass and watched them carefully. Their progress towards the fort seemed purposeful. When they caught sight of it, however, they drew behind some rocks and stayed out of sight. A sharp lookout for them was kept and after some time three of them emerged from cover and approached the fort. They came as far as Road Island which is about a mile from the site of the fort. Here they stopped. The men from the fort watched and listened.

"They're waving their coats in the air," observed one watcher.

"I think they're shouting," said another.

When all was still they could be faintly heard, the wind carrying their words of greeting to the fort. To hear and see better, several of the men, Mr. Potts among them, climbed onto the roof of the house and began to wave and shout in reply, "Chimo! Chimo! Chimo!"

The Eskimos came closer. They came right up to the *Eddystone*, a distance of some 200 yards from the fort.

"Get me my cutlass," ordered Mr. Potts as he scrambled down from the roof.

"I want my pistol, too," he shouted after the servant.

"Hector, you come with me."

All was now quiet. The snow-clad trees crouched against the hills. The wooden fort, tiny, unpretentious, seemed to shrink away from Potts and the boy as they moved towards the Eskimos. This was the kind of moment Potts loved. He was not afraid now as he strode out with rusty cutlass in one hand and pistol in the other. He strode out as England's representative, a man of the Company, a man destined to great things. He felt ten feet tall.

They walked resolutely until they were about one hundred yards from the Eskimos. The Eskimos then laid down their bows and arrows. Seeing this, Mr. Potts handed the boy, Hector, his gun and advanced alone towards them. He still gripped his rusty cutlass firmly. As he moved so did the Eskimos. They advanced in silence. The fort watched. Hector was ready. The pistol was primed. But there was no shooting, no fighting, for as soon as they met they all shook hands, smiled and made signs

of friendship. Mr. Potts walked back with them to the gates of
the fort. He kept them there for some time and before he let the
Eskimos into the fort he warned everyone to be on guard.

"Lay down your knives," he said to the Eskimos and signalled
what he meant as he spoke. They readily obliged.

"Come in. Follow me."

Once more the Eskimos were inside the fort. Mr. Potts took
them into his room and there he gave them bread and water.
They ate and drank hungrily.

Although these Eskimos had nothing to trade, Mr. Potts decided to give them a number of presents in an endeavor to persuade
them to become regular traders. He gave them knives, hatchets,
hand saws, files, flints, fire steels and a number of other things
which pleased them very much. Having surfeited them with
gifts Mr. Potts then tried to make it clear what things he wanted
and showed them fox skins and some whale bone. He then tried
to get across to them that he would like them to co-operate with
the Indians in the pursuit of whales at Little Whale River, come
summertime. It seems that he ran into difficulty when trying to
explain this for he remarked in his journal, "But I do believe
they did not understand me." Having written that, he then
makes a very interesting observation, an observation made even
more interesting because of subsequent events, "As for my boy,
he has lost the language."

By the time all the attempts at communication were over, it
was dinner hour and the Eskimos were invited to share the
venison. Following dinner Mr. Potts introduced the Eskimos to
alcohol. He writes, "I then ordered my boy, Streetor, to bring
me a little of Red Port of which I give every one of them about
a quarter of a glass which made them lick their lips and make
signs that they liked it much." After dinner the Eskimos stayed
for about two hours and then left for the Gulf.

During the next few days there were numerous encounters
with the Eskimos. These people, who had previously been so
difficult to meet on friendly terms, now seemed to be everywhere. They came to the fort and were courteously treated.
They were met on the trail and kindly greeted. It even seemed as
if a bridge of friendship was being built between such mortal
enemies as the Eskimos and the Indians. This was pointed up

when an Indian hunter in the employ of the Company at Richmond Gulf, met some Eskimos while out on the trail. This man, improbably called Robinson Crouses, was badly outnumbered when he came upon nine Eskimos and two sledges drawn by large dogs. The moment the Eskimos saw him they drove their sledges straight for him and halted a mere five yards away. As soon as the sledges stopped one person looked after the dogs and the other eight advanced upon him in friendly fashion, smiled and shook hands. Robinson Crouses had been primed by Mr. Potts about what to do if this sort of eventuality arose and he gave them four knives that Potts had supplied. They received the gifts with signalled thanks, then drove swiftly towards the Gulf.

Mr. Potts makes much of this encounter in his journal.

Meanwhile, at Little Whale River things had been very quiet. No Eskimos had been seen and no hunting had been done. For the men staying there the monotony was broken only by occasional visits of men from Richmond. Not until February 5th was Matthew Warden sent back there.

"I sent him there," Mr. Potts explains in his journal, "to cook for the men, working on the material for the addition to the house."

Apparently Matthew travelled back to Little Whale River with two men, one of whom was the carpenter who had come out bearing a letter to Mr. Potts from Henry Pollexsen. The letter merely told Potts that no Eskimos had been seen. With Matthew Warden's return to Little Whale River the stage was set for sudden tragedy. Matthew carried instructions from Mr. Potts warning the men not to relax their guard. Mr. Potts' unease never seemed to have left him. He was convinced that the Eskimos were potentially dangerous. He noted in his journal on Wednesday, the 5th of February, "Sent six men to hunt partridges not withstanding the great necessity there is in keeping our people at home for the safety of our fort on account of the Esquimaux."

Matthew arrived at Little Whale on Tuesday and the next day was busy with his cooking duties. The four men stayed close to the house. There was Henry Pollexsen, George Clark, Hugh Corston and the new man from the fort who is unidentified.

The day passed uneventfully. Thursday came and went in similar fashion. No Eskimos were seen. A constant watch began to seem unnecessary. The atmosphere of fear at the fort seemed to be losing its force. When Friday dawned it was clear and cold.

Before sunrise, first thing in the morning, while Matthew busied himself with breakfast, Henry Pollexsen dashed off a note to Mr. Potts. He had decided to send the man who had accompanied Matthew and the carpenter back to Richmond. "There have been no Esquimaux here since the second of the month," he wrote. "If any should come I will use them kindly and dispose of the goods you sent to the best advantage."

He was never to have the chance.

No sooner was breakfast eaten and the man despatched to Richmond, than the men decided that they had had enough of being confined to the house and more than enough of the tedious food that was their fare.

"Today we'll go hunting," said Henry. "I've had all I can take of that salt pork."

The carpenter, George Clark, and his helper, Hugh Corston, agreed wholeheartedly.

"I'll go down to the south and you two hunt back towards the east," said Henry, as he drew on his boots. "Now," he continued, this time talking to young Matthew Warden, "if any Eskimos come, don't let them in. If you see any approaching the house make the door and windows secure and," he added, "don't stray out of the house."

"No, sir."

It was 7:00 o'clock when Henry, George and Hugh strode out into the gloom. It was almost 4:00 o'clock when Henry made his way back to the house. Easily and confidently he strode towards the outpost. He was hungry and tired and ready for the few comforts that warm shelter and a good meal would afford. He was quite close to the house when he was brought up short.

"What's this?" he muttered, stooping down, "Grey goose shot? Flints?"

First he was puzzled and then frightened. He looked around keenly. The sundial was gone. Nails were scattered. From where he stood it was obvious the house had been plundered and what's more, in a moment of insight, he knew that someone was still in the house. Henry stooped low, cocked his gun and called out.

"Hello! Hello! . . . Who's there?"

At the sound of his voice there was silence. The forest brooded. The house grew sinister. Henry was afraid. Time stood still. Moments later there was movement in the house and Hugh Corston came to the door. Henry relaxed a little.

"What's happened?"

"Eskimos."

"Where's the boy?"

"I don't know. They've taken almost everything." It was George Clark speaking. He came out of the house and stood with his helper and Henry. Each of them gazed alertly around. There were just the three of them and they knew the Eskimos to be many.

"What shall we do?"

"I don't know."

"Let's see exactly what's missing. Did they kill the boy?"

"I think they carried him off."

"Wonder why."

Henry stepped into the house. What chaos! The bars had been savagely wrenched from the door and windows. Bedding was scattered everywhere and a sea chest had been ripped open and the handles torn off. Sealed provisions had been broken into and carted off and nearly all the trade goods were gone. The house had been viciously assaulted and comprehensively plundered.

The only thing they did not find, that each of them expected to find, was blood. It seemed that the Eskimos had carried Matthew Warden off alive.

"We'd better decide what to do quickly!" said George.

"I think," replied Henry, "that we'd better leave at once for Richmond Fort."

"I don't know. Don't you think we'd be better off staying for the night and getting some rest?"

"It would be too risky. We can't fasten the doors. The Eskimos have all the weapons except our hunting guns and one of us would have to keep watch. If we stay we're not going to get much in the way of rest."

"What about the boy though? Don't you think we might be able to discover where they've taken him if we wait till the light of morning? Perhaps we'll be able to follow the trail."

"We can't do that. We have to warn the fort. If we stay here our lives may well be forfeit."

So the discussion continued. George was for staying, Henry for leaving; Hugh Corston remained silent and neutral. Since Henry was in charge, the decision to leave was made and, although all three of them were very tired, they set out at 6:00 o'clock that night for Richmond Gulf. When they left, each was hauling a sledge. It seemed that the most prudent thing to do was to bundle up all the things they could and take them along. Travel proved too difficult after awhile so they stashed the sledges and walked on, carrying only their hunting guns. Naturally enough, they travelled by an inland route, being especially anxious to avoid any contact with the Eskimos. Shortly after 2:00 o'clock in the morning they reached a log tent, some 17 miles from Whale River, where some of the men from the fort were out partridge hunting. Here they stayed for the rest of the night and in the morning walked the seven remaining miles to Richmond Fort.

Mr. Potts was grieved to hear their news. His fears of the Eskimos now seemed justified. He immediately took every precaution he could think of to defend the fort. Partridge hunters were recalled; a regular watch was set; a system of rationing instigated. The blacksmith was put to work making bars for all the windows and the carpenter was kept busy installing them. By the following Wednesday Potts could write in his journal that the fort was now "put into a posture of defence".

Having made all these preparations, Potts now thought it time to engage actively in a search for Matthew Warden. He summoned everyone in the fort and, when they were all gathered, said, "I think it is now time to go in quest of the boy. In view of the fact that such an enterprise will be hazardous in the extreme and more arduous than we can imagine, I am not ordering anyone to go out and search but I'm asking for volunteers. The duty of the volunteers will be simply to recover the boy. They must discover his whereabouts and obtain his release by any manner at all. Will those of you who wish to volunteer sign your name to this proclamation."

Thirteen men signed right away. The first to sign was Henry Pollexsen and then John Stephenson, George Humble, George Clark and nine more. That night the thirteen men counselled together, laying plans for their safari in the snow. The task they had taken on was formidable. They must plan well.

Their plans were never put into execution. The next morning Mr. Potts cancelled the expedition. He had done some hard thinking that night and the next day called the men together. He describes it all in his journal: "Having seriously considered all the consequences that may attend such a dangerous attempt as to send out 13 raw, undisciplined men without proper clothing in quest of the boy, Matthew Warden, having no beaver coats in the factory to make their togs, mittens nor caps, to send these people out to sea among the islands in search of the Esquimaux (perhaps there may be hundreds of them) and not one drop of fresh water to be got, nor wood to melt snow to quench their thirst and should they be all starved to death with cold; we then would have but myself and seven hands with the two boys to defend the fort. And if they should be conquered by the Esquimaux and they got all our people's arms, if they with these arms, powder, ball, come and skulk about the fort for a few days behind the rocks we in the fort would be dead for want of rest and fresh water. This morning I called a council and gave my opinion as above."

Mr. Potts was persuasive enough in his presentation to impress John Stephenson although Henry Pollexsen was still all for going after the kidnappers. The weight of authority was against Henry so the expedition was stillborn. Out of their discussion, however, came a new plan. They decided that if any more Eskimos should come to the fort without bringing the boy they would capture two of them and hold them as hostages. This satisfied the most belligerent of the men and the fort returned to its state of fearful alertness.

In view of the fact that there were a number of oddments left at Little Whale River, Mr. Potts decided to send a well armed party of men there to recover all that remained. Henry Pollexsen, who seems to have been thirsting for action, volunteered to lead the group and Mr. Potts readily accepted his offer. Thus, on

Thursday, the 14th, just six days after Matthew's disappearance and Henry's frantic return to Richmond Fort, he was on his way back to the scene of the kidnapping. One of his chief jobs was to keep order among the band of men he was leading. Mr. Potts did not altogether trust the men but he knew that with Henry along nothing would be forgotten and he knew also that they would not all wind up drunk. It worried Potts that he had had to let them take a lot of brandy with them. Perhaps they needed some Dutch courage!

When the party reached Little Whale River they saw at once that the Eskimos had been back. The snow had been trampled around the house and what few things the three men had left behind were in even worse disorder. Every bit of iron work had been stripped from inside the house. Henry Pollexsen's bed was ripped open and some of the men's private belongings broken or stolen. Henry, when writing about it all later, said that the Eskimos did all the damage they possibly could to the house. The only further step they could have taken would have been to burn it. The men stayed there one night and returned to Richmond Fort on the Saturday.

For the next few days things remained fairly quiet at the fort. Fear of the Eskimos diminished and the desire for better food grew stronger. By Thursday, the 21st, grumbling about the salt pork rations and the lack of exercise was so insistent that Mr. Potts sent ten men out to the partridge tents. These men split into three groups and went in different directions. Those who went towards Elderton Forest, to the westward, had not travelled more than half a mile when they spotted some Eskimos. One came back to tell Potts who immediately signalled for them all to return. The three, however, who had gone to the east were out of sight and hearing. Potts deemed it unwise to send anyone in pursuit of them.

The fort was put into a state of alert and a sharp lookout was kept for the Eskimos. Mr. Potts was in high hopes that they would have Matthew Warden with them. Should he not be with them, Mr. Potts reasserted his intention to take two of the Eskimos prisoner. It was not until noon that the Eskimos were seen again. When they came in sight they were moving cautiously towards the fort. They reached Road Island and there stopped.

After a period of uncertainty and apparent deliberation they began to advance upon the fort again. Several times they paused to wave and call out "Chimo! Chimo!" Apparently they were approaching as friends. Like echoes from the forested hills the answering calls went out from the fort, "Chimo! Chimo! Chimo!"

About three hundred yards from the fort the three Eskimos halted. Seeing they were not going to come any closer Mr. Potts sent two men out to conduct them in. The factor watched. The two men walked confidently towards the Eskimos. Signs, friendly signs, were signalled to them. The men greeted each other and then all five turned towards the fort. Once inside the gates, the doors were closed. Mr. Potts now had his hostages. He took them to the guard room, used them kindly and then brought Mr. Pollexsen, Hugh Corston and George Clark to them. These were the men, of course, who had been at Little Whale River with Matthew Warden. In the presence of these men Mr. Potts endeavored to find out what had happened to the boy. They did not seem to understand. Indeed, they virtually ignored the questioning. Finally, exasperated with pointless questioning, Potts personally put two of them in irons and locked them together, right leg and left leg and set a guard over them. Before he left them he tried to terrorize them with bloodthirsty threats. He writes, "I then clapped my cutlass to their necks and made signs that if the boy was not returned I would cut off their heads and burn them in the stove."

It seems this threat was either not understood or not feared. The Eskimos remained unmoved.

Potts was determined to impress them, however, with his serious intentions and his formidable strength so he arranged for each man in the fort to walk through the guardroom several times. In between passages through the room they were to change clothes and thus by simple ruse give the impression that there was a large staff of men in the fort. Potts did not wish to provoke the Eskimos into an overt attack. A siege of only a few weeks would likely have crippled the fort.

Having done all he could to impress the three Eskimos he now liberated the one he had not enchained. He made it as clear as he could what he wanted from this liberated Eskimo and tried to impress upon him that no harm would come to the prisoners as long as Matthew Warden was returned intact. The Eskimos never spoke to each other and it was impossible to read their faces. Perhaps the message was understood. Perhaps it was not. The lone Eskimo walked swiftly away from the fort and disappeared in the snowy wasteland.

"I wonder if we'll ever see him again, Henry," Potts observed to Pollexsen.

Henry murmured a reply but Potts was not listening.

That night the prisoners gave no trouble. Not until six o'clock in the morning was there a change in their attitude. At this time Mr. Humble and the one other man were preparing to go out after the partridge hunters who had left the previous morning and whom they had not been able to call back. Humble reached for his gun and his snowshoes, as did the other men. The Eskimos could see them and they watched. The preparations seemed to disturb them. They began to talk angrily. Their attitude became defiant, hostile, threatening. The watch increased its vigilance. At last the Eskimos stood up, seemingly to stretch their legs. They took up a position against one end of a partition and there continued to stand for the best part of an hour. Henry Pollexsen was on guard and he became increasingly suspicious of the prisoners.

"Go and look behind that partition," he said to one of the watch. "I have an idea some small arms have been left there."

The man walked forward and endeavored to get by the Eskimos but they would not budge. Seeing this, Henry Pollexsen and George Clark, the other member of the watch, went to help him and they tried to push the Eskimos aside.

"Look out!" shouted Henry as one of the Eskimos lunged at Clark with a knife he had kept concealed in a coat sleeve. Clark dodged the blow and all three men withdrew to get their guns. As they back-pedalled furiously the Eskimos grabbed a couple of small arms which were behind the partition and began wielding them as clubs with frightful resolution and fury. The roof was low, the passage narrow and the melee fierce and wild. The Eskimos were out to kill the guard and, having seized the initiative, pressed home their advantage. They didn't realize the skull-crushing blows they aimed at the guards were being made with loaded rifles. At any moment those guns would go off and no one knew who would be killed. With dust, blood, arms, legs, shouts, grunts, the battle was waged. Then Christopher Smith took aim and with calm deliberation shot one of the Eskimos through the head. He was killed instantly. The other Eskimo, nothing daunted, stood his ground.

"Don't shoot him!" ordered Potts. "I want him kept alive." Again and again they attempted to overcome him. They hammered at him with sticks and fists. A knife flashed and cut off his thumb. Still he fought. So great was his rage and so effective his defence that Mr. Potts finally gave the order for him to be shot.

Now the fort had two Eskimo corpses and there was great alarm.

The alarm spread to Indians in the surrounding woods and some of them begged to stay within the environs of the fort for protection. Their request was granted.

The fort was put into a state of increased readiness for attack. The cannon were scaled and loaded and everyone was assigned to a particular duty and a particular post. It seemed like war.

At 10:00 a.m. on Saturday morning there was more excitement when an Eskimo sledge drawn by two dogs appeared. The dogs pulled the sledge to within a hundred yards of the fort and then sat down and waited. No Eskimos appeared. The driverless dogs curled up and slept. Three hours passed and then a few men went out from the fort to shoot the dogs at Potts' command but made so much noise on their way out that the dogs moved off, chained to their unguided burden. It was likely the small sledge that the two dead men had been using and which they had left out of sight of the fort .

So that day passed and the next. And Mr. Potts continued to protest his resolution to defend the fort to the last drop of his blood.

"What are you going to do with the corpses?" Robinson Crouses, the half breed hunter, asked Mr. Potts. "Are you going to hang them from a gibbet?"

"Yes. I'll teach them a lesson."

"I think it better not to do that."

"I'll teach them we are not to be trifled with."

"You do more harm than good, hanging them in chains."

"Why?"

"If they see their friends treated like that and the boy is still alive they'll kill him for sure and then they'll eat him."

"Do you think so?"

"I know so. Let me take those corpses. I'll get some of the Indians to come with me and we'll cut a hole in the river ice and drop their bodies through. They'll never be seen again."

So it was that down to the River Croquet they were taken and silently, swiftly disposed of. Before he let them go, however, Mr. Potts, with grisly intent, lopped one ear off each of them and notes in his journal: "this seemed to please the Indians very much." He further notes that he is going to send the Eskimo ears to the Indian captains at Moose and Albany. This was Mr. Potts' way of encouraging congenial relationships with the Indians.

After this episode things gradually returned to normal. No Eskimos were seen and with the passage of days and weeks and then months, the tension of the fort relaxed. Things returned to normal.

Not until May 25th did Mr. Potts learn anything more about the fate of Matthew Warden. On that day some Indians returned to Richmond Fort from Little Whale River. There they had discovered the remains of the boy, clearly visible now that the snow had gone. Not more than 200 yards from the house at Little Whale River the Indians had found bones, clothes, the stain of blood on the moss and some of the young lad's hair.

That was all that was left of Matthew Warden. It seems highly probable that he was murdered and partially eaten. Andrew Graham, a Hudson's Bay factor for many years and a copious writer, suggests in his notes that this is what happened. He comments on the fact that the flesh was apparently stripped from the bones. Should this be the case it still leaves the motive for the murder unknown. All we can do now is make educated guesses at the answer.

Could it be that some of the Eskimos had recognized the boy, Hector, the lad who had lost the language? How had he come into the service of the fort? Was the capture of Matthew Warden in reprisal for the abduction of Hector?

Perhaps, however, Dr. Diamond Jenness was right, who, when told the story, said, "Did you say there were Indians at the fort?"

"Yes."

"Did you say they were made to shake hands with the Indians?"

"Yes."

"Was it abundantly clear to the Eskimos that the Indians were friends of the white men?"

"Yes."

"Then that is why Matthew Warden was killed."

2
Probing the Mists

The Eskimos who made off with Matthew Warden probably had their camps and villages scattered in the chain of islands that cling to the east coast of the Hudson Bay. These islands are still part of the Northwest Territories although Richmond Gulf, Little Whale River and indeed the whole area of Ungava is now part of Quebec. The latter area has had a number of different administrations. At the time of Matthew Warden and Pollexsen it was administered, if that's not too grand a word to use, by the Hudson's Bay Company. It was not until 1870 that the Government of Canada took over Rupert's Land from the Hudson's Bay Company. It was then joined to the Northwestern Territories and the amalgamated area renamed the Northwest Territories. The Northwest Territories did not remain that size for very long. New provinces were formed and Ontario and Quebec extended and, in 1912, Quebec, Ontario and Manitoba stretched northwards and all the provincial boundaries were settled except those to the east between Newfoundland and Quebec.

The change in boundaries and the carving up of northern Canada made no difference initially to the state of the native population. Not until very recently has there been any real involvement of Eskimos in government processes. Without a treaty, without consultation and without any real awareness of his presence, the Eskimos' land has been divided up, explored, governed and exploited.

The size of the Eskimos' land can only be described as vast. It stretches as far north as the Arctic Islands and east and west right across the top of Canada. In the region of the eastern Arctic alone, there are mountains over 8,000 feet high, long stretches of marsh, plain and tundra, and lakes and rivers by the thousand.

It is a land through which the Eskimos have roamed for thousands of years. In the earliest days people identified as belonging to the pre-Dorset culture drifted across the continent from west to east. There is some evidence to suggest that these people reached as far west as Greenland around 2,000 B.C. They gradually gave way to the Dorset culture. It is likely that one of the greatest contributions made by these people was the invention of the snow house. It was a remarkable adaptation to their environment but of peculiar importance only to them. The rest of the world knew nothing of such people, such places, or such inventions. W.E. Taylor writing about the people of the Dorset culture in *Science, History and Hudson Bay** says: "Like so many others long silent the Dorset people had scant effect on the battered, clattering course of man's history. Nevertheless they occupied a large part of the earth's surface and did so for an impressive number of centuries." The Dorset culture existed from 800 B.C. to 1300 A.D.

About 700 years ago the Dorset culture began to give way to a new way of life practised by people moving in from Alaska. T. Mathiassen named this culture Thule. It brought to the Arctic a style of life that depended upon the use of domesticated dogs and the slaughter of the baleen whales. W.E. Taylor asserts that whaling more than anything else distinguishes Thule culture from earlier and later Canadian Arctic culture periods. Commenting on the tools and weaponry of the Thule period, Taylor says " . . . the arrow that struck Martin Frobisher in the buttocks as he fled to the beach of Frobisher Bay was delivered from a Thule bow by a Thule culture Eskimo whose unsuspecting ancestors had over slow centuries come all the way from Alaska for the event."

We have been slow to learn of these early cultures and, in fact, to learn anything about this vast northern area. As recently as the turn of the century, the Belcher Islands remained virtually unknown to the world. Hudson Bay charts showed them only as

* Beals, C.S. (Ed.), *Science, History and Hudson Bay*, Canada Department of Energy, Mines and Resources, 1968.

a narrow string of islands. It seems, judging by the maps, that ships' captains were aware of them as a hazard but had never attempted to sail their coasts and establish their sizes. Several ships have tangled with the Belchers and at least one disastrously.

In 1858, R. Hamilton, the Company factor at Great Whale River, in a letter to George Simpson, says that Captain Young, on leaving the Straits, held to the southward and eventually ran aground on the Belcher Islands which "extend 40 miles further south than laid down on the Company charts". Although Captain Young's ship was certainly in peril, the boat lost one anchor and only escaped the rocky coast of the Belchers by a hair's breadth, it did get through. His ship was luckier than the *Kitty* which sailed for Hudson Bay in 1859.

On the 15th of August, 1859, the Bishop at St. Boniface, in what is now Manitoba, sat down and wrote a letter to the factor at Moose Factory. The Bishop was beginning to get worried. Almost a year earlier he had ordered some things from England. These goods were supposed to be delivered by the Hudson's Bay Company's channel of communication that stretched from England, via the Hudson Bay, to Winnipeg and points west. In his letter the Bishop expressed his concern. James Clare, answering the letter on September 5th, said, "It is with much regret I have to reply that owing to the non arrival of the chartered ship *Kitty* in which all the private property was embarked at London, no pieces to your address have yet reached me."

The bishop was not the only worried man. Later in September, James Clare expressed his concern when writing to R. Wilson, stationed at Oxford House, "As the chartered ship *Kitty* having on board a quantity of the year's imports has not arrived in the country this season I have to impress upon you a strict attention to economy in the disbursement of your present outfit as it is possible I may be unable to renew your supply of some few articles until the arrival of the *Prince of Wales* next autumn." The *Kitty* was carrying on board a great variety of goods— everything from gunpowder, soap and hardware to two-thirds of the rum supply. The item that was the most serious loss, however, consisted of all the cod lines and twine.

On September 17th, James Clare still held out some hope of the vessel's arrival. On that day he wrote to T. Fraser, secretary of the Hudson's Bay Company in London, "I regret to state that nothing has yet been seen or heard of the charter ship *Kitty* but the season is yet too early to despair of her safe arrival."

Not until late in October was all hope for the *Kitty's* safe arrival abandoned. Clare notes soberly, on the 25th of October, "Winter is now upon us and nothing has been seen or heard of the chartered ship *Kitty*." With that news certain belts had to be tightened and any relish there may have been for the long winter was considerably diminished. For weeks and weeks everyone held on to the slenderest hopes. Eyes had grown tired looking for the *Kitty* and endlessly the question was asked, "I wonder what's happened to her." Not till almost a year later was there anything approaching a certain answer to that question. And even when the story is told there is much that can only be guessed at.

Chartered from London, the *Kitty* set sail in the summer for Moose Factory. She passed through the Straits and then, turning south, headed for James Bay. Progress was good. Ice conditions fair. All went well until she reached the vicinity of the Belchers. Perhaps the captain had the same trouble as Captain Young. The charts for that part of the Bay were so notoriously bad that a wreck on the hungry rocks of the Belchers was more than possible. The ship was either smashed on the rocks surrounding the Belcher Islands or wrecked north of them in ice. R. Hamilton, who was at that time in Great Whale River, thinks that whatever happened, happened fast. One moment all was reasonably secure and the next the boat was sinking. In the wild rush that followed to abandon ship, a few men managed to launch a couple of the ship's boats and get them safely away from the wreck. These survivors became separated. Those in one boat went towards the north-east while the others steered a southerly course and eventually sighted the Belchers. As they approached the Belcher Islands, clothed only in light shirts and trousers, they were spotted by a few Eskimos. The Eskimos watched carefully and kept their distance. The men in the boat did not see them. For the Eskimos, the appearance of these men from the north was a mystery. They knew the Hudson's Bay Company did not have any posts in that direction. These men must be strangers or spirits.

Out of the mists they came onto those incredibly inhospitable shores. The men found little to comfort them there. Apparently uninhabited, this was a God-forsaken stretch of land. As they beached their boat, stamped around, flapped their arms and tried to get and stay warm, they had no idea how carefully they were being watched. Had they seen a movement among the rocks perhaps their fate would have been different. It is more than possible that the Eskimos would have shared their food with them. Fear kept the Eskimos hidden and the white men never saw them.

They did not stay long on the Belcher Islands. Their condition was desperate and more than anything else they needed to make contact with the Eskimos. Their clothes were hopelessly inadequate. Their provisions were almost exhausted and all they had to hunt with was one pistol and one rifle. Pushing the boat out to sea again, they steered towards the north-east. They held steadily on course until they reached Smith Island. What happened on that trip and what happened on the island can only be guessed at. Their privations must have been terrible. The Hudson Bay can be ugly even for those well equipped, but for those inadequately prepared there is only the promise of slow death. Icy spume was flung over the open boat. Men thirsted, hungered, shivered and died. Corpses were dragged over the gunwales and dropped, unceremoniously, into the sea. They wished to God for something warm. It was cold, cold, always cold.

Wind, spray, mist, ice, snow, rain bludgeoned them, this way and that in the open sea. But they still managed to press towards land. No blue sky or pale sun could relieve their gloom. They needed human help and that right now. Their last few weeks were not without hope for, with remarkable luck, the three remaining men happened upon two more shipwrecked members of their own crew. The men in the other boat had drifted towards the east coast of the Hudson Bay and had eventually beached their craft on Smith Island. It was here that the two groups met. Each greeted the other with enthusiasm for each hoped for succour from the other. Their chance meeting was the pinnacle of their hopes and the end of their luck. Neither boat had much in the way of provisions and there was still only one rifle and pistol for hunting purposes. At first they searched eagerly for signs of habitation but all they could find was a deserted Eskimo camp right at the site where they had beached their boats. Scattered around the old encampment were the discarded bones of feasts held long before. In this setting the men tried to build some shelter and on this desolate shore they huddled together for warmth. Their plight was hopeless. Only a miracle could save them. They prayed for such a miracle but the sky grew greyer, the horizon lowered and the snow of fall began. Not many days passed before hunger's twisting pain gave way to numbness and the expectancy of a miracle gradually faded. The scattered bones they gnawed on were no use and the thought of the meat dripping with blood that had once clung to them was too hard to bear. One by one they died. By early fall five corpses lay in that old Eskimo encampment, stiff and cold. They may not have been long dead when a party of Eskimos came upon them. Those Eskimos had a surprise they never forgot for they had never seen white men before but had only heard of them. According to the story that eventually reached Hamilton at Great Whale River, these Eskimos had an abundance of venison with them at the time and would have been kindly disposed towards the shipwrecked sailors.

Hamilton had no sooner heard the story from some Eskimos who had obtained the story from some other Eskimos than he wanted to go and investigate the matter. He was unable to do so, however, because most of his Indians were away from the camp and he did not have a sufficiently good canoe to set off on a long and dangerous sea trip. As far as he could judge, from the information he received, the men had perished on or near Smith Island, some distance north of Mosquito Bay. That country was virtually unknown. Only the previous year, in 1859, a Mr. Anderson had gone north from Great Whale River to explore the coast and search specifically for rivers where the white whale fishing might be good. Anderson reported back that he had explored the coast as far as Mosquito Bay but did not go any further. He did not, apparently go as far north as Smith Island or the miracle the five men wanted and waited for might well have occurred. Those men were doomed to join the mounting number of men whose lives were claimed by Canada's north. The very year they perished F. L. McClintock returned to England and confirmed the fate of the Sir John Franklin Expedition.

If navigational charts had been better it is quite possible the *Kitty* would have made it to York Factory. But 120 years ago there was still a great deal of charting to do. Even in the better charted waters ships came to grief, as did the brigantine *Eagle* in 1836 and the *Nascopie* one hundred years later, in 1947. The *Eagle* nearly met her end in the Hudson Straits. On July 27th, 1836, the vessel struck a rock and rode up on it. The ship canted over on her beam end so steeply that no one could stand on her decks. Captain Charles Humphrey gave the order to abandon ship and take to the ice. On all sides open to the sea the ship was being pressed by heavy floe ice. For eight hours the crew remained on the ice and then Robert Steward and George Barton, the second mate, went back to the ship to get some dry clothes. Their intention was to be gone for a few moments and then return to the crew on the ice. As these two struggled below deck the ice around the boat shifted and, sliding away, left a large pond of water between the boat and floe ice. Robert Steward and Barton, for safety's sake, took to the rocks. They were uncomfortable but secure. They stayed there all night. By morning the crew had floated away on the ice and were a considerable distance from the ship. Fortunately the captain and crew had with them plenty of provisions and two of the ship's boats. Steward and Barton, now being entirely alone, offloaded a number of things onto the rocks, spirits from the ship together with a cask of rum and fifteen pairs of blankets. These articles they left on the rocks when they returned to the ship at flood tide. At that moment, a fortunate change of wind and a series of squalls released the vessel which then drifted amongst the ice. Not until the 5th of October, forty days after the ship stuck on the rock, did the captain and the rest of the crew rejoin the ship. By diligent use of the boats these men had finally managed to reach the *Eagle*. Captain Humphrey was not at all pleased with what he found when he did get back to his ship, for Robert Steward was hopelessly drunk on wine he had taken from the captain's cabin. No lives lost—just some spirits, some wine, some time and a few tempers.

The Hudson Bay, never the safest stretch of water, gradually became more easily navigated as the work of exploring was prosecuted right up to the present century. It was left to Robert Flaherty, who was later to become famous for his film *Nanook of the North*, to discover the size and extent of the Belcher Islands. In his book, *My Eskimo Friends,* * he describes his first journey there. A reproduction of a Hudson's Bay Company map in that same book shows that right up to the twentieth century the Company charts had the Belcher Islands very inaccurately recorded. It seems strange that no captain attempted to chart those islands. Perhaps this can be very simply attributed to the fact that they were in the Bay for the purpose of commerce rather than exploration and the season was too short for any dangerous and possibly unprofitable jaunts. So the Belcher Islands remained mysterious and unvisited.

In 1910 Robert Flaherty, the son of R.H. Flaherty, one of the most prominent prospectors for iron ore in Canada, was commissioned by Sir William Mackenzie to visit the Nastapoka Islands and prospect there for iron. Sir William Mackenzie, a far-seeing business man, reasoned that if the Government could ship wheat from the prairies by the Hudson Bay then iron ore could be shipped in the reverse direction too. In 1910 the Canadian Government initially agreed to a railway outlet to the Bay. Nineteen years later a branch line of the C.N.R. finally reached Churchill and Manitoba became the only prairie province with a direct outlet to the ocean.

Christmas of 1910 found Robert Flaherty approaching Great Whale River. He writes, "Sundown on Christmas day was our twelfth day of sledging and still no post could we see. Darkness came. The wind was bitterly cold. Long since I had given up hope of reaching the post that night. Shelter and scalding tea was all I could think of when the sledge shot out on a sheet of black glare ice. It was the river ice of the Great Whale. A single square of yellow light shone like a beacon through the darkness." That night Flaherty burrowed into his sleeping bag comfortable and warm. Outside he could hear the lash of snow against cabin walls, the dogs' mournful howls and the drifter's unending groan.

* Flaherty, Robert J., *My Eskimo Friends,* Doubleday, Page and Company, 1924.

A few days later he was on his way to the Nastapoka Islands. It was there that he expected to find iron ore. Occasional stories of mineralization had crept to the outside and it was believed that large workable iron deposits could be found on that string of islands.

In the vicinity of Great Whale itself, the Hudson's Bay Company had carried out some small mining operations to recover lead ore. On the first of May, 1858, R. Hamilton, the post manager, wrote to Sir George Simpson, "We were pleased to learn that the sample of lead ore shipped last autumn was of such good quality that I am in hopes that the mine may get to be of some profit to us." That same year Mr. Anderson had about five tons collected but it could not be brought out to the settlement until freeze-up so was not shipped to England until the following year. In desultory fashion high grade lead ore was sought, mined and shipped, but the endeavors were primitive and the returns small.

It was with high hopes that Flaherty began his search for iron on the Nastapokas. He spent five days prowling about the iron-bearing cliff faces of the islands, but the findings proved disappointing. He writes, "The result of my examination showed that the supposed deposits of iron ore of the Nastapokas were too hopelessly lean to be of the slightest economic importance. I had to face the fact that all the long journey had been for nothing."

Naturally enough, Flaherty was discouraged. He was going to have to return empty handed. As he was making preparations to leave, Nero, the Eskimo guide with him, pointed to the sea and talked of a big land over there. It was this remark that made Flaherty call to mind an earlier conversation he had had with a man called Wetalltok on Charlton Island. He had met this man while travelling up from Moose Factory to Great Whale. Wetalltok had been on the Belcher Islands. He spoke through the Company interpreter of ducks, geese, bears and islands more than a hundred miles long. At the time Flaherty had been intrigued by the story but until Nero pointed seawards and talked of a big land over there, the information had lain dormant in his mind.

Flaherty determined right then to pursue his enquiries once

he was back in Great Whale. This he did. He started with Old Harold, the Hudson's Bay helper, but Harold was skeptical about it all although he did concede that Wetalltok's story might be authentic. Harold's uncertainty did nothing to stem the tide of curiosity that was beginning to flood over Robert Flaherty. Long before he was back at Moose Factory, Flaherty was convinced that the islands were no dream but simply waiting for an explorer.

As early as 1885 there is written evidence of mineralization on the Belcher Islands. Dr. Robert Bell examined the area around the Nastapoka Islands and while there had some rock specimens given to him that were said to have come from the islands out at sea. What he saw made him think that the rock formation of the unvisited islands was similar to that of the Nastapokas. Quite likely, A.P. Low got hold of Bell's report for he, at one time, planned an expedition to the Belchers which was only cancelled because of inclement weather. In view of Bell's report, Low's interest, Wetalltok's story and Eskimo assertions, Flaherty felt that there was something that merited careful examination and exploration.

The following year he set out to reach the Belchers. At Moose Factory he secured the *Nastapoka,* a small ship, but in spite of a brave attempt, bad weather a few days out from Great Whale River almost wrecked the boat. The explorers were forced to limp painfully back to Great Whale where they had to admit to all the "told you so's" that they had been unable to reach the Belcher Islands in the *Nastapoka.* Flaherty decided to wait it out until winter and attempt a sledge strip across. Owing to the short supply of food at Great Whale he went down to Fort George to wait. That winter no Eskimos came over to the mainland. One day an Eskimo rushed into the camp where Flaherty was staying, with the news that between Great Whale and the Belchers there was open water and a dog team tangled in its harness had been seen trapped on floating ice. Some unknown Eskimo had come to grief in his attempt to get across. That season no one from the Belchers came at all and Flaherty had to return to civilization.

Sir William Mackenzie was determined that Flaherty should reach the Belchers and ordered him to get a ship. This he did.

And on the 14th of August, 1913, the *Laddie* sailed from St. John's. It was not much of a boat but it managed to fight its way through the Hudson Strait and as far as Amadjuak Bay—but no further. There Flaherty was forced to set up a winter's camp. Stores were unloaded and by the last week in September the *Laddie* was on her way back to St. John's, not to be seen again for the best part of a year.

It was the 19th of August, 1914, when the *Laddie* reappeared and Flaherty and his three men embarked for the Belchers. Plain sailing still eluded them, however, and they wound up wrecked amidst a "wild boil of reefs". By a miracle, the *Laddie*, though sadly damaged, still stayed afloat and with much hard work and able seamanship, the men managed to extricate her from her perilous position. Once free of the boulder-strewn sea the ship sailed towards a big island seen from a nearby promontory. The island proved to be Wetalltok's land and there they took shelter in a small rock-bound harbour. Unfortunately, Flaherty and his men could not stay there because they had tossed out a great deal of their cargo in order to drag the boat off the reefs. In addition, the boat was in desperate need of major repairs.

After a few days of rapid and temporary repair work, the *Laddie* left for Great Whale River. Three days later it was there. Darkness had fallen when they made their approach. Finding themselves unable to get across the sandbars at the river estuary, Flaherty and a couple of others launched a small boat. They missed their way and became entangled in sandbars and shoals. To signal for help, Flaherty fired his rifle repeatedly. No one came. Finally they managed to disentangle themselves and reach the settlement. Still no one came to them. A lighted building was entered. It proved empty. Things were odd. Not till Old Harold appeared was the mystery cleared up. He explained, "We thought you were the Germans."

It was 1914 and news of the war in Europe was fresh and frightening.

So it was that in 1915 the *Laddie* set out once more for the Belchers. This proved to be her last voyage. She reached the Islands without mishap but during the winter was crushed mercilessly by the ice. She never left those waters but remained an aging wreck in a storm-washed sea.

The winter of 1915-16 was a busy one for Flaherty and his men. They investigated, mapped, trapped, travelled, hunted and filmed. The truth of the Belchers was being uncovered.

It was these rarely visited islands, so difficult to reach and so inhospitable in appearance, that became front page news in 1940.

3
Religious Frenzy

Across the star-studded sky, like the flare of a rocket, a shooting star flashed. Mina, a small Eskimo woman on the Belcher Islands, saw the falling star and to her it was a sign. Often she had looked into the deep pool of night as the aurora rippled across it. Often she had watched magic figures appear, colours change and had felt the mystery of the universe around her. But never had the skies spoken as they spoke that night. She believed in God. She knew about Jesus and she knew, too, He was to come again. In the last days she had been told all kinds of strange things would happen. Some of these things she could not remember but as she watched that falling star she remembered part of the prophecy, "In those days . . . the stars will be falling from the heavens."

She watched the sky. Another meteor sprang into vision and burned its trail across the night. "Jesus is coming again. The world is coming to an end," she muttered. And so she became a key figure in the drama of religion and tragedy that swept across those sea-girt islands.

Shortly before this, Mina had been hearing about the strange behaviour of Charlie Ouyerak. It seemed that Charlie was leading a religious revival and was telling everyone, "Take no thought for the material things of this world." Some had heeded his words and destroyed both dogs and rifles. To find out more she left her igloo on Camsell Island and headed to the larger camp at the south end of Flaherty Island. When she arrived there everyone was in the grip of the religious mania. Many had seen the shooting stars. Charlie Ouyerak and Peter Sala, the most respected Eskimo among them, were leading a religious revival that was both violent and blasphemous. A horrible madness was everywhere. Mina loved it. She joined Charlie and Peter and became a staunch supporter. She even displaced Charlie's wife and became his mistress.

Not long after the new year had begun the evangelistic trio encountered stiff opposition. Although most of their friends and relatives had been cowed into belief, one or two refused to become a part of the movement. Opposition erupted during a gathering in a crowded snow house. At this meeting, Charlie Ouyerak and Peter Sala were in charge. For more than a week they had been asserting the imminent return of Jesus Christ. Now He was about to appear. In an atmosphere thick with the smell of unwashed bodies, untanned fur and partially cooked food, the Eskimos listened to Charlie.

"You have heard me tell you Jesus is to come. Well," he paused and everyone waited, hushed and silent, "He's here!"

"Here?"

"Yes, here. I am Jesus," he claimed. "And Peter Sala is God. That's right. Isn't it Peter?"

It was a declaration they had heard before but never with quite such force.

"Yes. That is right," agreed Peter. He was going to say more but Charlie continued talking.

"Can't you see our halos?" he asked rhetorically. "You must listen to us. You must obey. It is good that a rifle has been broken and dogs shot. The end of the world is near. We have seen signs in the heavens. Stars are falling. We have seen them. I am chosen," asserted Charlie.

"I am God," claimed Peter.

"It is true," cried Mina. "I, too, have seen the stars. I believe you, Charlie. I believe you, Peter."

"Ooooh, aaah," grunted the crowd.

Everyone was impressed. These simple people accepted the assertion of their leaders and believed that the Almighty had come again in a way they could all see and understand.

"We believe," they cried.

Slowly, all those gathered were being caught in a whirlpool of religious frenzy.

"You do believe?" said Charlie.

"Ooooo."

"You do believe," said Charlie.

"Oooooo."

"You do believe," said Charlie.

It was an incantation—a chant—a web of magic he was weaving.

"You do believe," and his voice rose.

Outside the wind moaned and the snow drifted blanket-white across the world. Huskies lay curled, nose to tail, in their holes of ice. These people lived in a land that gave them little or no peace. Merely to stay alive was a fierce, unending battle and there was not a solitary Eskimo adult who did not bear scars from the battle. The threat of hunger rarely left them. Diseases ravaged them. But now another enemy had come, an enemy from within, and a new sort of terror was to be theirs.

"You do believe," said Charlie.

"Ooooo," groaned the crowd.

"I don't believe you," said Sara.

Every eye turned in her direction.

"I don't believe you are Jesus," she asserted again.

"What?" roared her brother, Alec.

"And I don't believe Peter Sala's God, either," she cried.

"Did I hear you right?" asked Peter, grabbing her arm.

"You heard me. Must I say it again? Charlie's not Jesus and you're not God." The words tumbled out.

But it was too late for sense. Alec Apawkok believed Charlie and Peter. Angrily he struck at Sara.

"Fetch me a stick," he cried.

"Here," said Moses, handing him a piece of box wood.

Alec grabbed the wood and began to beat Sara.

Repeatedly he hit her across the neck and the head.

No one interfered.

"Sit down," he screamed at her and pushed her roughly to the floor.

Once she was down the others sprang to life. Four of them caught hold of her, struck her and, grabbing her by the hair, dragged her out of the igloo.

"Hit her with the stick!"

"Hammer her!"

Frenziedly they struck at her. But it was Akiinik who finished her off. She took hold of the barrel of a 30-30 that had no stock and, with a swinging blow, cracked her skull. In minutes Sara was dead.

Sara was only thirteen.

One person in that igloo was dismayed beyond measure by what had happened. Ketowieak. He disapproved strongly of the murder and was now convinced things had gone too far.

Like the others, Ketowieak was a religious man. But he was not sure that the claims of Sala and Ouyerak were valid.

Ketowieak had read the scriptures,* and read them more often than most because his wife was almost blind and she liked to listen to them. And it was now Ketowieak who spoke out against Charlie and Peter. Firmly, in the past, he had asserted that God would care for them, that they were all secure in Him. Now, Peter, their leader, was claiming to be God! Initially, in that strange meeting of song, prayer, preaching and madness, he too, had sung; he too had prayed; but now Sara was dead.

"I don't believe you, Charlie. This is not right," said Ketowieack.

"What's that you say?" said Charlie, moving towards him.

"I said, 'I don't believe you.' You are not Jesus or the Holy Spirit. You're Charlie! Charlie! Charlie Ouyerak!" Ketowieak's voice was rising. He was excited and frightened. Charlie lunged at him. Ketowieak lunged back and a fight began. During the scuffle Ketowieak's parka was torn but no personal damage was done. After a short tussle the combatants separated, glowered at each other and then Ketowieak turned and went out.

The body of Sara was in the snow porch of the igloo. Ketowieak looked down at the shadowed heap, stepped across it and in a sudden fit of anger partially destroyed the snow porch. Moving away to the left he threaded his way along a trail to an old snow house several hundred feet from the meeting house.

---

* Copies of the New Testament in syllabic script had been circulated among the Belcher Islands' Eskimos for years. Although no Anglican priest had been resident here, some had visited and two of the oldest Anglican Mission stations in the Territories were just across the water at Great Whale and Little Whale River. They had been founded there in 1876 and 1882 respectively. It was at Great Whale River that some of the earliest work had been done on the syllabic script of the New Testament by the Reverend E.J. Peck.

He stayed there for awhile and then, overcome by curiosity, went back to the igloo from which he had recently come. He paused uncertainly near the entrance and instead of going in, went round to the window. The window was a slab of clear ice set in the snow wall. The hole was too big for the ice and Ketowieak could easily hear what was being said inside and could make himself heard too.

He called to his friends and relatives, "I need your help. Won't any of you come to my side? Come on my side and believe in the true God."

Hardly had the last word been spoken than a piece of wood smashed cruelly into his mouth. Peter Sala had picked up a sleeping board and flung it violently and accurately at Ketowieak. Nobody moved to his aid, not even his wife. She was too blind to know what was happening. Ketowieak retreated to another igloo and stayed there the night.

Fear hung over the camp. Things were now in motion that no one could stop. It was now plain to all that they must believe in Charlie and Peter, or else . . . .

Deep darkness shrouded the igloos. Ketowieak tried to sleep but a wakeful restlessness was upon him. He was alone, terribly alone. Not even his wife was with him. He knew death was close. Had they not killed Sara? He knew he would not be spared. Slowly dawn crept upon them.

When morning had finally come, Peter Sala, watched by his apprehensive worshippers, approached Ketowieak's igloo with a harpoon in each hand. Ketowieak was crouching with his back to the entrance. Peter went in and prodded him with a harpoon.

"I am God! Do you hear me? I am God!"

Ketowieak remained unmoved. Peter continued to torment him with the harpoon and then suddenly leaned back and lunged forward, striking Ketowieak on the head.

"What are you going to do now?" Peter demanded. "I am God."

Uncannily, Ketowieak stayed silent and still, in the posture of prayer. He knew his end was near. Peter spoke to him again but Ketowieak made no attempt to answer. His silence frustrated Sala who finally could tolerate it no longer and, with the practiced accuracy of a seal hunter, pinned him with the other harpoon. Still alive, Ketowieak said nothing. Adlaykok, who had come behind Peter, climbed on to the top of the snow house and finished Ketowieak off with a rifle. No one intervened. Everyone knew that Ketowieak was being killed but they only listened and watched.

"I have shot Satan, Peter. I have shot Satan!" Adlaykok chanted excitedly.

They looked at each other and smiled. This was a good morning's work.

Later that day, the snow house in which Ketowieak's corpse rested was pulled down upon him. As they were about to do this, Adlaykok said to Peter Sala, "Lift up his hands and see if they're frozen yet."

"These hands will never freeze because they're in Hell's fire. He was Satan, Adlaykok," replied Peter.

Down tumbled the snow house and Ketowieak was buried until the police exhumed him during their investigation.

Slowly, the Eskimos gathered together their possessions, hitched up their dogs, and headed away from that tragic camp. But there was no hint of tragedy in their conversation, no sad light in their eyes. They were purified by the killings—delivered—liberated. Adlaykok, especially, was happy. Charlie must now know of his devotion. Had he not made it plain to the new Jesus? For he had killed Satan. He had actually asked Charlie for the cartridges to use on Ketowieak. He said his prayers to Jesus. He was the number one disciple.

Mina was happy, too. Peter was God. Charlie was Jesus and Mina was sleeping with him. Life was exciting, shot through with uncanny occurrences and supernatural visitations. Mina loved these ecstatic times.

With the slow deliberation of those who travel by winter, the small group of Eskimos crossed towards Tukarak Island. There they set up camp. With skill and ease snow houses were erected and the daily routine of life continued.

It was early in February before the strange religious frenzy that dominated Ouyerak, Sala and Mina flared into violence again. Day after day, Charlie had been insisting on the proximity of the end of the world and on his and Peter Sala's divinity.

Most believed—some fervently, some reluctantly and some with reservations. Alec Ikpak was one of the latter.

"Do you believe Charlie?" he asked his wife when snuggled together on their sleeping platform.

"I don't know. Do you?"

"No. I don't."

"Nor do I, really."

"I thought not."

"It's dangerous not to believe."

"I know."

"Tomorrow I'm going to tell Charlie. This madness has lasted long enough."

But Charlie was ready for Ikpak. He had already convinced the others that Ikpak was Satan.

"Ikpak is not a good man," Charlie insisted to Quarak, Alec's father-in-law, and a number of other Eskimos who were gathered in his igloo. "Such an evil man must not be allowed to live among us. What's going to happen to us in the last judgment if we tolerate Satan here? God threw Satan out of Heaven and he expelled the serpent from the garden. We must get him off these islands."

"What shall we do?" someone queried.

"He must be killed!"

"Killed?"

"We cannot have the devil in our midst."

"He must be killed!"

"Praise God! Hallelujah! Charlie, you're right. He must be killed!"

"Tomorrow," said Charlie, "when the sun is up."

"Tomorrow," murmured the court and Ikpak's fate was sealed.

In the morning of February 9th, Charlie Ouyerak went into Alec Ikpak's igloo.

"Have you changed your mind?" he asked Alec.

"No."

"I am Jesus, Alec."

"You are not Jesus. God is God and Jesus is Jesus and you are neither." Alec was quietly insistent although he knew his peril.

Eva, his wife, watched and listened.

"You are a devil, Alec. You belong to Satan. We all know you belong to Satan."

"I do not belong to Satan. I believe in God but I don't believe in you."

"He's not a devil," Eva interposed.

Charlie looked at her. Perhaps she, too, was a devil.

Alec spoke again and drew the attention away from his wife. "You've got to end this, Charlie. This has gone too far."

"Too far? Can you not see my halo? I am born of the Spirit. I am no longer Charlie, but Jesus."

His calm was weird and frightening. There was an intensity about his posture, his voice and his presence that was compelling. Alec resisted and reiterated his belief.

Suddenly, Charlie turned and left the igloo. Once outside he signalled to Quarak, Alec's father-in-law, to come over to him.

He then called to Alec, "Come on out!"

Silence.

"Come on out!"

Inside the igloo Eva and Alec exchanged glances and then slowly, as if bewitched, Alec stood up and moved towards the entrance.

"Walk over there," Charlie said to him as soon as he emerged, "and don't look around."

Alec walked steadily away, out on the sea ice.

"Shoot him!" said Charlie to Quarak.

Deliberately, Quarak raised his rifle, took aim and fired.

Alec stumbled and fell.

"He isn't dead yet," said Charlie. "Shoot him again."

Quarak moved closer and fired again.

"You'd better make sure. I think he still lives."

So Quarak shot him a third time, this time through the head.

Eva, who had come out of the igloo, had watched her father shoot the first two shots but turned her head as the third was fired. She was afraid.

"Hallelujah! Praise the Lord! Satan is dead! Let us be glad!" Charlie exhorted. Everyone smiled. Some clapped their hands. Quarak was a hero.

Not till Peter Sala came into the camp in the late afternoon did anyone do anything with Ikpak's body.

"Let us bury him," said Peter, after listening to an account of the shooting. "We will bring him to the beach and bury him properly."

The corpse was carried to a small hill a few hundred yards from the snow house and there covered with stones. Stones were hard to gather but the job was soon done. Charlie made sure no one was sad. Continually he exhorted them to be happy.

"How did you feel when Alec was shot?" Peter asked Eva.

"I was glad a little bit."

4
Death
on the Belchers

In 1940 there were only two white men on the Belcher Islands, the manager of the Hudson's Bay Company post, Ernie Riddell, and his clerk, Lou Bradbury. They lived silent, isolated lives. Every book in the post had been read several times and all the magazines were in tatters. They hardly knew there was a war on. Their only contact with the outside world was by morse wireless and that was not always reliable. The daily routine of post life had numbed them both. The winter had been long. Nothing unusual had happened. They had gone on occasional hunting forays, cooked their own food, kept their journals up to date, looked after their dogs and managed the business of the post. Now it was March and the gradual lengthening of the days made them restless.

"I think I'll go to Great Whale River to get the mail," said Ernie. "If I leave it any longer the ice bridge may be unsafe."

"O.K. Whatever you say."

It was quite usual for a trip to be made about this time of the year. They had talked about it during the preceding weeks and, in fact, looked forward to it. They were hungry for mail.

"I'll go and find Sala and see if he's ready to go right away."

Ernie found Peter Sala; told him that he wanted to go to Great Whale River and Peter agreed to go as the guide. From the Hudson's Bay Company post in the Belchers to Great Whale River is approximately 70 miles, not an enormous distance, but it was over sea ice and could be tricky. On a trip like that there was no better insurance than a good Eskimo guide and there was none better than Peter Sala. Ernie liked travelling with him.

Ernie, himself, was no stranger to the north and no stranger to rugged travel. He knew a good guide when he found one. By 1940 Ernie had been in the north almost a decade and had served in such widely separated places as Bathurst, Aklavik, Port Burwell and now the Belchers. An intelligent, able young man, he was well suited to the rigorous life he was leading. When he set out to see Peter Sala to make plans for the mail trip he had no knowledge of the strange religious frenzy that now gripped the native people. He found Peter and made the necessary arrangements in the usual way. It did not take long. Peter wanted to go and was glad to be asked.

On March 12th they set off. It was cold. Gusty March winds tugged at their parkas and stabbed at their faces. Eyebrows, nostrils and eyelashes were soon dusted with ice. They hunched into the wind and walked determinedly. The dogs, noses down, tails erect, pulled well but progress was slow. It was likely they would have to spend two nights on the ice before they reached Great Whale. Occasionally they stopped for mug-up. But Ernie was a pusher. He kept encouraging Peter to go a little bit further before the night. Finally Peter said, "That's far enough," and started to look around for suitable snow for an overnight igloo. While Peter set to work building an igloo Ernie tended to the dogs. Camp was put in order in double quick time. The little snow house was almost snug. Water was soon boiling, food prepared and sleeping robes stretched out. Ernie was just getting ready to settle in for the night when Peter said, "I'm a bad man."

"You're not bad, Peter. You're a good provider, a good hunter and a wise leader."

"No. Me, I'm a bad man."

Ernie continued to protest the reverse was true but Peter would not listen to him.

This puzzled Ernie because Peter would not say any more. It just was not like him to talk this way. Anyone who had had anything to do with Peter thought highly of him and it was recognized by them all that Peter was a leader; an intelligent, competent man, not given to dark moods or introspection.

"Why are you bad, Peter?" Ernie asked yet again.

"Oh, I am a bad man."

And that is all Peter would say. Peter could not bring himself to share with Ernie all the things that were happening on the island. So Ernie drifted off to sleep, mystified.

When they reached Great Whale River Ernie and Peter separated. Peter Sala went to see an old friend of his, Harold Udgarden, and Ernie went to the Hudson's Bay Company post. Tommy Carmichael, the manager at Great Whale was pleased to see Ernie, as was his clerk, Jimmy Lusk. They had lots to talk about. For Ernie it was almost like being back in civilization. The evening was far spent when Harold Udgarden suddenly burst into the room. Everyone turned and looked at him. Harold was excited. He was a half breed Indian who had worked for many years at Great Whale River for the Hudson's Bay Company and it is possible that he was the same Harold that R.J. Flaherty met at Great Whale in 1914.

"Have you heard about the murders on the Belcher Islands?" he asked in an extraordinarily deep voice. It was a voice so sepulchral that Ernie Riddell, talking about the event 29 years later, said, "I can still hear that voice asking that question."

All three men sat up straight.

"What murders?" they asked.

"Peter Sala's just been in to see me. He's told me about them."

"What did he tell you?"

Harold made himself comfortable and then told them the whole story. When he was finished the three Hudson's Bay men knew they had to take immediate action. Ernie Riddell got on the radio and sent a message to the Hudson's Bay Company in Winnipeg; "Have received information that three murders have been committed recently at Belcher. Advise immediate police investigation."

This signal was despatched to Ottawa and action began on it on March 15th. There was little more that Ernie and the other men could do. The radio message they received back from the police requesting more details merely served to emphasize their helplessness. All they had to go on was Peter Sala's story and the only way to find out more would be to conduct further investigations on the islands.

"I'll tell you what I'm going to do," Ernie said after a lengthy discussion with Carmichael and Lusk, "I'm going to go and see the Reverend Neilson. It's fairly evident some sort of religious mania is involved and I think we should talk to the missionary about it."

The others agreed to this.

The Reverend G. Neilson, a slightly eccentric Anglican missionary, gave Ernie a very careful hearing. He did not like the sound of what he heard and agreed to go back with Ernie to the island.

"I'll be ready to go whenever you're ready," said Neilson. "I think it's imperative I go."

This suited Ernie perfectly. He was sure the priest would be able to set things straight for the Eskimos.

Almost two weeks after their arrival at Great Whale River, Sala and Riddell, accompanied by the Reverend Neilson, were on their way back to the Belchers. They moved fairly quickly. Neilson was a good traveller. He handled a dog team well and was physically strong. He had a slight clerical stoop which belied his strength and accentuated his eccentricity. He was a good companion on the trail, and he brought along a batch of the tastiest home baked molasses cookies Ernie had had in years. As they approached the islands Ernie was close to Peter. They were keeping company with their own thoughts when Ernie suddenly spotted Quarak not far from them. He was out hunting.

They turned their teams towards him. Quarak saw them coming and waited for them to come up with him. Ernie was behind Peter. He saw Peter go up to Quarak, shake his hand and then he saw Quarak burst into tears. Ernie had never seen an Eskimo man cry before.

"What's the matter?" he asked Peter when Peter came back to him.

"Very bad. Very bad."

"But what's the matter?" Ernie pressed the question.

Peter just shook his head. Ernie watched Peter. And Peter wept.

Ernie was completely at a loss. He knew these two Eskimos better than any of the others. Peter was the leading Eskimo and his frequent travelling companion and Quarak was the man who had built him a kayak. In a special way Ernie liked and admired both of these men but now he did not know what to think. He did not really know them. Together they moved on towards land and Peter Sala's igloo. When they reached it they all went in. The Reverend Neilson was with them too. Peter's wife, Mina, was in the igloo.

"Where's your son Johnny?" asked Ernie. Johnny was one of Ernie's favorites. He referred to him as a real cute little guy. Mina did not answer at once. She looked straight at Ernie and then, turning to Peter, she said, "He's dead."

Peter looked as if he'd been struck. The silence was palpable.

"Where's Johnasie?" Ernie asked, trying to relieve the tension. "He's just the cutest little guy."

"He's dead, too," Mina answered flatly, unemotionally.

"Oh, my God," Ernie murmured. He could feel the hair on the back of his neck rise at this news and his stomach began to tie itself in knots. Ernie asked no more questions. As soon as he could, he left the igloo and dashed for the Hudson's Bay Company post. He filled his clerk in on the story and radioed via Port Harrison to the police, exhorting them to make an investigation.

By then the wheels of authority were turning. Preparations were being made to fly in an investigating party by Norseman aircraft.

That night the Reverend G. Neilson stayed at the Hudson's Bay Company post and the next day went on the trail to the various camps. When he returned some days later Ernie asked, "Well, did you get them all straightened out?"

"I don't think you'll have any more trouble," replied the Reverend Neilson. And that is all he said. Doubtless by now he knew the whole story but he was not about to share it with the Hudson's Bay men. He was anxious to protect the Eskimos from the white man's justice. A little more than a decade earlier two Eskimos had been hanged on Herschel Island. Neilson knew that and remembered. Justice had been injustice in the north too often and he did not want to see it happen again. Possibly he hoped the initial police investigation would uncover little and the R.C.M.P. would leave without seriously disturbing the people. But things had gone too far. Machinery had begun to roll and the events on the Belchers were too bizarre to be overlooked.

Neilson almost certainly knew the latest chapter that had been written in this macabre story, a chapter written while

Ernie and Peter were at Great Whale River. The most frightful chapter in a frightful series of events.

On March 29th, eight adults and their children were camped on Camsell Island. This island is a small turret of land that clings to Tukarak Island. The camp the Eskimos had there was only about five miles from the location of the other camp at Tukarak.

Morning came, a typically brisk one for March. A stiff wind was driving down from the north-east. It was no day for leisure and laughter out of doors. The sun glared from the surrounding ocean of ice but it did not warm the Eskimos. Summer was still a long way off. More than a month and a half had passed since Ikpak's death. During that time there seemed to be a diminution of religious fervor. Mina was back with Moses, her husband, and Peter Sala was in Great Whale River and Charlie Ouyerak was at another camp. (It should be explained, of course, that there were two Minas, Mina of the religious enthusiasm and Mina, the wife of Peter Sala.) A sudden eruption of maniacal religious violence must have seemed unlikely. March 29th was just another day. Certainly Quarak thought so.

"You come sealing with me today, Eva?" Quarak asked his daughter.

"I'll come."

Eva did not seem to hold it against her father for having shot her husband. Perhaps she too believed, or now believed more strongly, that her husband had been Satan. Whatever she thought about that she went sealing with her father. It could well be that if Quarak and Eva had stayed behind the approaching tragedy would have been averted. Or it might have engulfed them too.

Not long after Eva and Quarak had gone out onto the sea ice searching for seals' breathing holes, Mina began to act queerly. She talked to Mrs. Sala.

"I've seen a vision. I've seen stars shoot across the sky. I've seen signs. Jesus is coming again."

Peter's wife listened raptly. Mina was intense and hard to avoid.

"Jesus is coming again soon," she said.

And then to herself, and over and over again, head nodding in time with her words, "Jesus is coming again. We must get ready to meet him."

Peter's children stood close to their mother.

"We must go out onto the sea ice to meet him. We must be away from all these things in order to meet him. He comes to us. He's near to us. He wants us. He is for us. Let us be his. We must go and meet him."

The igloo was now crowded. Everyone in the camp was there.

"Come on. Let us go."

No one moved.

"Come on. We must go," Mina was excited and compelling. She went to the exit, beckoned to them all and went outside. The others followed. Out onto the ice they went. Mina like a dervish, dancing among them, running between them, shouting and then calling to Jesus. It was an unbelievable sight. Only Sara, Quarak's wife, hung back. She, with her children, scurried back into their own igloo. Mina seems not to have noticed. She was possessed. Everyone was afraid of her. Tirelessly she ran among them and forced them further and further out onto the ocean ice.

"Off with your clothes," she cried. "Naked we must meet the Saviour."

She made them all take off their parkas. Then she took the pants off the children. And, continually dancing among them, prevented them from reaching their clothes or putting them back on. The children struggled, whimpered and cried but they were powerless. Mina was deaf to all pleas. Such was her power that she forced both her mother and Sara Kumudluk, a widowed sister, to strip. The only ones who managed to escape her power were Moses, her husband, and Peter Sala's wife, Mina. Something brought them to their senses and they grabbed a child each and escaped to the shore. They and Mina were the only ones to come back with their lives. That night, lying dead on the ice, were four children and two women.

And Jesus had not come.

5
Belcher Islands Trial

On April 11th, 1940, the R.C.M.P. arrived on the Belcher Islands. This was their first visit for 21 years. In 1919 Inspector Philips and Sergeant A.H. Joy had gone there to investigate rumours of murders. They had arrived on September 30th and left twelve days later. During their stay on the islands they investigated the killing of Ko-Okyauk and Ketaushuk. These two natives were both killed because of deviant behaviour that marked them out as a threat to their society. No charges were pressed against the guilty persons. What Inspector Philips saw in the Belchers at that time horrified him. He wrote, "These people are the most destitute natives I have ever seen . . . . Not many of them own more than two to five traps. Their clothes consist of seal skins, dog skins and bird skins. The women and children are clothed in a combination garb of cotton, purchased in years when fur was plentiful, patched up with skins of everything procurable and in many cases not enough to cover their bodies. They have little bedding and in winter they sleep with their dogs to keep warm. Their real condition is inconceivable to one who has not seen."

It was into these circumstances that Ouyerak, Sala and Mina, the chief actors in the 1940 drama, were born. They were tiny children when Joy and Philips were there and were among the few to survive to adulthood.

Before the police left the island in 1919 the Eskimos asked them, "to approach the Government with a view to getting them a forty foot schooner by which they could move several families at one time from one hunting ground to another also to enable them to make a trip to Great Whale River in the summer in addition to finding new hunting grounds further out to sea which could not be done in a kayak. They also asked for tents, blankets, powder, shot, cartridges, size 44 Winchester, fishnets, 2½ to 3 inches mesh and six feet deep and gun caps." Inspector Philips makes the observation, "I noticed particularly they did not ask for any articles of food but only the means which would enable them to catch it." He concludes his report urgently recommending that these supplies be given them. But nothing was done. There was no adequate government machinery in existence to care for them and conditions remained the same.

In an environment of imminent starvation and daily peril, Sala, Ouyerak and the others matured. Life on the Belchers was lonely and routine. Things changed slightly for the better when the Hudson's Bay Company constructed a permanent post there in the thirties. Apart from Company employees the only white men to visit the islands were occasional prospectors and scientists. These were few and far between. Thus, when the police plane landed there on April 11th it caused a considerable stir. An aeroplane on the Belchers was almost unheard of.

Ernie Riddell was ready for it. He had carefully marked out a landing strip with coal sacks not far from the Company buildings. He was anxious for the aircraft to arrive for there was an uneasy air of tension among the natives. He had wanted it to come sooner for almost a month now had passed since the first message went outside. For days he had kept his dog team ready for the visitors but, unfortunately, he had had to send it away to Great Whale River for consumer supplies. He did not dare leave the last trip till later. The ice would rot any day now. So once more Peter Sala was away from the Belchers, this time with Lou Bradbury. Day after day Ernie awaited the arrival of the police patrol. It seemed ages since he had tapped out the first warning message. By the time April 11th had arrived Ernie had begun to think it highly likely that no patrol would get in till after break-up. Then he heard the engine. The Norseman made one or two passes over the Hudson's Bay Company post, circled the strip and dropped down. Ernie watched it slither to a standstill and strode towards it to meet the visitors. On board were Roy St. John, pilot, mechanic Corporal G.B. Swamey, Inspector D.J. Martin, Corporal Bill Kerr and Dr. T.J. Orford, the Indian Agent from Moose Factory and recently appointed Justice of the Peace. Inspector Martin made it clear to Ernie that speed was essential. "The ice is going out at Moose Factory so we have to get the plane back as soon as possible," he explained to Ernie.

"I'll see what I can do about dogs," said Ernie. "I'm afraid my team's away to Great Whale River."

That was easier said than done and not until two days later did they manage to obtain the services of one inadequate dog team. However, the investigators were able to reach Tukarak Camp, some six miles from the post, and there they discovered the body of Ikpak. Ikpak's wife told them where to find him. They uncovered the body and found it fully clothed. Dr. Orford examined it and found that two bullets had entered the back and one the head. The head was covered with a mixture of frozen blood and snow. It was a grisly sight.

The investigators worked methodically and quickly. By April 15th, Inspector Martin was able to report by radio that he had examined and identified seven bodies and of those seven bodies, one man was shot, one old woman and one young woman and four young boys had been stripped and driven out on the ice and frozen to death. He stated he had most of the culprits with him. The inspector does not fail to mention the other murders but states that although he knows where the other two bodies are they have not yet been recovered.

On April 16th the plane was ready to leave the Belchers. It took off with all the party that came plus three prisoners: Mina, Quarak and Adlaykok. Mina was charged with the deaths of the four children and two adults; Quarak with killing Ikpak, and Adlaykok with killing Ketowieak, whose body had not yet been found.

Ernie was sorry and a little uneasy to see the police leave. His position was now precarious. The Eskimos knew that he was responsible for the police arrival on the Belchers and that he was thus really responsible for the fact that some of their friends and relatives were taken away. Ernie sensed their animosity. He thought it highly likely that they would try to destroy some of the Hudson's Bay Company's equipment. In particular, he knew they viewed the radio machinery with great distrust. The Company had erected a small windcharger for the batteries so that communication could be maintained throughout the year. The Eskimos did not like that windcharger. They believed it was the machine that threw messages through the air. This was the machine that was used to tell the outside world about them. This would be a good machine to destroy.

The Eskimos talked this over in their igloos. Should they destroy the machine and the man? If we destroy one we must destroy both, was the voiced consensus of opinion. They vacillated when it came to killing Ernie. Ernie had not been a bad boss, a little odd, but a good boss. Ernie earned the reputation for being a little different soon after he arrived on the Belchers. Not long after he had settled in he went out to set some fish nets. A couple of days later he went to check them. He had not caught any fish but he had snared a couple of ducks that had been diving around. The natives noticed the new boss come back from fishing with two ducks but said nothing. Just a few days later Ernie took his .22 and went out to explore a little island. On his way round he came upon a little creek fed by a small lake. He followed the stream, hoping to see some fish. Luck was with him. Only a few hundred feet from where he first saw the creek he came on a small pool loaded with trout. "Gee, I'd like to get some of those," thought Ernie. "I'll try shooting them." He stood stock still on the bank and waited for the fish to swim close. Then he fired. The shot stunned the fish enough for it to come to the surface belly up. Ernie then simply scooped it out. When it came time to return to the post he went marching back with as fine a mess of trout as you ever saw. The natives saw him coming and this time they commented, "This is some boss. He goes to a fish net and he brings back ducks. He goes to hunt and he brings back fish. What kind of a boss do we have here?" They had a lot of fun with Ernie after that and would often mimic him. They would walk like him to the nets and pretend to come back with ducks and do the same thing with a rifle and fish. It was a big joke to make such fun of the boss. Ernie took it in good part and they liked Ernie.

But now things were different. The boss had sent three of their people away. What was going to happen to them? Who would be next? "Times are bad," they would say to each other, and nod darkly.

Ernie began to carry his rifle with him everywhere although he knew perfectly well that if they wanted to pick him off they could, just whenever they chose. "They should have left a policeman on the islands," Ernie said to Lou Bradbury as soon as he got back. "I don't think we are safe." Lou agreed. They even took their rifles with them when they made a trip to the outside toilet. These journeys became trips they dreaded. It was a long way to the little shack and the path was exposed.

"I didn't like that walk," Ernie recalls nearly thirty years later.

But nothing happened. The discussions in the igloos and arguments in the camp did not result in action and Ernie and Lou were spared.

Although the tension gradually eased, Ernie was delighted when all the necessary arrangements were completed and court was ready to open on the Belcher Islands.

It had been decided to try the accused on the Belchers near the scene of the crimes and among their own people, rather than fly everyone who was needed to Moose Factory. There was great rejoicing among the native people when Adlaykok, Mina and Quarak came back to them. It was more like a village fair atmosphere than the setting of the stage for murder trials. Much had happened since these natives had seen each other. Mina had been as far away as Toronto where she had been cared for in a psychiatric hospital while Quarak and Adlaykok had passed the time at Moose Factory.

The police arrived ahead of the judicial party and arrested Ouyerak, Sala, Apawkok and Akiinik. Now there were seven prisoners. During the time that had elapsed since the first investigations the bodies of Sara and Ketowieak had been recovered. Anawak, the Eskimo who had acted as guide to Inspector Philips, had undertaken to recover these bodies and bring them back to the vicinity of the Hudson's Bay Company post and rebury them there. This he had apparently done.

The judiciary party, headed by Judge Plaxton of Toronto, arrived on the Belcher Islands on Monday, August 18th, at 5:00 o'clock in the afternoon. They had been a long time en route from Moose Factory owing to extremely rough weather. It was so wild that for a week they had had to seek refuge at

Great Whale River. At one time it looked as if the Norseman would have to be used to ferry in all the party. Eventually the weather eased and the party was able to take the S.S. *Fort Charles* across the open water safely.

Fortunately for the course of justice, a few extra jurymen were readily available because a Mr. Holzman of Toronto who had chartered the *Dorothy,* was prospecting in the area and he and his crew were on the Belchers and willing to serve at the trial. When the jury was finally selected the following men served: Mr. Holzman, mining engineer, Jack Rubie, prospector, James McCook, newspaper reporter, Canadian Press, William Kinmond, newspaper reporter, *Toronto Star,* E.J. Cadney, ship's engineer, *Fort Charles* and E. Riddell, Hudson's Bay post manager. The trials were conducted in a large police marquee that had been brought for the purpose. Wooden benches had been built for the prisoners and jurymen and a special dais for the judge's chair and table. Witnesses squatted on the moss and proceedings began.

Everything was done in order with full formality and procedure. The trials began on the 19th and ended two days later on the 21st. By the time they closed a great deal of discussion had been provoked concerning the Eskimos, their ways and the white man's laws, their responsibilities and the white man's responsibilities, the place of the church and so on. Opinions varied and a wide range of views were stated. Some people in the outside world thought that the Eskimos should be whipped rather than punished by imprisonment or any of the other penalties normally demanded by the law. There was sufficient talk like this to prompt the commander of the Eastern Arctic Patrol, Major D. McKeand, to write to the Deputy Commissioner of the Northwest Territories, Mr. R.A. Gibson, "There has been a lot of loose talk about whipping Eskimos convicted of criminal offences . . . . If a white man attempts to ridicule an Eskimo before his fellows, tragedy will follow as day follows night. I reported to you that I saw negroes whipped by white men in South Africa forty years ago but the negro has a tribal system and moreover has been the slave race since the dawn of history. Eskimos have no tribal system and the family is the independent unit. In time, to ridicule or inflict whipping on the Canadian

Eskimos would bring forth a vigorous protest from all white persons who know them personally."

There always seem to be advocates of violent punishment in society although better judgment held sway in the Belchers. As early as May 31st a senior solicitor wrote to Major McKeand expressing the real need to find the right judge, "I think someone conversant with native psychology, customs and habits should be in charge." He also points out the necessity there would be for serious consideration regarding sentence should a verdict of guilty be handed down. He goes on to say, "As it is unthinkable that a native would receive capital sentence the further question of detention and punishment will also arise. Detention at any of the penitentiaries would, I think, be equivalent to execution by slow torture but detention at any of the northern police posts would be equivalent to a holiday with pay and the matter must be carefully considered." Perhaps that's why some advocated the whip.

In his charge to the jury, Judge Plaxton spoke at considerable length. He was anxious both to uphold the law and to act mercifully. He said, "You are called upon to perform a task which is at once delicate and difficult. The task involves the application of the criminal laws of Canada, the white man's laws, to the primitive Eskimos of these islands. It is a delicate task because these people, though in some respects of their behaviour are very childlike . . . in many other aspects are very childish—of low mental growth judged by our standards."

He went on to examine briefly the origin of the people and their relationship with white people. He pointed out that the only law they had was that of "time honoured custom":

Untutored in our ways of life, uninfluenced by any form of alien culture, these "children of the twilight" carry on today as did their ancestors through countless generations; in this bleak, inhospitable region a ceaseless struggle for existence, grim and merciless in its character. A struggle perhaps unequalled by any aboriginal people in the quality displayed of ingenuity, endurance and fortitude . . . . A people must naturally be viewed in the lot of its environment and the conditions under which they have lived and had their being. These Eskimos are in fact still at an early stage of evolution as human beings. We should also bear in mind that life in this desolate region, exposed as it is to the cruelest conditions and ever on the verge of extermination is not conducive to excessive gentleness. Moreover the terrible uncertainty of life in this region may account to some extent for the childish superstitions and mysteries with which they invest the earth and the universe.

Notwithstanding all this, the King's Writ reigns in these islands as our presence here attests. The criminal laws of Canada apply here as well as elsewhere throughout Canada. They are applicable no less to these aborigines than to the other inhabitants of the Dominion . . . . The laws of Canada are fair and just. To every citizen is secured the protection of life and property and the pursuit of happiness . . . . There may be some among you who entertain the view that our code of punishment for crime, most particularly in the case of major crimes, is not suited to the conditions of these people and as applied to them will fail to attain the prime object in view, namely to deter the commission of crime among them. There may be some merit in that view. As to that I express no opinion. So far as these cases are concerned, gentlemen, you and I are bound to take the law as it stands.

The jury did as it was bid. At the close of the trial Alec Apawkok was found not guilty and sentences were passed on the other six prisoners, all of whom were found to be in some measure guilty. Quarak was released on a two year suspended sentence and entered into recognizance to keep the peace and be of good behaviour and to protect and provide for the families of Sala, Ouyerak and Adlaykok during their terms of imprisonment. The remaining five prisoners were disposed of: Mina, found insane; Akiinik, insane; Adlaykok, one year's imprisonment; and Peter Sala and Charlie Ouyerak, both two years' imprisonment. These prisoners were put aboard the *Fort Charles* which left the Belchers on August 22nd. Before leaving the islands, however, orders were issued authorizing the Hudson's Bay Company to provide a weekly ration to the wives of the three male prisoners until further notice. An order was also issued on the Company authorizing the issue of ten rounds of ammunition weekly or equivalent value in shot and powder to those natives who promised to provide meat and fish for the families of Sala, Quyerak and Adlaykok.

Although the prisoners were now in custody and the trial a matter of record there was still a lot of talk about the Belcher Islands and the Eskimos in general. It is perhaps instructive for us to read now what was being said then. R. Olmstead, the Crown Prosecutor at the trials, in a memorandum to the Deputy Minister, Department of Justice, dated October 11, 1941, summarizes the thinking of many.

It is my opinion that it would be very difficult to secure a jury of white men in the James and Hudson Bay districts who would convict an Eskimo of murder arising out of the killings of last winter or any other time. White men resident in these areas appear to have what amounts almost to an affection for the Eskimos. They understand that he is probably the friendliest, happiest aborigine anywhere in the world and that he lives in a country and under conditions far more rigorous than existence elsewhere outside the Arctic region . . . . Any killing that may occur is due very rarely to malice but has behind it some motive, belief, transgression, or tradition which justifies it in his eyes. I am satisfied that hanging would not have a deterrent effect as it is supposed to have among white men, even if it were carried out on the site. The motive, whatever it may have been, which prompted an Eskimo would still be a motive in the minds of the other Eskimos and I do not believe that with their short memories the lesson intended to be taught with hanging would remain long with them . . . .

Similarly with regard to punishment. It is not understood as punishment unless it is associated with physical pain. It is the only form of punishment he knows. He whips his dogs frequently and hard when he thinks they deserve it. To take him away and shelter, clothe and feed him for months on end, meanwhile giving similar treatment to his family is not his idea of punishment. Being complacent and easy going by nature, a term of imprisonment is a holiday about which he will be able to talk the rest of his life . . . . In fact one of the accused was begging to be taken away before the trial. He frequently asked, "Moosonee, me, plane?" He actually gloated and beamed with pleasure when he learned he was to go.

After commenting briefly on the sentences handed down by Judge Plaxton, Olmstead goes on to make recommendations.

I recommend and strongly urge that never again should the provisions of the Criminal Code be applied to the Eskimos. The cap of Canadian criminal jurisprudence cannot be made to fit the head of this primitive people. The Criminal Code is not applied to white children of tender years . . . . Evolution in primitive man is slower in some cases than others and it ill behooves the most advanced race to apply its rigid rules of conduct to another race which by reason principally of geography has made little or no advance in the last two or three thousand years.

The Eskimo is still a child. His attitude to life, his customs and traditions have been handed down to him through countless generations. He is said to be free from guile, excepting in the hunting, predominantly honest and unconcerned about provision for the future. When he is hungry he goes hunting and gorges himself on the kill . . . .

I contend that it is unfair to treat as equals these members of the aboriginal race who, up to 25 years ago, insofar as the Belcher Islands is concerned, had never seen a white man nor had any knowledge of his standards of conduct . . . . They are not naturally killers unless they have been deeply provoked when the killing is to them really a form of self-defence . . . .

The Eskimo can become a problem to Canada if they choose to intervene to any extent in his life. His existence is not essential to the welfare of the country except as a source of furs. He could be entirely ignored and still thrive . . . . It is gross cruelty to him to attempt to assimilate him into our way of life. The Eskimo is many thousands of years behind us in development. Our problem is not how we should deal with the Eskimo. It is more correctly should we interfere with him at all. Personally I am strongly against intervention of any kind. If, however, it is felt that some intervention or supervision is indicated for humanitarian reasons then its extent must be carefully watched so as to interfere as little as possible with their normal and natural way of life . . . .

It would be almost impossible and inordinately expensive to bring all Eskimos under the watchful eye of the Government officials. It is true that in certain localities, including the Belcher Islands, the Government is supplying relief rations to certain Eskimos. This practice tends in my opinion to make an independent people dependent . . . .

I suggest that should another crime occur in the future the R.C.M.P. as soon as they hear of it should take the perpetrator away to a police barracks and place all the evidence before the Commissioner of the Northwest Territories who should be authorized to prescribe at his discretion, a proper period of detention.

Mr. Olmstead then examines the trading practices of the Eskimos and the nature of the Hudson's Bay Company post on the Belchers. This post was only opened there according to Mr. Olmstead because of government pressure on the Company. The Government wanted an avenue through which some help could be filtered to the Eskimos. In spite of the fact that the post was not profitable to the Hudson's Bay Company it had been kept open—though not without protest. Olmstead writes,

I understand further that the Company does not exactly appreciate its position as a Government relief agent charged with the responsibility of supervising the welfare of the Eskimos in sickness and in health and policing them in the event of infractions of white man's laws. I heard it said that if the R.C.M.P. would establish a post on the Belcher Islands to take over relief and police duties, the Company might consider keeping the post open, but unless this is done the Company would find it more profitable to close the post, appoint one Eskimo to take charge and make an annual call at a previously designated point to pick up furs the Eskimos brought together for trading . . . . "

Mr. Olmstead then discusses putting government agents on the islands.

Personally I cannot see why two white men should be asked to live in that region at great expense to their Government in order to supply certain commodities to a few dozen Eskimos who might or might not need them.

These Eskimos should not be on these islands and should not be allowed to remain there. If the Government insists in supervising their welfare then it should move them to localities where they would have a better chance of avoiding starvation, where R.C.M.P. posts are already established and serviced, where it would cost less money to supervise them and where there are more of their own kind . . . .

In a sombre mood Olmstead then has something to say about

the criminals,

Further, Peter Sala, Charlie Ouyerak and Adlaykok should not be regarded upon their return from a delightful holiday as reformed criminals. They are all mean and left to themselves will probably be disposed of by others. Charlie Ouyerak particularly carries a grudge. Many years ago his father was killed in a series of murders. Anything may happen when these three schemers return to the Belchers. They will have become accustomed in the meantime to many things which are in the Hudson's Bay store. They will have suffered no punishment for murder committed; they will be heroes among their own people; they will want things in that store and being excellent shots with a rifle will take the easiest way of getting them quickly as in the case of the Eskimo who murdered the priest for his rifle.

I most strongly urge that the Eskimos now held under detention, except Mina, be returned next August and not held for two years; that the Hudson's Bay Company be closed as a permanent post; that unless and until some church considers it worthwhile to the Eskimos to place a missionary permanently on the island, no sporadic attempts at religious instruction be made; that these people be left entirely by themselves so far as government intervention be concerned and, lastly, that under no circumstances, should the Eskimos on the Belchers or elsewhere in the Arctic be considered amenable to the Criminal Code.

This was written less than thirty years ago. Before it was written and while it was beginning to boil in Mr. Olmstead's mind, Judge Plaxton was encouraging Eskimo dependency by causing largess to be distributed. He delved into his own pocket and passed on $20.00 to the Reverend Mr. Neilson, to be spent in such a way that it would in part alleviate the native distress. The Reverend Neilson was grateful for the donation and he and a few newspaper reporters heard the Judge say, "That's the best $20.00 I ever spent." It was with some chagrin, therefore, that the Reverend Neilson later received a request from the Judge for a receipt for the sum of $20.00. The Reverend Neilson thought Judge Plaxton had decided to charge it to expenses.

6
Nascopie Wedding

Charlie Ouyerak did not last long in detention. Soon after he was sentenced and taken to Moose Factory he became sick and Dr. Orford diagnosed pulmonary tuberculosis. He died a few months later. The others survived the term of their sentences and all of them continued to live in the vicinity of Hudson Bay. Peter Sala was for some time in Great Whale River, as was Adlaykok. Mina was released and became something of a traveller. She spent a short time in several different communities.

In 1946 she travelled by open boat along the east coast of Hudson Bay in the company of Peter Sala and one or two other Eskimos. They stopped and camped whenever they wished and gradually worked towards Port Harrison. When they reached Port Harrison Mina was delighted to find Corporal Kerr living there. Corporal Bill Kerr had looked after her following the trials on the Belchers. She had become very fond of him and was thrilled to discover him again. She was so pleased that she let the boat go on without her and moved in with Bill and his wife, Norma, as their housekeeper. They did not need a housekeeper. They only had themselves to look after and a dog but that made no difference to Mina. She had found Bill again and she was going to look after him. It's not quite clear how she regarded Norma but apparently Norma was her friend too. By this time, six years after the murders, Mina was a different person. Although occasionally moody, on the whole she was a cheerful, handshaking, smiling woman who wanted to please and be useful. Mr. and Mrs. Sam Dodds were in Port Harrison at that time and they always referred to Mina as Blitzkreig Bessie. It was a nickname that fitted. She descended on Bill and Norma without invitation, and she moved into their house and into the community like a single-handed invasion. On the whole people enjoyed Mina. Bill and Norma kindly tolerated her ministrations.

All this was very new to Mrs. Dodds who had only been in the north a matter of a few weeks. In fact she had not long been Mrs. Dodds. She had come north that year to get married to Sam, the weatherman. Sometime during the previous winter, Sam said, he put in a requisition for one wife. It is highly improbable that he only put in a requisition a few months before the summer. The Government usually did not fill its requisitions that quickly! Anyway, on board ship that summer were Miss Wanda McNeil who married Wulf Tallborn and Miss Didi Keightley who married Sam Dodds. Both of them were heading for Port Harrison where their bridegrooms were working. The *Nascopie* had a fairly straightforward run that year as far as Cape Smith and then ran into ice. Ice so thick they could do nothing about it but wait. From Cape Smith to Port Harrison was usually a comfortable day's journey so when they got that far the girls began to get really excited and make final preparations for their weddings. The night before they expected to arrive at Harrison they curled their hair, did their fingernails and made themselves look as lovely as possible. When their toilet was finished the boys on the boat said, "Come on. Let's have a party. This is your last night of freedom. Let's live it up." So they had a party. It was a lot of fun, a good party with which to end single life. Next day dawned. Sleep slowly left.

"I wonder where we are," one of them murmured.

"We'll be pretty nearly there."

Not long after they were dressed they met the captain.

"Sorry girls, you're no nearer Port Harrison than you were last night. The ship is stuck in the ice."

So that night there was more primping, powdering and polishing and then another party. This went on for seven consecutive days until the ship finally got underway again. In the meantime, Sam was getting impatient.

"Come on in, girls," he signalled. "Don't be shy."

Wanda and Didi replied, "Well, coax us some more. Maybe we'll walk."

Everyone on board had a lot of fun at the expense of the two ladies. They were more than anxious to see the great reunion when it took place. As the ship closed with Port Harrison a peterhead came out to meet it with Wulf and Sam in it and every camera was ready. The decks were lined with people. Mr. J.W. Anderson, the Hudson's Bay Company's manager for the Eastern Arctic District, and Mr. J.G. Wright, officer in charge, saved the girls. Mr. Wright called Didi aside and told her to go into his cabin and Mr. Anderson volunteered the use of his cabin to Wanda. After all, the poor girls could get no privacy. They shared their cabin with two other ladies, a Mrs. Woodrow and her daughter, Freddie. The boys were escorted to the respective cabins by Mr. Anderson and Mr. Wright and there the great reunions took place. Everyone was mad about this because they could not get any pictures.

Didi and Sam were married a day or so later at the Anglican Mission, a Canon Shephard officiating.

It was some honeymoon. Early that first evening everybody in the community showed up and sat around on packing cases. They stayed until 2:00 or 3:00 in the morning. Fred Woodrow, the radio operator, kept singing Sweet Violets at regular intervals and Mrs. Woodrow played the accordion. Didi could not even serve coffee. She didn't know where the coffee was, where the cups were, or indeed, where anything was. Everything was just pushed into the house. There were packing cases everywhere. There was no warehouse and no storage place. All the winter supplies were there including 680 cans of soup, a pig and half a cow.

It was very nice to have all that meat but there was no way to keep it refrigerated and there were no jars in which it could be preserved.

"What am I going to do with all that meat?" Didi queried of no one in particular.

"It's easy enough to preserve," said someone. "All you need is a wooden barrel."

"A wooden barrel?"

"Yes, a wooden barrel. What you do is this. You fry all the pork. Then pour the fat into the barrel and place the meat in that. It'll keep if you cook it and store it in its own fat."

Didi wanted to do the right thing so as soon as the chance

came she set to and started frying the pig. It took a long time, a whole week in fact. Every drape, stitch of clothing and utensil in the house smelled of frying fat. The air was greasy with pig. Finally it was done. The barrel was loaded with fatty fried pig. In a week or so it was rotten. They salvaged what they could and gave the rest away to whoever wanted it. The Dodds did not fancy rotten meat although both Eskimos and Indians had had to settle for such meat at times.

New brides in the north were bound to be confronted with crises very different than those a young bride would meet outside, and to run into situations both amusing and surprising. Unlike some women, Didi did not try to force outside ways into a northern context. Some ladies did.

When the *Nascopie* had brought her and Wanda north the boat called at Lake Harbour. There, to the astonishment of most people on board and the two girls in particular, the wife of the local Hudson's Bay Company post manager came clambering over the rocks to the ship, wearing the latest in fashions. She was complete with high heels, tight skirt, nylon stockings and a glorious mass of hair swept up and piled. Not many women in the north at that time took quite so much trouble.

Next year, however, Didi was in for another surprise, this time at Arctic Bay. She and her husband, Sam, were transferred there with the Department of Transport. When they arrived Canon Jack Turner was there with his wife, sorting out their supplies and getting them ready to take to Moffet Inlet. Mrs. Turner, a pretty, delightful Englishwoman who had joined Canon Turner in 1944, invited Didi to tea. Didi accepted the invitation and at the appointed time went over to Mrs. Turner's tent. In spite of the fact that they were deep in the Arctic, in spite of the fact that they were thousands of miles from England and in spite of the fact that to get into the tent you had to crawl, Mrs. Turner had carefully prepared the afternoon tea. She had laid out a white cloth on top of a blanket on the ground and neatly decorated it with a beautiful tea service.

"Tea?" she asked Didi, lifting the silver teapot.

7

Jack Turner - the Real Man

Jack Turner was a big man. Although not a tall man there was a bigness about him that was inescapable. He was big in character, personality and spirit. The Eskimos called him the "real man". There was a no-nonsense determination about Turner that made itself felt. In a way rarely achieved by white men he won the Eskimos completely. They loved him. More than twenty years after his death, Eskimos, who knew him, light up when his name is mentioned. Those who were married by him are proud of it. Those who travelled with him have never forgotten it and those who were baptized by him feel somehow specially blessed.

Jack Turner was an Englishman, a member of the Bible Churchman's Missionary Society and a dedicated Evangelist; a single-minded man who knew what he believed and why he believed; a man who knew he was right.

In 1929 he turned up at Pond Inlet with Harold Duncan, another missionary, to start the Anglican work there. It seems that right from the start they ran into competition from the Roman Catholic Church.

Jack Turner did not like Roman Catholicism and he made no bones about it. He was an outspoken opponent of what he called "Popery". In 1931 he reported to his headquarters, "The Roman Catholics have been more active this year and just recently I felt led to give a direct warning against them . . . . When I learned of definite attempts on the part of our adversaries to pervert the people—and you are not ignorant of Rome's devices—I felt the time had come for something more aggressive. We have always, of course, exalted the Scriptures, and this is where we have a great advantage over any false teaching."

Maurice Flint comments in his short biography of John Turner, *Operation Canon**: "It is a hard thing for primitive Eskimo to see white men, professing to follow the Lord Jesus Christ who will not shake hands or greet one another. Bribery, untruth, misrepresentation and baser methods are not new to students of history but to isolated natives of the Northern Darkness they provide nothing but misunderstanding and a hindrance to full spiritual development. Old native men and women in these Arctic wastes, by nature given to hospitality, friendly and happy, have found themselves threatened with eternal punishment if they entertain a Protestant missionary. New Testaments and Prayer Books have been confiscated and burned by the servants of Rome."

John Turner notes in his diary for March, 1946, "Those who have been asked here why they follow the priests have acknowledged that they have no desire to do so but simply respond to pressure. The priest tells them all that unless they follow him they will die. His latest story is that the great chief of Protestant teachers (presumably the Archbishop of Canterbury) has now become a Roman Catholic so it is foolish to follow the teachers." Maurice Flint observes, "Roman Catholic priests in the North have been known to support such claims by showing pictures of the hierarchy of the Protestant Church, extracted from daily newspapers of civilization, in which they are wearing vestments which the priest claims are essentially Roman."

Criticism of the rival churches flashed between them. The Roman Church was especially pained by the success of the Anglican Mission at Pond Inlet because it felt it had been one-upped. Writing of Pond Inlet in the *Eskimo Quarterly*,** a Roman Catholic Publication, Father Rousselière says, "It was there that Father Girard and Bazin had founded the Sacred Heart Mission in 1929. The establishment of this mission originally scheduled for 1927 had to be postponed when the supply ship *Bayrupert* was ship-

* Flint, Maurice, *Operation Canon*, Bible Churchman's Missionary Society, 1949.

** *Eskimo Quarterly*, Oblate Fathers, Hudson Bay Vicariate, Churchill, Manitoba.

wrecked. The following year a Protestant bishop, aware of this project, rapidly arrived to baptize a group of local Eskimos after a very brief course in religious instruction and exacted their solemn promise that they would never become Catholics. The two founders, expecting to find a favourable environment, were bitterly disappointed."

Doubtless the Anglicans would see the hand of the Lord in the non-arrival of building materials for the Roman Catholic mission in 1927.

As the course of events turned out, the four missionaries all arrived at Pond Inlet together—Fathers Girard and Bazin, the Roman Catholics, and Turner and Duncan, the Anglicans. They had travelled together on the *Nascopie* so each party was fully aware of the intention of the other. Jack Turner viewed them with suspicion and spoke minimally to *Mr.* Bazin and *Mr.* Girard. John Turner never, ever, referred to them as "Father".

According to one unverified story told by Mr. Alan Robertson Scott, a Hudson's Bay manager in the Arctic for many years, the rivalry between the two churches was brutally emphasized from the very start. As soon as the *Nascopie* docked, unloading operations began. Both missions had on board supplies for the winter and sufficient equipment to build small mission houses. Naturally enough, these four men wanted the help of the natives. The Roman Catholics knew of the Eskimos' great fondness for tea so they supplied the natives with it and managed to get their building well on the way. A little work on the building, a little tea. The Anglicans decided to run some competition to this. They also offered the Eskimos tea. Now this was great for the natives. Tea at both places and not too much work. They played the two pairs of men off against each other. Apparently the Anglicans got wise to this and instead of offering lots of little tea parties one of them said, "When you finish the job we'll have one great big tea party." When the Eskimos heard this they were not too impressed so they stopped working for the Anglicans. After all, the Roman Catholics were giving them parties all along. Do a little bit of work. Have tea. The only trouble was that the rations had to last a whole year. Gradually the rations the Roman Catholics had on hand began to peter out and it looked as if it would be unwise to continue the parties on such a scale so they eased up. The Eskimos did not like this. Slowly they ceased work and went back to the Anglicans who had not been quite so prodigal with supplies. They finished the mission and then had a great big bash as promised. By then the Roman Catholics still were not finished.

Pond Inlet was captured by the Anglicans and in spite of strenuous, dedicated and constant efforts on the part of the Roman Catholic priests, the Eskimos remained faithful to the Anglican Church. John Turner must be given full credit for this. No one could help but admire him. He was a man of steel.

Turner was the greatest Arctic traveller of all time. He travelled when no one else would. He travelled where no one else would and many, many times he travelled alone.

Alan Scott remembers him arriving at Arctic Bay more dead than alive. When Jack had set out from Pond Inlet he had had 18 dogs with him but on the way he ran into a howling blizzard. The Arctic sky lowered and held him fast. Food ran out. Jack prayed and waited. He fed the weakest dogs to the other dogs until there were only two left. With these two he managed to reach safety and comfort at Arctic Bay. This happened more than once, but he always managed to pull through. He would say, with a confidence some found naive, "I have no fears. The Lord will provide." And He did.

Jack Doyle, a member of the R.C.M.P. who spent a number of years in the Pond Inlet area, remembers Turner well. "He always called me Mr. Doyle. I always called him Mr. Turner." There was something about Jack Turner that made familiarity difficult. Something of a recluse, a man of great depth, he seemed to keep the castle of his soul inviolate. On one occasion Doyle and Turner were travelling together from Clyde River to Pond Inlet. They had set out late in the season from Pond with one team of dogs. They had pooled their best dogs. The trip to Clyde was uneventful but the return journey was awful. The weather turned warm. The snow became mushy and travel became next to impossible. One night they built a small overnight igloo out on the sea ice and turned in. While they slept the ice floe shifted and when they woke they were far out at sea and could barely see the land.

"This is a pretty how d'ye do," said Doyle, looking at the

horrifying stretch of black, black water that reached from the floe edge to land. The floe ice was in such a position that they were able to keep travelling on it so they kept pushing on, as near as they could judge, to the north and west. They travelled all day and then before they knew it they were in soft snow again. It was push, pull, drag, haul—exhausting, unrewarding work. By the end of the day no land was in sight. Jack Turner looked the situation over and said, "Mr. Doyle, we will have to pray."

"Go ahead," said Jack Doyle, "It can't do any harm. As a matter of fact I think I'll do a little praying myself."

Jack Doyle is a Roman Catholic.

Turner kneeled by the side of the komitik, uncovered his head, bowed and prayed out loud. He asked the Lord to shift the winds and arrange the tides in such a manner that they would be brought to land. It was a simple, direct request, uttered with confidence by a man of deep faith. Following a firm "Amen" Turner looked up and said, "Let's make camp."

They camped. They slept. Next morning they were back on land.

"It was miraculous," says Doyle. "Miraculous. Jack Turner's confidence was so impressive. Turner maintained the Lord had looked after His own and that was that. It was that simple."

It took them all day to get off the floe ice. Where land and ocean met snow and ice had piled up into a frightful, chaotic jumble of ice blocks and drifts. The ledge, as such a place is called, was a treacherous spot to be. The cliffs were sheer and in places black water glinted as the low sweeping sun shot fire across it. They had to get up onto a cliff in order to get round a point of land. Once around that point they thought the going would be much easier. It was. In fact, for a while, the trip became enjoyable again. They were on solid ice once more. Seals were plentiful. There was lots of daylight. Nothing to worry about. That is, nothing but the sun. When they were about 35 miles from Pond they ran into heavy wet snow. The going became impossible. The dogs could not even haul the komitik with the few supplies they had.

"It's no good," said Doyle to Turner. "We'll just have to let the dogs loose and leave everything behind."

Turner agreed. They each took their rifles, turned the dogs loose and took enough food to last them the 35 mile walk. On their way into Pond Inlet they met a few Eskimos. They told them exactly where the komitik was left and said that if they brought it in they would be handsomely rewarded. Fortunately the weather changed. The temperature dropped a little. Snow and ice firmed up and within four or five days the Eskimos had recovered Doyle's and Turner's belongings. Jack Doyle had abandoned four or five hundred dollars worth of equipment, sleeping bag, silk tents, rifles and ammunition. When the Eskimos came back with all this stuff Jack gave them a couple of tins of flour, lard and tobacco.

"The fellow I handed it to felt like a wealthy man," said Doyle. "Mind you it must be remembered the year was 1939 and, at Hudson's Bay Company prices, what I handed out might well have cost more than $100.00."

Turner viewed the incursion of civilization into the north with a jaundiced eye. He loved the Eskimos as they were and hated to see them spoiled by whites. Maurice Flint writes, "John Turner in his wilderness environment was not only to be opposed by the forces of heathendom alone but also at times the influence of white civilization were not conducive to the progress of his missionary work." Captain J.E. Bernier wrote in 1910, "I cannot too strongly emphasize the duty of the white man to save a race they have done so much to destroy." Bernier was referring, of course, to the contact the Eskimos had had with the whalers around Baffin Island.

Flint cites one incident in which Turner was dealt with deceitfully by white men. It was on Christmas day. Turner and his missionary companion were invited to the festivities at the Hudson's Bay Company post. Turner declined but the invitation was pressed and finally when it was made clear that in deference to the missionaries there would be no smoking or drinking during the meal, the invitation was accepted. Before the meal was over first one man and then another excused himself and did not return. The longer they were away the more suspicious Turner became. It seems he sensed something was wrong. He excused himself, went back to the mission house and found the two men with two Eskimo girls the missionary had been caring for. The girls were orphans. The men were unprincipled. This kind of thing incensed Jack Turner and certainly made him unpopular with some white men living in the north. In his diary Turner actually says, "Missionaries are by no means popular generally speaking." It was inevitable that his rigidly enforced code of morals would meet with both opposition and criticism, a fact that daunted him not at all. Bishop Archibald Lang Fleming, in his book *Archibald the Arctic,* * says of Turner, " . . . he feared neither man nor beast nor cold nor death. He knew right well that his was a lonely pilgrimage in the frozen realms of Arctic Canada. He was one of the few people I have known who would have gone to the stake cheerfully for his convictions."

Turner was unique among the hardy men who forced a living out of the hostile Arctic. His travels were phenomenal. Year after year he would go far in excess of a thousand miles and during one memorable season he went close to four thousand miles. In 1941 he made a trip from Igloolik to Fort Ross over a route that has probably never been travelled before or since. That year Jack Doyle was on patrol in the Igloolik area when he ran into Jack Turner. Canon Turner was, at that time, planning to head out to Fort Ross. A day after he left Igloolik Doyle followed him and caught him up at the Fury and Hecla Strait. They hunted together for a little while, got a couple of seals and then Turner said that he was going on to Fort Ross.

"I'm going to go in as direct a line as possible," he explained coolly and confidently.

"That's impossible," Jack expostulated. "You'll get into floe ice and come to grief for sure."

Jack's words fell on deaf ears. Turner had made up his mind. The journey he contemplated was horrifying. Ice is always on the move in the Gulf of Boothia. Eskimos did not travel the way he planned.

Doyle said to him, "Well, you do as you like. I'm not going to take any chances."

Doyle and Turner separated. Doyle went up the west coast of the Brodeur Peninsula. Turner hit out across the Gulf of

* Fleming, Archibald Lang, *Archibald the Arctic*, Saunders of Toronto Limited, 1965.

Boothia. He went alone and he made it. How he got across no one will ever know. It took him about a week or ten days and during that time he was adrift on floating ice, had to manhandle the sledge over ice ridges and fight his way through wet snow. He reached Fort Ross long before Doyle and was on his way again prior to Doyle's arrival there.

"He left a few days before I got there," said Jack Doyle, "and went down to Pelly Bay, to give Father Henry some competition, I think."

It is certain that Jack Turner went down to Pelly Bay but whether or not it was that year or the following one is not clear. According to Maurice Flint, the journey as far as King William Island was not made until the 1941-42 season. Whichever year it was that he went he had a rugged trip. By the time he reached Pelly Bay his dogs were starving and he too was hungry.

Father Henry met him.

Pelly Bay was a Roman Catholic settlement. The Roman Church had done all the pioneer Christian work in that place and not until Turner arrived had a Protestant church attempted an invasion of that particular area. The spearhead of the Roman Church's advance there had been Father Henry. Father Henry was the stuff of which pioneers are made. He had done incredible things in that barren stretch of Arctic coast. Often alone for years, he had become an integral part of that Arctic area. Almost singlehandedly he had made contact with the very primitive Eskimos of the Pelly Bay region and almost singlehandedly he had built among them a stone church, now a famous landmark in the Arctic. It was the 30th of May, 1935, when Father Henry arrived there. He had taken six weeks to make the journey with his Eskimo guides from Repulse Bay. Armand Clabout describes Father Henry's arrival. "The little group of travellers reached the final heights overlooking the east coast of Pelly Bay . . . . Father Henry stopped for a long moment to contemplate this frigid scenery of the barren land. The Bay was held under its heavy shell of ice. Myriads of tiny islands spread all the way to the horizon like little grey pegs protruding through the snow. In the distance, chains of rocky mountains undulated like serpents on the glistening snow . . . . This was Pelly Bay. The goal had been reached."

The way was not smooth for Father Henry. He was laughed at when he tried to catch fish with a net. Spears were better. He was often hungry and even had to hide the small amount of fish he had been able to catch so that he would not have to share it with those who had much more. During the first winter his breakfast was often only a cold cup of tea. When Canon Turner met Father Henry he was meeting a man who was no stranger to hardship and a man who certainly had been motivated by a desire to serve his Lord. However, when they met they were cast in the role of opponents. On the one hand was the Anglican zealot, belonging to a missionary society scarcely as old as himself and on the other hand was the priest with the tradition of the Roman Church and liturgy of the Roman Church written deep in his soul. They were both dedicated men.

Turner moved in towards the settlement. No one greeted him. Even the dogs seemed silent. Father Henry had got wind of his arrival. He was ready. Robed in his priestly vestments, Henry strode down towards Turner, a lone black figure in a landscape of white. A short distance from the priest Canon Turner stopped. Henry spoke.

"If you will agree not to propagate your message here and leave without disturbing the peace and faith of the native people I will find meat for you and your dogs."

There was a note of threat in his voice. Their eyes met, the eyes of two men who had to do battle because they held so fast to their convictions.

"Sir," replied Turner, "not only will I preach here the gospel of the Lord Jesus Christ to every single native I can but when I am finished in this place I intend to go to Gjoa Haven and spread the message there too. I have no need of your meat. The Lord will provide."

It was a great moment and a sad one. For seconds silence hung between them. Then Father Henry turned on his heels and strode back to his dwelling and began to make preparations to go to Gjoa Haven. This man, Turner, was threatening to upset so much that he had worked for. With anger in his heart he drove his dogs to Gjoa Haven.

Turner did as he said he was going to do. He preached the gospel. He opposed, with a bitterness which seemed unreasonable, the activities of the Roman Catholic Church. Having stayed in Pelly Bay for a short time he left in pursuit of Father Henry. A little way out of the settlement he shot four polar bears and thus had more than sufficient meat for himself and his dogs. Deep inside, Turner was glad that Father Henry had gone to Gjoa Haven because he did not know the way and the fresh trail was an enormous help.

Canon Turner went everywhere he could and everywhere he went he had only one ambition and that was to convert men and women to Jesus Christ. It is sad that the two branches of the Christian Church in the Northwest Territories could not have worked in harmony.

Turner not only confronted the Roman Catholic Church but the Government of Canada as well. Under the Migratory Birds Act it was, and still is, impossible for the natives to molest any of the geese that come in the thousands to nest on Bylot Island. The geese are in the vicinity of Pond Inlet only when they are out of season. By the time it is legal to shoot them they have been on their way south for weeks. Turner decided to test the law. He and Maurice Flint, who was in Pond assisting Turner at the time, went over to Bylot Island and collected a number of eggs. They ate the eggs and then took the shells to Jack Doyle.

"Here," said Turner, "I've broken the law. Charge me."

Neither Doyle nor Len Corey, the other R.C.M.P. officer, had a great deal of detachment experience but Jack had had a little more than Len so he laid the charge. Eventually when the ship came in Turner was brought up before Major McKeand and fined $5.00. Somebody dug down and paid his fine.

An outside newspaper got hold of this story and headlined it, "Missionary Shoots Goose While Nesting".

"It wasn't that way at all," says Doyle. "He just collected the eggs to show how stupid the law was. The law is fine in the south but an ass in the north."

In 1944 Canon Turner was married. His wife came over from England and the wedding took place at Pond Inlet on August 29th, 1944. They did not stay in Pond Inlet but went to Moffet Inlet where Turner had built a small outpost. There was not a settlement there but Turner chose to build in that location because it afforded a place of quiet and a place where he would be able to instruct the Eskimos in the things of God without any of the distractions usually present in a settlement. The Moffet Inlet house was to be the centre for serious Bible study and translation work too. This house Turner built in 1929. It was greatly loved by him and it was here he did his last hours of work.

On September 24th, 1947, the weather was unsuitable for outside work so Jack continued with jobs inside the house. While he worked in the attic two young Eskimo girls, Rebecca and Elizabeth, were busy replenishing the water supply with pails of broken ice. As they worked they spotted a seal in the shallow water near the shore. They shouted the news to Turner. He quickly grabbed his .22 rifle, which he knew was in need of minor repairs, and hurried after the seal. On his return he met Elizabeth carrying a large pail of ice. John tucked the rifle under his left arm and helped Elizabeth with her burden. They mounted the steps to the house and just as he reached the top step the rifle went off. The bullet went through his head and lodged at the base of his skull. He fell backwards down the steps and lay unconscious on the snow.

He lived for more than two months and died in Winnipeg. A remarkable air rescue operation was carried out to bring Canon Turner to the finest medical help available. But Turner was beyond the help of mortal man and died on December 7th.

Maurice Flint says, with a touch of poetry, "No longer do the cruel biting winds tear into his flesh or the cold drifting snows blind his vision. No longer can fatigue destroy his vitality or cruel sinful men belittle his beauty. He rests from his labours. He did his work well."

Turner is now a legend. Turner, the "real man".

8
Arctic Bay

The tiny settlement at Arctic Bay lies on the east coast of Admiralty Inlet. The approach to the settlement down Admiralty Inlet and Adams Sound is past sheer cliffs of sandstone and limestone, buff, sepia, red and white, rising from heights varying from 800 to 1200 feet. The settlement itself is set in an amphitheatre of encircling hills, open only to the inlet. It is beautiful country, a land of plunging rivers, beetling cliffs and hanging glaciers.

The origin of its name is a matter for some doubt. According to "Community Sketches", specially prepared by the Government for the Government, it was named after the Government ship, C.G.S. *Arctic*, which, under the command of J.E. Bernier, was frozen in there during the winter of 1910-11. However, in the book, *Arctic Canada from the Air*, it is maintained that the Bay was named after the whaling ship *Arctic* which visited there in 1872 under Captain W. Adams. Support is given to the latter contention in *Settlements of the Northwest Territories*, a series of volumes especially produced for the Advisory Commission on the Development of Government in the Northwest Territories.

It was to this country that Alan Robertson Scott came in 1936 to open the Hudson's Bay Company store. Strictly speaking, he re-opened the post because in the middle of the twenties the Company had established a post there and called it Tatkik the moon. It had to be closed in 1927 in accordance with a new Arctic Islands Preserve Act which came into force at that time.

When the Eastern Arctic Patrol had called at Arctic Bay in 1937 Alan Scott had asked the Hudson's Bay Company manager for permission to go outside to get married. He had an arrangement with a girl back in Peterhead, he explained. The manager refused. "All traders and post managers have to stand to their jobs this year. I'm afraid you're going to have to stay here."

That was enough for Alan. If he could not go outside to get a wife then he would bring the bride-to-be to Arctic Bay. The moment the chance arrived he wrote a rapid note to ask Eileen if she would come to Arctic Bay and be his wife.

"I'm coming," she wired back.

The message eventually reached Alan in Morse code via the radio station at Nottingham Island. Alan was thrilled. It would be a year before she arrived but at least it was now certain she both wanted him and was willing to come into the far north. The year went slowly by. Alan kept busy but he kept one eye on the calendar too. He crossed the days off like a soldier awaiting demobilization. Finally, summer came. The ice moved out and the day of Eileen's arrival was but a month or so away. Alan busied himself with all kinds of scrubbing-up chores. He painted. He mended. He organized and arranged. He even made curtains for the windows.

When Eileen's arrival was a matter of a mere two weeks or so away, Alan's routine was suddenly interrupted and for several days he hardly thought of her. Living in a tiny mission at Arctic Bay at that time was the Reverend Father Cochard. He had been on his own there for a few years and three weeks before the *Nascopie* was due to arrive in 1938 he became very ill. For several days he lay in his tent alone, without heat or warm food, too ill to move and too sick to help himself. It was early in August, a time when the weather, although not bitterly cold, was still cool.

Alan Scott found him. He noticed the absence of smoke from the priest's tent and then he realized he had not seen Father Cochard around recently so he asked one or two of the natives about him and they seemed to know nothing.

"I'd better go and see how the Father is," Alan said to the clerk as he strode off towards the priest's tent.

Alan was in for a shock. Father Cochard looked close to death. He was in great pain, quite unable to lie still for a minute, writhing on the bed. Alan asked him a few questions, made him as comfortable as he could, and then went back to the Hudson's

Bay Company post.

"We'll have to bring Cochard over here. He's very ill," Alan explained to his clerk. "I need you to help me get him over here. As soon as we've done this I'll radio for help. It's just possible the Roman Catholic mission will be able to send their aircraft. I don't think he'll last until the ship gets here."

They went and fetched Father Cochard. Alan did his best to ease his pain and settle him down and the moment radio schedule time arrived he asked for help. "Father Julien Cochard very ill for 9 days. Temperature 105 degrees. Severe pain left side. Takes no nourishment. Please help." This message went to Nottingham Island and was relayed to Bishop Clabout on the *Nascopie*. At that time the *Nascopie* was in Churchill preparing for its voyage to northern Baffin Island. A few hours after the message reached the ship the news filtered through to Father Schulte, the flying priest. Immediately, he volunteered to go. If gasoline had been delivered the previous year to Igloolik as he had requested then he would have a fuel supply close enough to Arctic Bay to make the trip. Igloolik is 270 miles by air from Arctic Bay. Father Schulte was able to establish for certain that there was gasoline at Igloolik by using photographs that had been taken of the settlement since the visit of the supply ship the previous year. Having examined the pictures he set off. He carried with him Brother Beaudoin, his mechanic. When Father Schulte left Churchill it was his intention to pick up Dr. Melling at Chesterfield Inlet but Dr. Melling was sick with a throat infection and unable to go. He gave Father Schulte instructions and some medications and wished him success.

The journey Father Schulte embarked on was no piece of cake. Navigation is tricky in that part of the world. Maps were hopelessly inadequate and inaccurate and no one had ever before flown that route. This was a hazardous enterprise but life was at stake. Father Schulte was an extremely competent pilot and he managed to get to Arctic Bay on the second attempt. The first time, headwinds had forced him to return to Igloolik, refuel and snatch a few hours sleep. By the time he reached Arctic Bay two days had elapsed since the radio message had been received at Churchill. However, Father Schulte was in time. Father Cochard was terribly ill but still hanging onto life. The pain in his side was unrelieved and, to add to his discomfort, his back, elbows and legs were covered with bedsores. For days he had had nothing to eat but took, with the gratitude of a hungry child, the orange Father Schulte offered him. Oranges! It had been four years since he had seen one.

Alan Scott was more than relieved to help load Father Cochard on the plane. It had been a terrible strain watching this man get worse and being unable to do anything for him. He was glad to learn later that Father Cochard reached Chesterfield safely and there began an effective period of recuperation.

It was this same Father Schulte who came under suspicion shortly after the Second World War was declared. It was rumoured that the priest was working for the Germans. Alan Scott recalls one strange incident when Father Schulte would not give him a lift to Churchill. At this time Alan Scott was working at Chesterfield. "It seems odd," said Alan, thirty years later, "The request I made was simple and fair. I expected him to say 'Certainly. Come along', but he didn't want me. Shortly after that I received orders to destroy all the gas caches he had set in my area. Orders like this went to all the Hudson's Bay Company post managers in the area he flew. I have an idea that the day I wanted a ride he had a rendezvous with the enemy."

There may have been no truth in the rumours that circulated concerning Father Schulte but they were certainly believed by many.

When Alan waved goodbye to him in 1938 his mind was not on affairs of international importance but upon the now imminent arrival of Eileen. When the excitement of the priest's evacuation had died down time began to drag. Not so for Eileen. Everything for her was new, interesting and full of adventure. She was glad she had decided to say yes to Alan's proposal. It had been a big decision. This was a big step for a Scottish girl to take, a step she was sure was the right one although, at the time, her mother thought she was crazy. On July 20th, 1938, she left Scotland in the *Letitia.* Before she actually embarked her mother and relatives, her friends and acquaintances all filled her with good advice. "Never speak to a strange man," said one well-wisher. "If any man speaks to you, walk away," said another of the worldly wise. "Never put your handbag down." "Watch out for your suitcases." And so on. She was so loaded down with advice that she could barely think straight. Thirty years later she said, commenting on the ocean trip, "I walked around in a self-made prison for the first three of four days. The ship must have been half way across the Atlantic before I began to act like a human being."

They were only about two days out when the inevitable happened. A strange man spoke to her. "I was standing by the deck rail looking out to sea," she says, "when an elderly man came alongside me. He looked at me. In fact, he frankly looked at my face. I turned away from him, shot sidelong glances in his direction and wished he'd go away. After a while, the man, who didn't seem to realize he was getting the cold shoulder, said to me, 'How old are you?' 'What's it to you how old I am?' I replied and stalked off. Gee I was pleased with myself. That was my first difficult encounter—victoriously negotiated. Dirty old man, trying to get fresh with me. Later that same day the captain asked me to be hostess at a tea he was giving and lo and behold when I arrived at the tea I was introduced to this old gentleman. It was Ralph Parsons, the Fur Trade Commissioner for the Hudson's Bay Company in Canada."

For many years Mr. Parsons had been the key man in the Arctic for the Hudson's Bay Company. J.W. Anderson, writing in his book, *Fur Trader's Story**, says, "Ralph Parsons was the man responsible for the development of the fur trade with the Eskimos in the Eastern and Central Arctic. He was known at the height of his northern Arctic march as the King of Baffin Land."

Eileen did not know that.

By the time she reached Arctic Bay she was a much more poised young woman. The *Star Weekly* told the story of Alan and Eileen's wedding in an article published on March 1st, 1941. "It was Sunday when the *Nascopie* hove off Arctic Bay post. And there plunging out to meet her from the shore was the post manager's little engined whaleboat with the bridegroom aboard. But you can't marry on Sunday, bishop or no bishop, so the *Nascopie* had to lie an extra day, while the scows were lowered

---

* Anderson, J.W., *Fur Trader's Story*, The Ryerson Press, 1961.

and the bales went ashore and the bales came off from shore, full of white fox, blue fox, ivory and whale hide . . . .

"In her wedding gown and veil Eileen was married to Alan aboard the *Nascopie* by Bishop Fleming. The wedding cake was cut and found seasoned and rich with all its journey from Scotland. The wedding was at 10 a.m. The ship sailed at 12 noon. There were joyous and hasty wedding celebrations aboard the ship and then the bride and groom went down the companionway into the whaleboat and ashore. That was Monday, Aug. 29, 1938. By Friday the first snow fell."

Soon after the *Nascopie* left, Eileen did what nearly every other woman would have done under similar circumstances—she wept. But she soon got over that and settled into Arctic life. The only things she really did not like were the Eskimo dogs. They terrified her. Not long after she arrived there Canon Turner brought her a little pup. It was a bitch, just a few weeks old. Eileen loved that little dog. Everywhere she went she carried it with her. One day she went for a walk along the beach. The pup was in her arms. The Eskimo dogs were not tied up and, as she passed a native shack, they got up and came towards her. In a moment she was in the centre of a menacing circle. Teeth bared, hair up, tails down and heads lowered, the dogs gradually moved in on her. It was a dangerous moment. Alan, who was far behind Eileen, yelled to her, "Throw the pup away!" Eileen clutched it tighter. "Throw the pup away!" Eileen was numb. She knew they would tear the pup to pieces and she knew too that if they jumped her and she fell they would tear her to pieces too. She found her voice at last and screamed. Nearby Eskimo hunters heard her and raced to her aid. Alan arrived almost as they did and together they beat the dogs off. And they really beat them. No quarter was given at all. It was no easy job settling that pack of dogs now that their blood was up.

"Here," said Alan, "in future when you go out, take this with you," and handed her a big ivory cane with a wicked looking knob on it. It was quite a weapon. Eileen had such a scare from that pack of dogs that from then on she never took any chances. Not long after that she was strolling around the camp when a dog came near her and lifted its head to look at her. It gazed at her in such a way that it scared her and she promptly banged it on the skull and knocked it cold.

"When I think back on it," says Eileen, "it was cruel but I was scared and not prepared to take any chances."

Eileen was wise. More than a few people have been savaged by dogs in the north and some have been killed. The wife of R.C.M.P. Sergeant Clay was attacked by dogs at Chesterfield Inlet and died shortly after. It was a terrible moment in the police work of the north. At the time of the attack Sergeant Clay was away from the settlement on patrol. When he returned an emergency operation with inadequate tools was carried out on Mrs. Clay. One of her legs was amputated but the attempt to save her failed. Eskimo dogs are not pets and are never to be trifled with. It was well for Eileen that she learned this lesson quickly and thoroughly.

Eileen was not going to be caught again. She never went out unprepared. On one occasion she was washing dishes near the window when she saw a dog coming towards the house. It was summertime and the window was open. Eileen watched the dog. She watched it carefully because at that time there was a rather virulent disease going through the dogs and many were dying. The disease caused the dogs to run round in circles and behave oddly in other ways. When this particular dog was close to the house Eileen shouted and yelled at him. He took no notice. Eileen was anxious to get him away because nearly every morning they were finding dead dogs lying about the house. Right at her elbow Eileen had a basin of very hot water. "I thought I'd slosh this water on him," Eileen relates, "I picked up the basin of nearly boiling water and swooshed it on top of this poor animal. When I threw it I did not realize it was so hot. What a panic! I felt the cruelest person ever born. That poor half dead scalded dog went howling through the settlement as if demented. He got better, though. It must have done something to him. He didn't die of the disease."

One of the times Eileen looked forward to and yet dreaded was the first Christmas. Homesickness would certainly be her companion and yet when the time came she prepared for it and had a marvelous time. More than thirty years later she remembered it vividly.

"My first Christmas was marvelous. We had a big party for

the Eskimos. Alan made a Christmas tree for them with a broom handle and he bored holes in it and stuck sticks in it. I bound each part with green wool and made stars and baubles to hang all over the tree. We gave little parcels to all the kids too. These also hung on the tree to make it look even more attractive. We gave them sweeties and brooches and other stuff we had in the store, baubles and trinkets and the likes. Come Christmas day we had a great big meal. We put one big table in the kitchen, clearing everything else out. For four or five days previous to Christmas I baked caraway buns, doughnuts and bread. I just put all these in sacks and took them outside to freeze. For a main course we made a huge boilerful of caribou tongues and beans, supplemented with canned bacon and tomato sauce. What it amounted to was a huge stew pot full of everything we could think of. For dessert I made a big plum duff, old fashioned plum duff, the kind designed to fill you up. How the Eskimos came and how they ate! They even finished off the bottles of sauce. We put bottles of tomato ketchup on the table and there wasn't even a drop of ketchup left when they were finished. I gave them all a plate and a big spoon and the pot in the middle of the table and they helped themselves. They washed it all down with quarts of tea and belched with great satisfaction. After the meal we danced. I shall never forget it. They smelled like blubber—ten months old. The women put on clean print dresses over their fur pants but the men, when they started dancing, they started stripping. First they pulled off one parka and then another and then the fleece lined shirt they sometimes wear, that came off and I was up dancing with them. I'd hang onto their arms to be given a swing and they'd be slippery with grease and sweat and everything. It was wonderful. The atmosphere was unbelievable but everyone was so happy. To climax the evening everyone went outside to the beach and quickly a huge bonfire was built and lit. It was a glorious blaze with which to end the best Christmas I've ever had. Christmases in civilization are tame after one like that."

It was not many weeks prior to that Christmas that Eileen had had a bad scare. She had, by that time, settled in fairly well and was beginning to make friends with the Eskimos. She felt at ease with them all. Alan did not think she needed him around all the time anymore so he often went seal hunting. He had a dog team to feed and needed the meat. On one occasion he had gone away for the day and Eileen was alone at the post doing her ordinary household duties when suddenly she looked up and saw an Eskimo man looking through the window at her. She could not remember having seen him before. He had long lank black hair hanging down to his shoulders. He looked somehow shifty-eyed. The man stared at her. Eileen smiled a signal. The man made no response. After several seconds of deadpan staring the Eskimo turned away from the window, walked round the side of the store and entered the house. Eileen heard him come in the door. She listened as he strode across the kitchen and came into the living room where she was standing. He smelled strongly of walrus. Eileen's nose twitched at the stench. Without looking at her he walked over to the rocking chair, gave it a little push and watched it rock. His head moved in time with the chair. All was silent. The chair stopped moving and he sat down. With a push of his heels he swung the chair again, backwards and forwards like a granny at her knitting. He did not speak. Eileen broke the spell, "Tea? Do you want tea?" Her voice was taut. He made no answer. Just sat there rocking, tugging at his long black hair as if he was pulling nits out. Eventually Eileen went out and brewed tea. She was brewing it for a man who had stood trial for murder. It was as well she did not know that. The tea was soon ready and she took it in to him, a big steaming mug of it. Still he did not speak. He sucked at the tea and, holding the mug in one hand, continued to tug at his hair with the other. Eileen watched and waited. At last the tea was finished and she asked him to go. She signaled him to go. He took no notice. "Scram!" she said in an unladylike fashion. It had no effect. "Get lost!" she said with more determination. He did not move. Finally Eileen went in search of one of the girls who often came to help her in the kitchen and this girl managed to persuade him to leave. She knew him well, of course, "That's Ahteetah," she said to Eileen.

Ahteetah was a difficult man. He frequently created problems for Alan. He came in one day hauling a big bunch of fur and it was a great pile and it was all dirty, very dirty. There were foxes that had not been skinned and those that had looked a mess. He dumped them all on the floor of the post for Alan to look at.

"Do you want to trade fur?" asked Alan.

"Mm hm," grunted Ahteetah.

"Then, you'd better clean this lot up. I'm not going to accept it like that. If you don't clean it up that's fine but I'm not going to trade with you."

This made Ahteetah angry. He sprang across the pile of fur at Alan and took him by the throat. Instantly Alan's Scottish ire was raised. He shook Ahteetah free, grabbed him by the back of the neck and the seat of the pants and threw him out of the store.

"Don't you come back in this store again," he said to the sprawling man. "If you have fur to trade, send your women to do it for you."

This was a very insulting thing to suggest to Ahteetah. It was bad to suggest that a woman do a man's work.

"The quicker he learns I'm boss around here the better," Alan said as he went back into the store. The remark was directed to Ahteetah's two grown sons who had witnessed the whole encounter. They said nothing and did not seem to disapprove of Alan's actions. Silently they took out Ahteetah's pile of fur—and what a pile it was! He must have had hundreds of pelts. Alan wanted those skins.

Ahteetah must have had some second thoughts because after a while Alan saw him going off to collect some stone to use for cleaning the furs. The stones he brought back, according to Alan Scott, were slightly phosphorescent. Whatever they were they were particularly good for cleaning fur. Not many days after he had fetched the load of stones Ahteetah turned up at the store again with his fur. He did not send his women. If Alan Scott had insisted on that his pride would have been stung too much. Alan examined it all carefully.

"This is what it's worth," said Alan and as he spoke he spread out in front of him the amount of money he would give for the fur. Ahteetah's eyes gleamed and then Alan Scott asked, "How much do you owe the post at Pond Inlet?" Ahteetah's face fell. "Thirty fox." Alan Scott picked through the pile of pelts and lifted out thirty of the best, gave him credit for them and then paid him for the rest.

On the first occasion Ahteetah only brought in about 40 furs but then he kept bringing them in. He was a good trapper and had been a very successful one. Gradually Ahteetah became more at ease and began to make protestations of friendship to Alan Scott. Everytime they met he would shake him by the hand and say, "You my friend. You my buddy." One day Alan told him that he was planning a trip to Igloolik and Ahteetah volunteered to set out meat caches for him. When Scott made the trip he found that Ahteetah had kept his word for all the caches were in order, all the way to Igloolik. However, the course of their friendship was not to be smooth for Scott was to cross him one more time. While the Scotts were at Arctic Bay their first child was born, a little girl, Evelyn. She was quite the event in the community. None of the natives there had ever seen a white baby girl, or even a white baby. One day when Ahteetah came in Evelyn was sitting in the room. He was carrying a large bundle of fur. Throwing this on the floor and looking at the little girl he said, "Me take." He wanted to buy her with pelts.

Scott said, "That's not enough."

"How much you want?"

"There's not enough fur in the north to buy her," Scott explained. "She's not for sale."

Ahteetah did not like this. It seemed as if Alan Scott was saying to him you are not good enough to be her father. This angered him and he took a long time to get over it.

"The whole episode was a little strange," Alan Scott says in retrospect, "because he wanted a girl and girls do not figure too largely in an Eskimo's way of life."

9

Pangnirtung

Prior to his stay in Arctic Bay, Alan Scott had spent about ten years in the Eastern Arctic. It was 1929 when, as a young man of twenty three, he had felt the urge to leave his native Scotland. He was fed up. Life lacked excitement. He itched for change and adventure. The farm job he had was not challenging enough nor were the prospects bright enough. His mother urged him to join the police force. She wanted him to be a policeman because his father, who had died when he was a young boy, had been a policeman. Alan was not too keen but he did apply and actually went to sit for the necessary examinations in London. On his way through Aberdeen he read in the local newspaper the Hudson's Bay Company's advertisement for young men to work in Canada's north. The advertisement held his attention and gripped his imagination. He applied but so did at least 65 others. They were all interviewed and Alan was among the selected few. The day before Alan set sail for Canada he received a letter from London accepting him for the police force. His mother pleaded with him, "Please go to the police. Dinna' go to that foreign country awa' there in the cold." Alan, who already had an older brother in America, was unmoved by her pleading.

"Now, Mum, look, I'd rather go. If I don't like it I can always come back."

Alan had made up his mind and Alan was not one to vacillate. Like many before him, Alan was sent to Montreal. There he met Mr. Ralph Parsons—the gentleman his wife was to meet eight years later aboard the *Letitia*.

"During the time we were in Montreal," Alan Scott recalls, "We, that is all the new HBC boys, worked very hard helping to pack boxes for the *Nascopie*. We worked six to seven weeks on that before the *Nascopie* was ready to sail with us on board.

"Before the ship left, Ralph Parsons invited all of us to a rather sumptuous meal. It was much higher class stuff than any of us were used to. At the beginning of the meal he asked us what kind of wine we would like. I said I'd like a nice sweet wine. Parsons did not take kindly to that suggestion. 'What do you fellows know about wine, anyway?' he asked, 'You boys don't know anything about wine. I'll order the wine.' So he ordered three or four bottles of his own selection. It eventually arrived, was tasted and served. I took one sip of the wine and that was one sip too many. The stuff was just like vinegar. 'Don't you like it?' asked Parsons. 'Sorry, no I don't,' I said. I said it with a little too much emphasis and then felt embarrassed. I then noticed that nobody else liked it either. Leastways no Scotsman liked it. The only person who drank it was the lone Englishman. 'Maybe you should drink everyone else's if you like it so much,' said Mr. Parsons to the Englishman. I think he said it a little wickedly. The poor Englishman drank the works, said he liked it and vomited comprehensively afterwards."

When the *Nascopie* left Montreal Alan Scott still did not know what post he would be stationed at. The ship went to camp after camp. Stores were offloaded and furs were onloaded. Alan was kept busy with strenuous manual work. After they had passed each post Alan began to think the next one would be his but it was not. He had started to think that he was not going to be put anywhere at all but taken back to Montreal. Finally the boat nosed its way into Pangnirtung Fiord. "Well, lad, this is the last post," Parsons said to him. "I hope you'll like it. If you don't like it, well, we'll take you out again."

Alan liked it.

Pangnirtung is a magnificent place, the fiord strikingly beautiful. It boasts some of the finest mountain scenery to be seen on Baffin Island. Behind the settlement rises the Mount Duval and two and a half miles across the fiord the bleak, dark cliffs of unnamed peaks stretch towards the skies.

The fiord itself acts as a natural wind tunnel that on many occasions has caused memorable gales. G.C. Barr, who was in the R.C.M.P. stationed at Pangnirtung, recalls a few of them.

"We used to call it Pang's Effort," he says, "I've seen days when the wind would roll 45 gallon drums around like beach balls in a breeze. The worst wind I ever witnessed took place in the late 40's. Behind our warehouse we had a small backhouse full of reindeer hides. These were sent over from Reindeer Station, in the Western Arctic, as relief supplies. Pangnirtung Eskimos were not too keen on these skins. I don't think they disliked them because they were reindeer so much as because they came from Eskimos on the other side of the world. They did not want charity. So these skins were left year after year, piled high in this old backhouse. One night a gale began to blow. It hurled itself on the settlement as if wanting to destroy everything. It picked up the small storage room and tossed it, full of skins, into the air and carried it some 28 paces. When it landed it disintegrated. Then the wind had sport with the skins. Helterskelter they rolled, tumbled and flew through the settlement. A few days later Eskimos were bringing skins in from five miles away."

It's not hard to imagine what a wind like that can do to a tent or to a frail Eskimo tupik.

Wind has frequently been a problem in Pangnirtung and, since the era of flying, has been a special hazard to pilots. There are such serious downdrafts near the settlement that light planes are not advised to attempt a landing should there be a wind of more than twelve miles an hour. At least one aeroplane has come to grief in the fiord and for some time was one of the mysteries of the area.

In 1958 Corporal Barr was some way down the fiord visiting a small winter camp when he noticed a piece of aircraft was being used as part of the floor in one of the Eskimo snowhouses.

"Wherever did you get that?" he asked. "It's a piece of an aeroplane, isn't it?"

"Yes, you're right. It's from an aeroplane. I got it from the wreck in Abraham Bay."

"Wreck! Abraham Bay? What wreck?"

"Oh, there's been an aeroplane wreck up there for years. In summertime at low tide you can see the tail fin sticking out of the water. I've seen it many times."

Corporal Barr took note of as much information as possible

and opened an investigation. He went by dog team to Abraham Bay and managed to find some parts of the aircraft. He took all the parts back to Pangnirtung and managed to reassemble part of the aileron. From these recovered parts experts were able to identify the aircraft as a Beechcraft, a small twin-engined plane used frequently during the Second World War. American authorities were informed of this discovery and they disclosed that in the early forties a Beechcraft had gone missing between Chrystal 2 and Chrystal 3. These were the names given to the airstrips at Frobisher and Padloping. Although this solution seemed adequate, the R.C.M.P. were instructed to visit the site of the crash and conduct dragging operations. These were undertaken by Constable Alexander a year or so after Corporal Barr had been transferred from Pangnirtung but the operations were unsuccessful.

The file was closed with the fairly firm conviction that the identity of the aircraft had been satisfactorily made. Further investigations were not thought worthwhile.

The very first aircraft ever to land at Pangnirtung was checked in and out by Constable Hugh Margetts. The aeroplane was flown by Parker D. Cramer, an adventurous American. He and his companion, Pickett, flew up from the States to Canada and then moved on to Greenland, aiming ultimately to fly into Germany. On the way they stopped at a number of tiny Eskimo settlements in order to refuel, among them at Pangnirtung. In 1930 there was no aviation fuel, as such, available there, but the aircraft Cramer was flying was powered by a diesel engine which would burn fuel oil. Cramer had deliberately chosen that kind of engine because he figured he would be able to obtain suitable fuel at scattered Hudson's Bay Company posts. He was right, although Margetts had to do a lot of scrounging to round up enough for him at Pangnirtung. He went to the HBC post, the Anglican hospital and to the doctor, himself. In all he managed to gather barely sufficient for Cramer's needs. Cramer, however, was very pleased with Margett's efforts.

It had looked for a little while as though Pangnirtung was going to be the end of the trip. When the plane touched down on the water of the fiord it hit rather hard and some damage was done to the propeller of the main generator. It was slung below a wing and simply driven by an exposed propeller. The large supply of, for those days, very sophisticated radio equipment was dependent on the operation of this generator. Cramer told Margetts his problems. Margetts was able to help him. The previous year he had had a new Model A Ford sent in to Pangnirtung. It had arrived packaged in pieces and Margetts and a few others had a great game assembling it. Hugh Margetts' original scheme had been to convert it into a snowmobile of some sort. This was not successful although he did get the car running and used it for some time to haul fresh water from the river to the detachment. A road was actually cleared as far as the Duval River just for this stripped down Ford. In later years the engine was used in a variety of boats and the remains of the car hauled behind a dog team in both summer and winter. It was probably the only six dog-powered Ford in the world. The presence of this car proved a real asset to Cramer.

"I think," said Margetts, "you can probably do something with the fan from our Ford."

"You have a car?"

"There she is," said Margetts, taking him to its station by the detachment.

It did not take them long to remove the fan and start adjusting it for the generator. Cramer was very handy and skillful with machinery. He cut the fan, twisted it and carefully adjusted the pitch. After a lot of work Cramer was happy.

"I'll give it a try."

Margetts watched the experiment.

"It works fine," said Cramer when he touched down and came ashore.

He was really pleased with himself then, although his companion was nothing like so delighted. He had been trying to persuade Cramer to abandon the trip. Alan Scott, who was working for the HBC at the time, remembers distinctly that there was tension between the two men. He says, "Pickett would stand around with a vacant look on his face and leave all the talking to Cramer. They seldom spoke to each other and when they did they argued. I remember them arguing, for example, about the route. I never thought they would make it. Things were really stacked against them when they left Pangnirtung. The R.C.M.P.

and I, and one or two others, tried hard to persuade Cramer to give up the venture." Like Hugh Margetts, Alan Scott remembers how they scurried around for fuel. "At that time we were very low on coal oil and they wanted, if I remember correctly, three drums of fuel. All we could find was about two and a half drums and it was not in very good shape. The drums had been lying around for years and had drawn a lot of condensation so a good part of the contents was undoubtedly water. I offered Cramer a chamois to filter it into the tanks but he said it would take too long. 'Just pour it in,' he said. So that's what we did."

When they took off they had been in Pangnirtung four or five days. They didn't have enough fuel for safety, and it was poor quality. Then too there was a rift between the two. Things looked bad.

"I really don't think they'll make it," said Alan to Margetts as the plane slid out of the fiord.

Scott was right. The aeroplane crashed not far from the Orkney Islands, on the last leg of their flight to Great Britain. It was tough luck for by then, as a matter of fact, the worst of their trip was over.

A year after Cramer had left for Europe Alan Scott began to wish there was a quick and easy way to get to Scotland and back or even to and from a large city in Canada. He was the subject of a minor but irritating accident. Air transportation would have been a real help for him. When Alan had joined the Hudson's Bay Company in Scotland one of the questions he was asked was, "Are those your own teeth?" to which he had replied, very firmly, "Aye. They're my own." But the question had been misunderstood. When the query was made the questioner simply wanted to know if Alan had false teeth. Alan, however, thought they wanted to know if they were paid for and only the previous day Alan had paid in full the bill for his new set of false teeth. The denture was most definitely his. "Yes," he reiterated, "the teeth are mine."

This misunderstanding had repercussions. One morning in the summer of 1932, when the skies were blue and the sun was shining and the air was crisp and clean, Alan Scott was out on a whaling trip. When he awoke he went down to the net he had set the previous night and pulled out a few Arctic char.

"What's better than a good fish breakfast?" thought Alan as he walked back to his tent. The fish looked delicious. The Arctic char is a beautiful fish at any time but to a hungry man it looks even better than beautiful. Alan gutted one of them, steaked it and slapped it in the frying pan. A dash of salt, a sprinkling of pepper, a few minutes, and the fish was ready. Alan tucked in. He ate a lot—in fact he ate too much. But it was good.

As soon as breakfast was over they set out on the whale hunt. The sea was calm. The sun was warm. The smoke from the exhaust hung lazily in their wake. They were picture postcard moments. Alan was enjoying it all. There was not a break in the sea. The boat just swayed quietly on the gentle swells. Alan felt good but all of a sudden he came over queasy. Colour drained from his face and with one or two glorious heaves he returned his breakfast to the sea. It was a convulsive movement. He had no time to think about anything but getting his head over the side of the boat. His Eskimo companions looked at him and smiled. Suddenly Alan realized that not only had he lost his breakfast but he had lost his teeth as well.

"My teeth!" he yelled, "My teeth!"

The boat was travelling very slowly, towing a whole line of other boats.

"My teeth!" Alan yelled to an Eskimo in the second boat. "Can you grab my teeth?"

Alan could see them floating away. Gradually they sank, drifting backwards and forwards in the water, like a gently falling autumn leaf.

The man in the second boat was sharp eyed and quick witted. He spotted the teeth floating amidst the remains of Alan's breakfast and, grabbing a harpoon, reached for them. He tried to pick them up. Once, twice, he made a stab at them. Alan watched so anxiously that he hardly felt sick anymore. Each time the Eskimo actually touched the teeth but only succeeded in knocking them further away. Alan watched them drift out of sight. Everyone but Alan thought it was a huge joke. The Eskimos all wanted to peer into his mouth to be convinced he really had vomited them all out. Some sickness that! He had not only brought up his breakfast but spewed out all his teeth, too. "What am I going to do now?" Alan murmured to nobody in particular. "Sops, sops and more sops, I suppose."

Alan Scott's plight was the joke of the trip for everybody but Alan. The moment he was back in the settlement he went around to the doctor to ask him for help. The doctor was attached to the Anglican Mission that had opened its hospital there in 1930.

"I know the Company will send me out if I explain the situation," Alan told the doctor, "but I don't want to go out. Do you think we could get an impression that we could send out to my dentist in Peterhead?"

"I guess I could try. What shall we use?"

"Let's try some plaster of paris."

The doctor thought that was a good idea so he mixed some up to what he thought was the required consistency.

"Open up," he said to Alan, "Let's see what we can do."

Alan opened his mouth wide. He had no reason to be anything but confident. The doctor took a good sized wad and began to work it over Alan's toothless gums. Things did not go too badly for the first few minutes but the doctor had the plaster a little too thick and worked a little too slowly because it hardened so rapidly and firmly that Alan was stuck with a mouthful of rock-like plaster.

"I'll never get that out in one piece," said the doctor, "It just isn't possible."

"Ugh – ugh – ugh," Alan grunted.

"Don't get excited," the doctor said encouragingly as Alan began to wiggle as if suffocating. As he spoke he was trying to pry the plaster loose. "It went in easily enough," the doctor said, almost to himself, "but it sure doesn't want to come out." He picked at it with his fingers without success.

"I'm going to need some tools, Alan. You'll have to wait a minute."

Alan waited with his mouth full of plaster.

The doctor returned with a chisel and actually had to chisel it all out. When it was all out Alan rinsed his mouth thoroughly and said, "Let's give it another try."

The doctor was game so another batch of plaster was mixed. This time he tried to alter the consistency so that he would be able to recover the mould and not have to use a chisel. He was only partially successful. Certainly chisels were not necessary but the mixture was now so soft that it kept breaking in pieces and Alan was swallowing so much powder that it began to feel like a golf ball in his belly. The doctor was persistent and Alan was very patient but try as they would they could not get a decent plate impression.

"It's no good, Alan. We're going to have to think of something else."

"Have you got any ideas?"

"Nooo. Let me think."

"Could we melt wax candles?" suggested Alan. "We may be able to get a wax impression."

The doctor thought that this was a good idea so they tried it. Soon Alan had a large gob of wax in his hand to give it a try. He pressed it hard into his mouth.

"Get it all in," the doctor encouraged.

Alan jammed it all in.

"Don't forget to take a bite," the doctor reminded him, just as Alan had thought of it for himself and just before he was going to take the wax out. Alan bit. He bit hard.

"Now all we have to do is lift it out," said the doctor.

This was easier said than done. The wax was in tight and stiff. Carefully the doctor eased it loose, using lots of cold water on it. Finally he managed to pull the impression out. It looked good.

"That's fine," said Alan. "I'm sure it'll be good enough for the dentist."

Hardly were the words out of his mouth when the impression split in two. The men looked at it.

"That's still all right," Alan insisted," I've been nearly suffocated three times already. I'm going to send it like it is."

"The impression is still plain," the doctor said, a little doubtfully, "Maybe it'll be o.k."

Alan packed the wax impression in a small box lined with cotton wool. In view of the fact that the *Nascopie* had already called, the impression would not get outside until dog teams began to travel. It was well on in the winter before the box finally reached Peterhead. By then it had been carried by several dog teams, had accompanied a number of police patrols and had travelled many thousands of miles further than the shortest distance between Pangnirtung and Peterhead. For Alan that winter was miserable. He did not starve but he certainly grew hungry for meat. It was a dull diet of soggy bread, soggy hardtack and thick porridge.

When the *Nascopie* steamed into Pangnirtung in 1933 it brought Alan a beautiful set of teeth. Douglas Cain, the dentist in Peterhead, had done a marvelous job. Alan slipped the new set of teeth into place and they fitted like a charm, only one small spot had to be touched up with a file.

By now, of course, the story of Alan's teeth had leaked out to the Hudson's Bay Company headquarters and, to quote Alan, "I got hell for not stating that I had false teeth. I was told in no uncertain terms that I was a lunatic not to have a spare set with me."

Douglas Cain, the dentist, was so intrigued with the wax impression from Canada's Arctic that, when he heard some years later that Alan was on holiday in Peterhead, he was anxious to see him so sent him an enormous bill for the teeth. This infuriated Alan who had already paid the bill.

"What do you mean by this?" he demanded of Mr. Cain, waving the bill at him.

"Take it easy, mon. I just wanted to see you. I reckoned a bill like that would bring you here more than fast. I was right. Wasn't I?"

"Aye. You were that," Alan said, a little shame-faced.

"I'd like to hear the whole story. Do you mind sharing it with me?"

So Alan told him everything. He was interested in the north.

"You should be here assisting me," he said when Alan had finished. "Anyone who can make that good an impression with wax candles would make a great dental mechanic. And, incidentally," he said, "if you hadna' taken that bite I couldna' done a thing for you."

Whaling trips like the one Alan Scott was on when he lost his teeth were often hazardous. The mammals they were after could sometimes cause trouble and then there was always the threat of sudden storms. Each year the entire population would involve itself in the pursuit of the white whale, which is, strictly speaking, a porpoise. A whole fleet of little boats would enter a fiord where it was known there were white whales and proceed to shepherd the whales into shallow water. As the fleet moved in on the animals the Eskimos would make as much noise as they could, slapping the water and banging the boats to prevent the whales from attempting to pass them and head for open water. They were not always successful in containing them. Sometimes the whales would make a break for it and rush past the advancing armada.

Alan Scott recalls how they escaped from one such attack. Things seemed to be going well. White foam was being lashed up ahead of them by the twisting frightened whales. "Just a little further and they will strand themselves in shallow water," thought Alan. He was more than glad because what he saw ahead would provide enough meat for the dogs all through the approaching winter. But he was in for a disappointment. All of a sudden the whole herd of whales stopped, turned, and, led by an old fellow, came right for the boats. It was a bad thing. Try as they would the men could not hold them. As they passed they could be felt butting into the bottom of the boats. The Eskimos needed those whales. Alan Scott is of the opinion that the whales got wise to the methods of hunting they were using and the only way hunts would be successful in the future was to try new methods. As a matter of fact, as a last ditch effort to get a few whales that season he did something that was doubtless highly illegal. Together with a number of Eskimos he went on one last whale hunt in an attempt to get dog feed only this time he took a few home made depth charges. He rounded up a few lemonade bottles with screw tops, half filled these with sand, then topped them up with blasting powder. To these he attached underwater fuses. Using this method he managed to drive a number of whales ahead of him and keep them ahead of him in the fiord. It was this invention and contravention of laws that enabled him to have one successful hunt that year.

On one of the very first of these drives that Alan Scott went on, an Eskimo was drowned. The fleet of boats had just come around Duval Island when Kullulu fell into the water. There was a heavy sea running at the time and he had lost his balance while cutting the scow loose from the boat.

The moment he went overboard several Eskimos cried out

and Constable Moore plunged in after him. It was a brave thing to do. The storm was bad and the water cold. Moore managed to get hold of Kullulu who had been kept partially afloat by the air trapped in his clothes. When the Mountie caught hold of him they were right at the base of a cliff, and surrounded by jagged rocks. Kullulu was so terrified that he started to fight with Moore, clinging to his neck and dragging him under. The Mountie shook himself free and went after the Eskimo again and managed to grab him. Three times he got hold of Kullulu but was unable to control him. Finally he could find the Eskimo no more. He dived several times but without success. Without hesitation Moore had risked his life in a wild sea near a rock strewn shore. It was a courageous act. He just made it safely to shore himself. It was not until then that he discovered he had a bad gash on his face. According to the police report regarding this incident the Eskimos thought nothing of Kullulu's drowning but were very nervous when they saw Moore in the water. They were quite sure he would drown too and then they would be unable to face Sergeant Petty, the R.C.M.P. officer in charge of Pangnirtung.

Alan Scott says, however, that the natives were extremely disheartened by the accident.

The pursuit of whales across the centuries has cost many lives. Whaling for many years was a hazardous undertaking and there are numerous tales that come from the shores of Baffin Island, and the Hudson Bay, of wrecks and near wrecks, of survival in open boats, and of sudden death from drowning and slow death by exposure. The environs of Pangnirtung and Cumberland Sound have witnessed the death of many a fine ship and the gradual destruction of not a few fine men.

10
The Whalers

It was the whalers who probed their way across the Davis Strait and began to map, in elementary fashion, the coastline of Baffin Island. They had been preceded by Norsemen and occasional adventurers who had visited some parts of that dramatic land. But it was left to the whalers to start the thread of history that unwinds to the present.

In the early part of the eighteenth century whalers penetrated to the Davis Strait and then, almost exactly one hundred years later, Sir John Ross, a British sea captain, sailed down the east coast of Baffin Island and opened up the possibility of whaling there. Captain Ross was in charge of one of four ships that were sent out from England on voyages of discovery. It was he who named Melville Bay and it was he who named many of the coves, bays and inlets on Baffin Island's coast. On this particular voyage he made one interesting mistake. He believed a range of mountains blocked the end of Lancaster Sound and he named them the Croker Mountains. It is quite probable that he saw only icebergs.

Captain Ross was one in a long line of explorers who set out to find the Northwest Passage. As early as 1516 Martin Frobisher was contemplating a route to the Orient via the north west and in 1576, 1577 and 1578, made journeys that took him into what is now Canadian territory. He was followed, in 1611, by Henry Hudson who perished in the bay named after him. Not to be deterred by the failure of these men, Luke Foxe set out in 1631, penetrated the Hudson Strait and went on into the Foxe Basin. The Northwest Passage would not yield to these adventurers and it was not until the Second World War that a boat managed to smash its way through the ice-barred passage.

Long before this event, however, whalers and adventurers of many different nationalities had sailed in the northern waters which now belong to Canada. Danes, Americans, Norsemen, Dutchmen and Englishmen had all cast their nets in these seas long before Canada emerged as an entity and began to assert her sovereignty. Had it not been for the very active whaling industry emanating from Great Britain and the extensive voyages of exploration undertaken by her sailors, Canada's claim to Arctic sovereignty would be extremely shaky. From London, Hull, Peterhead and Dundee the whalers came. Not in one's and two's but by the score. Year after year they dared the dangerous waters. It was not until the present century that these exciting days came to an end, and in scattered corners of the globe a few men still live who remember fondly the last of these days. These whalers were the first men to take western civilization to the Eskimos of the far north and the first to carry Eskimos back to their own lands.

Mrs. Curtis of a Dundee whaling family, remembers an Eskimo called Shoodloo who was brought back on the whaling ship, *Active*, in the late 1890's.

"I mind him well," she says. "He had a bear on a chain and he used to just hum a tune to the bear. It wasna' a song. There were no words. The bear danced about and the crowd threw money to the Eskimo. That's one of the things I remember as a wee girlie."

It was John Innis, Mrs. Curtis's father-in-law who introduced many Eskimos to the mouth organ, the whistle and other elementary musical instruments. Every time he went out he took a large collection of these instruments to barter with the natives. He took other things, too, but the musical instruments were much favoured by the Eskimos.

When the whaling days ended and there were no more scenes of drunkenness, excitement, laughing and crying at the great whaling ports of northern Britain, there ended one of the most adventure filled occupations in the world. Even today in Peterhead, Dundee, Hull and London, whaling stories are told. The remains of the wrecks of some of their boats can still be seen in the north. Indeed for many years such shipwrecks were the only reminder to the Eskimos that there were strangers across the sea. Some of the shipwrecks were too far north even to be seen by the Eskimos.

One such was the wreck of the *Windward* which took place in the year 1907, a year described as disastrous by a Dundee newspaper published at that time. It was not only disastrous because the *Windward* was lost but because the ships returned without whales. The *Diana,* for example, cruised over 1400 miles and returned with one small whale, two bear cubs, a score of skins and a few walrus hides. Such poor seasons forced the ships to go further and further afield for cargo. That is what took the *Windward* as far north as the Cary Islands where she met her end.

When news of the wreck reached Scotland the Dundee newspaper outlined the history of this famous ship: "Built in 1860 at the Peterhead the whaler was of staunch and hardy structure and stood the severe test of many arduous voyages to the Arctic seas.

"In 1895 to 6 the *Windward* was engaged with the Jackson — Harmsworth expedition in Franz Josef Land and in the year 1896 the whaler conveyed Dr. Nansen to Vardo on the great explorer's return from his famous dash to the North Pole.

"Subsequently the *Windward* was gifted to Lieutenant Peary, the intrepid American explorer, and wintered for a year at Cape Durville. After the lapse of a year the *Windward* was acquired by Norwegians and was engaged in seal and whale fishing. Four years ago this historical craft was purchased by a Dundee firm and since then has made regular voyages to Davis Strait with varying success."

The islands on which the *Windward* met her end lie 77 degrees north latitude — further north than the habitation of any Canadian Eskimos. They are lonely ice-bound specks in one of the world's most treacherous stretches of water.

The last voyage of the *Windward* was dogged by misfortune. On the fifth day out one of the seamen went mad and leapt over the deck railing into the sea. Although a boat was immediately lowered they had little or no hope of recovering the man for it was pitch dark. Just ten days after this happened the ship caught fire in the bunkers. It took five hours to bring the fire under control and put it out. A few days later six whales were seen and the pursuit was scarcely in progress when the whole world was obliterated by thick fog. The chase had to be stopped and the boats returned to their mother ship without having fired a single harpoon. On the 14th of June, after the ship had successfully completed the dangerous passage of Melville Bay, engineer Donald Wilson died. He had been in bad health but his death came as a shock to the ship's company. Preparations were made to bury him on land but ice conditions made it impossible and he had to be slipped gently into the waters of the Davis Strait. Just ten days later the final disaster struck.

James Henderson, the carpenter, tells the story of the wreck in graphic fashion. It was a story he loved to tell and one his son, who still lives in Dundee, has heard him tell many times. Henderson was a seaman of rare quality and one who had travelled frequently into the Arctic. He had sailed on both the *Active* and the *Snowdrop*, ships that had had rare associations with Canada's northland. It was not surprising that he was level-headed enough to keep a private log of the events and was in charge of one of the ship's lifeboats.

At 5:00 o'clock in the afternoon of June 25th, the *Windward* sailed into sight of the Cary Islands. There are about sixteen islands in this group, some of them being little more than tide-washed rocks. About 10:40 p.m. the *Windward* struck a submerged rock. A sounding revealed there was twelve feet of water but, although the engines were reversed and everything possible done to refloat her, it was of no avail. The tide receded and the ship listed heavily to port. Soon it was almost impossible for the crew to stand on the steeply canted decks. When in this position, the ship slipped aft about four feet and, striking heavily, was badly holed about the stern part. The donkey pumps were unable to stem the rush of water and in time the boilers' fires were drowned out. Boats were launched and provisions were taken to one of the large islands about two miles distant. The crew stayed on the island the night of the 26th and early next morning went back to the *Windward* to obtain as much more in the way of provisions as possible.

In the boat commanded by James Henderson there were three ordinary seamen, a steward and one boat steerer, six all told. At 8:00 o'clock in the morning of the 27th of June the

The annual supplies arriving at Pangnirtung.

Ernie Riddell, manager of the Hudson's Bay Company post on the Belcher Islands at the time of the religious murders.

Peter Sala believed he was God. He is shown preparing a mug-up on the trail.

The Reverend G. Neilson, Anglican missionary who aided in the investigation of the Belcher Islands religious murders.

Quarak received a two year suspended sentence for his part in the religious murders.

Mina and Akiinik, followers of Charlie Ouyerak and Peter Sala, were pronounced insane by the jury.

Typical scene from a northern trial —
administering the oath to a witness.

Sergeant A. H. Joy and Eskimos, investigating the Belcher Island murders
of 1918 and 1919.

The R.C.M.P. schooner, *St. Roch.*

A wedding on board the *Nascopie* — the bride and groom, Eileen and Alan Scott; Bishop A. L. Fleming; and guests.

Natives at River Clyde settlement, Baffin Island, awaiting arrival of *Nascopie* for transportation to homes in Arctic Bay and Fort Ross.

Whaling station at Cape Haven, southern Baffin Island, 1903.

Eskimos unload scow bringing supplies from *Nascopie* anchored off shore at Arctic Bay.

G. Gely, N.F.B.

Eskimo cutting open a spotted seal.

Preparation of seal skins — Pangnirtung, Baffin Island.

boat set out for Pond Inlet, some 300 miles away as the crow flies. Henderson's boat became separated from the others, which had stood off the islands to the southwards to avoid a strong northwesterly. Pulling towards the shore of Ellesmere Island the boat was set on a course for Glacier Strait. Fortunately the wind eased and shifted a little making it possible to use the sail to the very best advantage and skirting along the floe edge they moved fairly rapidly southwards. At 11:00 a.m. on June 29th the sail was pulled in and the boat heaved up onto the floe ice. While here, James Henderson, who had the forethought to bring tools with him, set to work and built a rudder out of some pieces of board on the boat. This done, it was possible to steer and mind the sail at the same time which was much more convenient than guiding the boat with the oar. On June 30th they started on their passage across Lady Ann Strait. During all this time, Henderson, who was in charge, had done all the steering. He notes in his log:

"I am done up for want of sleep. I have not had any since the morning we lost the ship. I have been so long without it that I cannot fall off. My mind is wandering at times. The younger ones seem to sleep all right sitting in the boat with their blankets over them but the anxiety of my mind keeps me from it."

Not long after this entry was made Henderson sighted the other five boats coming across the Strait. He waited for them at Cape Horsburgh. The flotilla set off at 8:00 a.m. on the first of July and made good progress. Not until half way across Lancaster Sound did they run into serious difficulty. The wind freshened. The sail was double reefed and the boat rolled wildly. Henderson managed to get to some ice behind which he took shelter. He was soon followed by the captain and the rest of the boats. Their position was precarious but, temporarily at least, they were safe. Next day they were on their way again. It was July the second. For James Henderson it was almost his last day. He notes in his diary:

"Towards 7:00 p.m. launched the boats from the ice floe and took in two reefs and were about to get underway when a large piece of ice came in unnoticed by any of us, jammed the boat's head and walked right over us, filling us right up with water. I thought it was to be the last of us and the last of all we had for a home. The ice eased off and the boat floated flush with the surface of the water. Thank God for it. I never thought she would right with the water that was in her. Everything was soaked. Bread was damaged and nothing was dry. It was hard looking at our wrecked home. We got the water out and examined her and found that our rudder was broken beyond repair. Proceeded to load up again and finished at 8:20 and launched the boat. Set sail and ran northwest with two reefs in our sail — four boats of us towards the land — in blinding sleet."

Henderson only mentions four boats here. Presumably two of them had already moved off. In the next few days they were in daily peril from smashing ice floes, wild winds and gale blown seas. Noses, cheeks and lips were frozen. Feet and ankles were swollen. "At one time," writes Henderson, "a swell came in and broke the floe on which we had taken refuge, threatening to swallow us up, boats and all."

With frantic endeavor the shipwrecked men managed to save one of their boats by manhandling it over the hummocked, tortured ice. "We hauled the boats over the tops of high pinnacles of ice till sometimes they were only bearing on the centre, sometimes standing on end." Fortunately for them the squall moderated and they were able to relaunch the boats. Not long after this hazard was safely negotiated Pond Inlet was reached and the shipwrecked sailors taken aboard the whaler *Morning*.

The voyage in the open boats had taken twelve days, twelve long days, twelve days Henderson never forgot, twelve days from which only one man never recovered. He was Hans Neilson, a Swede, who died on board the *Eclipse*. The *Eclipse* was one of the three whalers among which the crew of the wrecked *Windward* was distributed.

The crew of the *Windward* was fortunate. Not often have such perilous journeys in open boats been made with such small losses. The fate of many whalers caught on ice floes, swept by blizzards and battered by gales, had been less happy. Alfred Basil Lubbock, in his book *The Arctic Whalers*,* recounts some

* Lubbock, Alfred Basil, *The Arctic Whalers,* Brown Son and Ferguson Limited, 1937.

barely credible tales. In 1826, the *Jean* was wrecked. Ice cold water flooded the decks. It sloshed across, and into, everything. The wind lashed the hulk and men tried to take refuge from its tearing blasts behind the protective awning of the sails. Still the water came, a freezing wet nightmare. The searing cold slashed across their faces and drove to the very marrow of the bone. A few men of spirit kept on the move and by brisk activity tried to stay alive. For them there was hope, but for those who sprawled in a mass on the deck the end was near. With the selfishness of fear each man tried to reach the warmest place in the centre of the kicking, struggling heap. Knives were drawn and amid the howling of the storm a wild free-for-all developed. It was every man for himself and not many of them lived.

An unpleasant story, but for sheer, quiet, blood-chilling horror it would be hard to find a more stirring one than that told of the loss of the *Shannon*. At one point, the few remaining crewmen watched the surgeon tap blood from a man called O'Neill. They watched in silence as the blood flowed slowly into a shoe. Drip, drip, it came, then faster. Taking the shoe full of blood the surgeon held it to the lips of the dying O'Neill but he could not drink it. Slowly the light left O'Neill's eyes and life slipped quietly from him. The surgeon then passed the shoe to the other men and they drank and lived. They drank the blood of a man they watched die and they drank their own blood, too. For what the surgeon had endeavored to get O'Neill to do he persuaded each of the other men to do. A strong solution to the problem of starvation but incredibly it worked.

There were many young men who went north and west in search of the whale, who never returned. They died of cold, exposure, drowning, hunger and thirst. Yet, in spite of such perils and perhaps sometimes because of them, the whaling fleet was never short of men and many a modern sailor regrets that he was born too late to sail when the sea was a challenge, the whale a treacherous monster, and the great land of Canada's north was a fierce uncharted enemy.

11
Cape Haven

One adventurer who just managed to share in the closing days of whaling in Canada's northern waters was Osbert Clare Forsythe-Grant. He came onto the scene shortly after the turn of the century and died a decade later in the wreck of the *Seduisante*.

He was a striking man to look at and a remarkable man to know. Bishop Fleming, in his book *Archibald the Arctic* describes him as "an intense man, intense in his love of justice, equally intense in his hate." Fleming was impressed with this man. He seems to have been drawn to Grant in spite of himself. When he went to visit Grant at Cape Haven on Frobisher Bay his arrival earlier than anticipated caused some embarrassment. "The truth was," writes Fleming, "that he had an Eskimo concubine, a fact which he would have liked to conceal from me." Such an arrangement was hardly likely to encourage the admiration of a missionary but Fleming could not help himself. He writes further, "Grant's personality dominated all else . . . . He was unlike the usual Arctic trader. He stood about six feet in height, had a clearly chiselled profile, searching eyes, slightly hollow cheeks, sensitive mouth expressive of both wit and sarcasm and a very determined chin."

There is a touch of devil-may-care recklessness about Grant's career that would evoke the hero worship of more than a few small boys. Once Forsythe-Grant entered the Arctic, adventure was his constant companion.

Originally, he had intended to enter the British army but

Sandhurst and he did not get along too well so he bought himself out. He visited Canada, voyaged on a whaler, fell in love with the Arctic and purchased the whaling ship, *Snowdrop*. It was as owner and operator of this ship that Osbert Clare Forsythe-Grant ran afoul of the law. He was taken to court by the company of Wrightington and Sons, of Boston, Massachusetts.

In 1903 the tangled skein of events that led up to the litigation began. In that year, Charles Wrightington wrote on behalf of his company to Captain W.J. Jackson. He expressed grave concern over their operation in the Arctic. The company had a fur trading post and whaling operation at Signuia (Cape Haven) on the east coast of Baffin Island, just north of Cyrus Field. This station had been left in the charge of a Mr. Jensen. It seems from correspondence that Jensen first went to the post in 1897 and came out six years later in 1903. In 1897 the company had sent up two years' supplies on Rear Admiral R.E. Peary's ship and arranged for Peary to call again in 1899 to re-supply and pick up products. The Peary Arctic Club refused to redeem the promise made by the explorer because it was afraid of becoming a common carrier. This decision came so late in 1899 that Wrightingtons could send no other vessel that year. There was nothing the company could do to relieve Jensen. Like it or not, he would have to stick it out for another winter.

By the time the next sailing season came round, the company realised that it was not only imperative to relieve Jensen but that they must get some return from their trading post. The schooner *Lily of the North* was chartered at Halifax and supplies shipped to her from Boston. This done, the company directors felt a little easier. They settled back to await news from the Arctic, each one eager to learn if the investment had been a wise one. Disaster struck. The *Lily of the North* and cargo were completely lost and, to make matters worse, none of the supplies were insured.

The position was now desperate. The moment the bad news was heard another ship was chartered. This time the company hired the S.T.R. *Kide*. To the relief of all concerned, this boat made the round trip to Cape Haven in thirty days without incident.

The following year the company arranged for the *Forget Me Not* to call at the post during its Arctic tour. A few supplies were sent up and products were expected back. By the end of the summer sailing season the ship had not turned up and was presumed lost. Hence, in 1902 the *Windward* was engaged to carry cargo to and from Signuia. The owners were paid $700 in advance. When the *Windward* arrived in Frobisher Bay the *Forget Me Not* was discovered there and its captain, W.J. Jackson, refused to hand over the goods he had already collected from Signuia. Wrightingtons had paid both the owners of the *Forget Me Not* and the *Windward* in advance for their services. Charles Wrightington bemoans this fact in a letter to Captain Jackson. He says, "Freight was paid twice on the products of the Station."

Because of this run of very bad luck the company wanted to recoup some of its losses. Charles Wrightington engaged Captain Jackson, formerly of the *Forget Me Not* to take over from Jensen. In a letter to Jackson dated June 9th, 1903, Wrightington catalogues the disasters and then says: "Because of all these things we want to see an active successful year this year." He tells Jackson that Jensen wants a year's leave and then makes it clear what he expects of Jackson, "Our idea in making this arrangement with you to go to our Station is to relieve Jensen and enable him to return home for a year and while we want to get all the information we can as to ways in which the business can be developed our primary object is to catch whales, etc. and we want to see more money out of the Station before putting more money into it so we trust you will do your best to make the Station pay this season a good return. We would not send you out to return on the ship."

The company made a fair deal with Captain Jackson, offering him free transportation from his home in Dundee, two pounds a month to his wife and one-fourteenth of the net proceeds of sale of all bone, fur, oil, walrus hide, etc. He was happy with it and set sail for Cape Haven with an easy mind.

Jackson, however, was not to have his easy mind for long. In the proceedings from 1904 till 1907, when the legal battle between Wrightingtons and Forsythe-Grant was begun Jackson emerges as a coward and a fool. When in the Arctic he seems to have acted irrationally and when back in Scotland he was an Arctic blowhard; a blabbermouth, one unfriendly critic labelled him.

Captain Jackson, who became a key figure in the trial involving Grant and others, had led an interesting life. He had first sailed to the Arctic Ocean as a lad of 17. A few years later, in 1896, he was on a trading expedition to Siberia and the following year he sailed with the *Forget Me Not* to Baffin Island. The *Forget Me Not* was frozen in that winter and during that time Jackson established a small trading station about twenty five miles from the one owned by Wrightingtons. His first acquaintance with the latter station was when he called there in 1901. This was, of course, during the time that Jensen was looking after the post and Jackson was the man who would not give up the products of Signuia to the captain of the *Windward*.

It is therefore apparent that Jackson had a good knowledge of the area in which he took up residence in 1903. He already knew the post owned by Wrightington Company and had some knowledge of trading. In spite of this, however, once he began to live at Cape Haven things did not go well. Jackson spent a miserable winter there. According to him Jensen had left a clean swept station. The amount of stock that Jackson had to work on was small and by the time the summer of 1904 came round he was desperate for a boat to relieve him. He waited in vain. On August 21st he decided to make for Blacklead Island on the Cumberland Sound. He knew he would get some help there. The Anglican Church had maintained a tiny mission on the island since 1894. The missionaries had built a mission house and a hospital, neither of which was much more than a tar paper shack, but the Anglicans were justly proud of them. Those little buildings represented their first mission outpost in Arctic Canada.

The Anglican mission had established itself near a whaling station run by a Mr. Noble from Aberdeen. This station was run in conjunction with the one of nearby Kekerton. For these stations, as for Captain Jackson at Cape Haven, the season of 1903-4 was an extremely poor one. Not a single whale was brought to any of the stations in the summer of 1904. A.P. Low, writing about the Cumberland Gulf Whaling Station in the

government report *The Cruise of the Neptune** makes it clear
that times were particularly bad. "At Blacklead," he writes, "we
were visited by the Rev. Mr. J. Peck and the agent of the whaling station and learned from them that the past year had been
very unprofitable to whalers and disastrous to the natives.
Owing to the quantity of broken ice that had been jammed into
the gulf throughout the summer and which prevented the boats
from reaching the open water, no whales had been captured,
though a few had been seen. A succession of heavy easterly
gales occurred during the winter causing a heavy swell which
from time to time broke up the solid ice in the bay and prevented the natives from going as usual to the edge of the open water
on their winter chase of seal and walrus. Many consequently
were in a chronic state of starvation during the winter. The
same cause prevented relief reaching them from other stations,
dog-travelling being impossible. Late in the autumn a heavy gale
in conjunction with an extra high tide swept away several tents
and other belongings of the natives who were camped on the
lower part of the island, the tide rising twenty feet above the
ordinary high water mark. In March the heavy swell broke up
ice three feet thick on which 40 Eskimos were encamped. During their retreat to a place of safety three of these people perished from exposure. All the survivors escaped with their lives
only, leaving all their belongings on the ice."

It was through these treacherous waters that Captain Jackson
went towards Blacklead Island at the end of August, 1904. The
distance from Cape Haven to Blacklead by sea is some 150
miles.

Captain Jackson set out with two boats. For days on end
they battled against the wind, snow, sleet and ice but they were
unable to reach Blacklead Island. Finally, Jackson gave up and
returned to Cape Haven. He had been away sixteen days. When
he got back he was frustrated beyond measure to discover that
only six hours previous to his arrival the *Neptune* had called.
The natives told him the boat was going to return in seven to
fourteen days but Jackson did not believe them. Jackson could

---

* Low, Albert Peter, *The Cruise of the Neptune,* Ottawa, Government
Printing Bureau, 1906.

see no reason why it should return and said as much in a letter he addressed to Mr. Noble at Blacklead Island.

This letter, written on September 3rd, reveals a thoroughly frightened man. He wrote, "Dear Mr. Noble: I am stranded here without boat or food and if you will allow your ship to call here for me and if possible for the small freightage, 36 small, 3 large casks of oil, about 150 walrus hides and 12 bear pelts, I should say you have a good action at law for substantial freightage against Mr. Wrightington. At any rate surely you will not see a fellow left in this God forsaken country without an effort to relieve him."

Although Jackson had spent sixteen days in an unsuccessful attempt to get to Blacklead Island he then had the nerve to say, "It is all plain sailing and easily get-able. You can have my boat's crew to pilot you and a good lookout will be kept for your entering . . . . Peradventure that the *Neptune* shall return here I shall of course return with her . . . (but) they do not know the predicament I am in." To try to make sure that Noble will come, Jackson then adds, "If she (the *Neptune*) comes I shall not take the produce in her and you have my full authority to ship it in your vessel at a remunerative freightage and hold it as security until your demands are satisfied so that you cannot lose financially. If I am away I shall leave the keys and full instructions to natives to deliver it to you and will meet you on your arrival home. God bless you dear boy. I am in a hurry to get the boat away to catch you. Yours, W.J. Jackson."

Two weeks after this letter was written Jackson wrote to his employers. It is a gloomy piece of correspondence written by a despondent man. " . . . on September 3rd I despatched a boat with a letter to you craving Mr. Noble's son to call here with his ship and take myself and produce home, as I have been for some time without fuel, food (white man's) or salt for preserving hides and am now out of caps and lead for reloading ammunition.

"Whether I go home or not there will be no more produce as natives will migrate up Frobisher Bay where there are more seals and every shot will tell." This sounds almost petulant and there is more of it to come.

"You ought to have sent a vessel for myself and your produce even if you sent no provisions to keep on the station. . . . At any rate I in no way blame you. Morally Jensen is the one to blame for not having kept you fully informed of matters and I trust you will in no way blame yourself if anything disastrous happens to me though it would be only just if you gave my wife and family pecuniary assistance.

"Having waited thus long for the steamer's return I start again for Blacklead on the remote chance of catching the ship there. If she has left I will stay there with the missionaries until the ship comes out next year." Jackson concludes this touching note with a strange sentence. "Mr. Suffling, 1 Portsdown Rd., London W. is in a position to advise you best as to the relief of this station, as I do not expect this letter to reach you I will conclude. Your obedient servant."

Why give Mr. Suffling's address? Why bother with the letter at all? Why does he think it unlikely that he will ever get back to civilisation? Had he been threatened?

Having despatched this letter Captain Jackson made another attempt to reach Blacklead Island but was unsuccessful. He tried several more times and finally he made it. When a ship called there in the summer of 1905 he embarked on it and returned to Peterhead, arriving there in November. Before he had left the post at Cape Haven he promised the natives that he would return and bring them gifts. "Don't worry I'm not deserting you for good," he assured them. "When I return I'll bring you all manner of good things, nets, knives, rifles, cloth, salt and so on."

It must be said for Captain Jackson that he made an effort to redeem at least part of his promise. He did set sail on a ship that was destined that season to call at Cape Haven. But by the time the boat reached Canada, Captain Jackson had deserted his post.

Early in 1906 the paths of Grant and Jackson crossed. Osbert Clare Forsyth-Grant asked Jackson to go back into the Arctic as master of the *Snowdrop*.

"I was unwilling," Captain Jackson said later at the trial, "but Grant pressed me."

On April 9th, 1906, the *Snowdrop* sailed for the Arctic with the skipper, Captain Jackson and the owner, Forsyth-Grant on board. The object of the voyage was ostensibly walrus hunting on the east coast of Davis Strait. According to Jackson, Mr. Grant had been told about the station at Cape Haven and was fully aware of how much Arctic produce had been left there.

The voyage of the *Snowdrop* proved to be a memorable one. Things went fairly well until the ship was entering Holsteinborg on the west coast of Greenland. As the *Snowdrop* made its approach it hit a rock and sustained considerable damage to its keel. At the time this happened things had already come to a pretty pass on board. The crew was so unruly that once the ship was damaged they wanted no more to do with it. A few of the members persuaded Captain Jackson to approach the Danish authorities at Holsteinborg and ask them to inspect the ship. Jackson complied with their request and asked two men, the Captain of *McClintock's Fox*, a coaster in that part of the country that was not permitted to cross the Atlantic, and a mate in the employ of the Greenland Company. These men examined the *Snowdrop* and, although not condemning her out of hand, declared her unseaworthy.

As soon as Jackson heard this he quit the ship. His example was followed by nine men which left Grant with only five of the original crew. Forsythe-Grant was highly incensed by the action of Jackson, the crew and the Danes. He was particularly maddened by the Danes because although they did not condemn the boat they would not make available to him the necessary help to repair her and make her seaworthy. "Even if we bring her onto the beach," they said, "we cannot repair the chaffed keel because the two carpenters now helping you must finish a house here and then they have to leave directly for Egdesminde."

Hearing this, Grant went to the Governor of Holsteinborg. "My boat is declared unseaworthy," he said. "You cannot make available help to repair her. Will you, therefore, buy it on behalf of the insurance company?"

"I am afraid I cannot do that," replied the Governor and that was that.

Grant was more incensed than ever. He wrote to W. & O. Taylor & Sons Co., the people handling affairs pertaining to the trip, in a letter dated June, 1906.

Dear Mr. Baxter:

You will be astonished to find two-thirds of my crew landing in Britain about the time you get this. We got on a rock coming in here and some of the men who are I think over insured induced Captain Jackson to get the Danes . . .

to survey us . . . .

Grant, having explained to Baxter what he tried to do, then contemplates what would happen if the *Snowdrop* were abandoned there for the winter.

. . . If we left her here the chances are that with the ice in January, February and March and the Christianity filled but not overly scrupulous Eskimos there would be very little of her left by next summer.

Grant was in a very difficult position. If he set out and any disaster actually overtook him he was no longer covered by the underwriters. Whereas if he deserted the boat and waited another year for repairs there would, quite likely, be only a hulk left, not worth repairing. Grant decided to run the risk of crossing to Canada.

Five of us are going to take it to the Hudson Strait and head for the Bay and if we find we can do nothing else with her, we will run down the Labrador shore to St. John's, Newfoundland. I do not think there is anything seriously the matter and as I write she is bumping on the beach and against the quay and we scarcely get the water we put into the pump out of her. I am satisfied that we run no more risk than ever before — have seen the ship opened up and know how much there is left of the keel. We have 56 very large walrus hides on board and also 5 seals. This is the chief part of our catch so far . . . .

I feel sure I cannot do better than leave you an open hand to settle re the Captain and crew who have left . . . . I do not know if we shall try and cross the Atlantic. If she is satisfactory we shall do so but for safety's sake write me a line to St. John's, Newfoundland and tell me whom you think I had better employ there. As far as I know St. John's is not over honest in some transactions. Either write to the G.P.O. (to be left to call for) or to your agents there and tell them to come on board with your letter as soon as they hear of our arrival.

Between you and me Captain Jackson is not an expert

fisher in this part of the country. He does not care to be in ice out of sight of land and to me appears to have something on his conscience. God knows I do not wish to do anything foolhardy but I do pray that I may never be so afraid to endure a few days in a boat or even to meet my end if necessary. I think all the fishing he has done has been to collect stuff shot by natives in Frobisher Bay or thereabouts . . . .

Still hoping and trusting to make a good voyage which should not be too difficult with the help of Eskimos and with kind regards, I remain,

Yours sincerely,
O.C.F.G.

Shortly after this letter was written Grant's problems were made even more difficult when two more of the crew deserted, leaving him only three.

Mr. Baxter replied to this letter on the 11th of July, 1906. His letter, headed Very Private & Confidential, contains a number of extraordinary and interesting things. He wrote:

I deplore the very unhappy accident to the vessel which helped to cause such a split among the crew but it looks to me from the conversation I have had with Captain Jackson that it has been a case of sheer funk and fright so far at least as he was concerned and no doubt the men were influenced by him greatly in what he did. I cannot express too strongly my opinion on the cowardly desertion of Jackson and his mates and it would be a matter for grave consideration whether on your return the case should not be taken before the Board of Trade. Jackson seems a man all jaw-blabbing to everyone he meets — newspapermen as well, of the chaos, insubordination and lack of discipline on board the *Snowdrop*, etc. etc., and in particular he has a mortal horror of the mate who, to his astonishment, also came home by the same steamer. Ritchie I have not seen yet.

After some words on how he is going to handle the matter of the crew's wages Baxter continues,

I am greatly concerned at the very unfortunate situation you are now in with so few hands to assist you even with the ordinary working of the vessel but I do most sincerely trust you will come out of the ordeal with flying colours and get back safely home with the ship and cargo . . . . I have had very anxious enquiries from the underwriter on ship and cargo and I am not just very clear as to your position now that the Captain and the bulk of the men have come home, the former bringing with him a certificate *which I have* signed by the parties you referred to that the vessel could not be made seaworthy. The U/S on the hull although the ship is lost after leaving Holsteinborg cannot be in any worse position than they would have been had you abandoned her there. But the U/S on cargo may turn around and say in the event of claims that the hides at least might have been landed or sent home from Holsteinborg and both sets of underwriters may set up an objection that the vessel was unseaworthy on leaving Holsteinborg not only in respect of the damage received but by reason of being undermanned. These points all occur to me and I do trust your safe arrival will do away with any necessity for such questions being raised.

Baxter goes on to tell Grant to deal with Bowring Brothers in St. John's and concludes, "I shall be very anxious until I get further news from you and can only hope on concluding that all is well with you and the *Snowdrop*." Baxter then adds an intriguing post script, " . . . Jackson has been writing to your father, I learn, about Ritchie's evil influence over you, etc., but I wrote to Ecclesgreig today telling Mr. Grant not to attach much if any importance to anything he writes."

It seems as if there were wheels within wheels on the *Snowdrop*. The picture that emerges is fascinating. There is blabber-jaw Jackson, a man with an uneasy conscience, less knowledge of seafaring than he claims and a coward. Then there is Osbert Clare Forsythe-Grant, son of a Scottish landowner, a man with a public school education, a love of adventure and a powerful personality. Finally, like a shadow, looms the figure of Ritchie, a man about whom little is said, but enough to conjure up an image of evil power.

Grant, however, was left with just three others to continue his voyage. It seems from newspaper reports and other documents that quite possibly there were two men named Ritchie on board, the one who wielded the influence seems to have stayed with Grant. Before Jackson and Grant parted company, however, Grant is supposed to have quizzed the captain about the

affairs at Signuia (Cape Haven). According to Jackson, Grant
wanted to know what Mr. Wrightington was like and what he
would do should he, Grant, pick up the produce at the station.
Jackson is supposed to have answered these enquiries by assur-
ing Grant that Mr. Wrightington was an honourable man and
would deal justly with him. Later on in court, Jackson said, "At
the time I left he (Grant) indicated to me that he was going to
Signuia. He did not tell me that but I knew it perfectly well."

Grant did manage to go on to Cape Haven and what took
place there eventually led him into court. He dealt with the
natives for the produce that was apparently in the store at
Signuia and took it with him to St. John's, Newfoundland. He
made the trip with three of his original crew and a few Eskimo
helpers.

Once in St. John's things began to get difficult. When resalt-
ing some of the hides there Grant discovered a company stamp
on a few of them. This, supposedly, took him by surprise. He
maintained then, and later, that he had purchased the bales in
good faith from the natives believing their story that they were
theirs to sell. Wrightington's representative, however, a Mr. R.
Kinnes, who had agreed to have his ship, the whaler *Active*,
collect the produce at Signuia, insisted Grant knew perfectly
well where the hides came from and that he had only confessed
to being in possession of a number of goods belonging to
another company when he knew someone was on his track.
Grant denied this. Kinnes threatened to take him to court and
actually instructed his agents to arrest the goods when they
came to Liverpool.

"If you don't give up your claim to these goods Mr. Grant,
there is no other recourse for me but to take you to Court,"
Kinnes said, acting on behalf of Wrightington & Company. This
was said directly to Grant.

The attitude Kinnes adopted incensed Grant. The backs of
two fighting men were now up and unless Grant could settle the
matter out of court directly with Wrightington he was in for a
lot of trouble. Grant recognized this and wrote a lengthy letter
to Mr. Wrightington on January 14th, 1907.

I saw Jackson in Brighton on the 10th inst. and gave
him an account of what I did in the neighborhood of your

station and told him that I was quite ready to settle with you on reasonable terms. On Friday the 11th inst. he told me he had wired you and you replied Kinnes had full powers to settle with him.

I have however no desire to go to Kinnes and suggest a settlement — nor do I suppose for a moment he would accept a reasonable offer for he is fighting his own battle with your money. This I had ample proof of during my first interview with him on my return to Dundee in November last — for on my admitting I had some skins with W & Co. on tags attached to them, also some boiled oil, etc but refusing to be drawn as to how I got them, he threatened me with all sorts of dire things and on my asking if he was sure he could do all this he burst out with more.

I may here state that I am looked upon here in Dundee as an interloper for I have little to do with the other ships. I have nothing in common with their owners — besides all the Dundee whaling captains and officers have long known one another for the younger generation has always seen service under the elder and they are all hand in hand and I am a stranger and an unknown quantity. I am also in the eyes of the Dundee whalers an undesirable person in the Arctic and one who should if possible be got rid of. Need I point out that the present opportunity is just what some of these connected with Dundee whalers desire . . . a chance of causing me a certain amount of annoyance . . . and possibly expense.

. . . May I give you a short statement of what took place and attempt to settle with you, for I scarcely wish you to think I want to steal your produce and a lawsuit is seldom certain in anything except expense.

Jackson told me before he left *Snowdrop*, your station — I think he mentioned two — was in the Frobisher district and that the natives would be up Frobisher Bay as the food was more plentiful. I could not get up Hudson Straits on account of ice so went in towards Frobisher where I fell in with an Eskimo boat who took us up Newgumilant Bay where another boat joined us and they wanted to take us to the anchorage near your station. This was, however, too unprotected a berth as the ice was not far off and a shift of wind would have brought it on top of us. I explained this to the natives and they took us to a harbour containing salmon which Jackson recognized from my description. We were well protected from ice by many islands outside us. I asked the natives as soon as I had supplied their immediate wants what they had to barter and they said they had very much and brought me two boat loads of walrus hides and 13 bear skins. I was absolutely unaware at that time that these hides or some of them had tags on them and only found this out in St. John's, Newfoundland when we opened the hides to resalt any places that required it. In my asking if they had any more to barter they told me a quantity of oil — about 9 tons — for which they said the white man had not paid them nor for the work they did in connection with it. They further said that the white man had told them to keep the oil and skins which they had when he left them and that the white man would send them boats and rifles and all they needed for their livelihood but he had not done so — so of course they bartered me the lot.

Grant goes on to describe how pleased the natives were at seeing him and how desperate their plight was. "The natives were completely out of ammunition. They were using the head of a common red wooden match to fire a rifle four times and digging out old bullets from any beast killed. Their clothing was pitiful for they had very little deerskin." To help them in this regard Grant describes how he took them over to Meta Incognito aboard his ship for a deer hunt. "The number of deer they shot was extraordinary making adequate meat and clothing immediately available." Grant became a hero to the natives, who apparently treated him royally. He writes, "When we left the natives on 2nd October — I say it with pride sir — there was hardly a man or woman or child with dry eyes."

Grant tried to persuade Wrightington to meet him in a compromise. "I would have done so in St. John's," he writes, "but the way the thing was put before me I confess considerably ruffled me for Bowrings on hearing from you asked me if I wanted freight or salvage and on protesting that the goods were bought by me in good faith seemed to hint that they were not my property but stolen which of course put my back up and I told them that I wanted nothing but the goods which were mine in every way."

Grant asked Wrightington how much he would accept as a settlement and also expressed a wish to purchase the station at Cape Haven. He said, "I have no intention of being driven out of the Arctic by Kinnes or anyone else and I could easily call at Cape Haven every year."

Grant closed this letter with a final plea. "If you do not consider my offer a fair one will you let me have your idea as to figure by cable when I will do my best to meet you."

This plea was rejected and the whole matter reached the Court of Session on the 14th of March, 1907.

12
Wrightington vs. Grant

On a blustery day in March, Lord Salvesen took his seat in the Court of Session in Dundee. Kinnes and Grant faced each other in court. Kinnes was seeking, on behalf of Wrightington and Sons, delivery of 195 walrus hides, 29 bearskins, 300 sealskins, fox skins, 51 casks of oil, walrus tusks and other goods which he claimed were illegally taken from the post at Signuia. Osbert Clare Forsythe-Grant, on the other hand, replied that these goods were derelict and that he acquired them in good faith from persons entitled by the trading customs of the Arctic to dispose of them. In addition to this, Grant claimed that those who sued him had absented themselves for an unconscionable length of time from their post at Signuia and thus no longer had any claims upon the goods there.

Lord Salvesen, the presiding judge, who was a man with a keen sense of humour and no knowledge of the Arctic, listened to the opening gambit of both sides and then was instructed and entertained by the star witness for the defence, none other than Captain Jackson. As it turned out, Captain Jackson became the accidental creator of much amusement. Some of the things he said are barely credible. During cross-examination he was asked about a letter he wrote to Wrightington telling him that white men had been to the station at Signuia and looted it. (The "men" in question was apparently "man" and the man was a missionary.)

"Why did you write this letter?"

"To help Mr. Grant."

"Was the letter bluff?"

"Yes, partly. I had taken up a position to help Grant. I knew that he had committed a commercial error and I wanted to help him out of it."

"You thought by this letter to make Mr. Wrightington believe others had taken produce from the station."

"I did not write what I thought but what I wanted Mr. Wrightington to think. I was trying to help Mr. Grant. Everything in this letter is right except the word 'looted'. That must have slipped in."

"Did you deliberately charge a missionary with looting the station?"

"There is no missionary mentioned there. The missionary had written himself and told me he was there."

"And you took it upon yourself to write that the station had been looted?"

"That is a slip of the pen. I did not mean looted and I never meant it. I never dreamt such a deliberate falsehood. It was nothing to benefit myself."

"Was it to benefit somebody else?"

"Well, it looks like that."

Lord Salvesen instructed the witness to write the name on a piece of paper so that the name would not get in the press. (The missionary concerned was most likely the Reverend Mr. Greenshields.)

Captain Jackson wrote the name down and handed it to the Clerk of the Court.

"Sometimes I make mistakes when I write," he said as he handed it over.

Mr. McClure, the Counsel for the Defence, said, "You write down anything?"

"Yes."

"That's what I thought."

Everyone but Jackson laughed. Jackson chose to ignore the comment and continued to peruse the letter that he was being questioned about. Suddenly he observed to the Court, "I came across another falsehood here, but you have not picked that one out."

Everybody in court burst out laughing.

Captain Jackson, quite unmoved by the laughter, said, "That rifle which I said was given to me by the Canadian Government was given to me by a missionary. That's a falsehood for you."

"It was a mistake," Lord Salveson injected acidly.

Mr. McClure then referred Captain Jackson to other letters. "In this letter you refer to your anxiety to get out of this God-forsaken country. What was the matter?"

"I was in bad straits when I wrote that. I was out of ammunition and could not get any. To stay in the country any longer was to waste a year of my life. I was almost out of white man's food."

"You were tired of walrus beef?" Lord Salvesen asked rhetorically.

"Did I understand you had no ammunition?" asked Mr. McClure.

"That is figuratively. I was not without some. I left ammunition there when I came away."

McClure then shifted his attack to yet another piece of correspondence. "What do you mean in this letter when at one time you say the station is denuded and in the next breath speak of stores on hand?"

"I don't know what I mean," said Jackson, more than a little nervous. "I must have been writing of another station. This must be a letter I wrote and flung away. Mr. Grant must have found it somewhere else and taken it to the station at Signuia."

"It says the station was denuded and it says there were stores. Explain!"

"I must have been practicing writing when I wrote that."

When order was restored after that remark the cross-examination shifted direction to life in the Arctic and trading practices there.

"Did you find life dangerous in the Arctic? Were you ever afraid some disaster might befall you?"

"In the Arctic regions you are liable to disaster at any time. You go out for a stroll and never come back again."

"That did not happen to you?"

"No. I took care of myself."

"You have always done that?"

"Yes."

"Was there any other white man at the station while you were there?"

"No."

"Were you ever afraid of the Esquimaux?"

"I might have said on occasion that I thought some of the natives were plotting to kill me. I was especially unpopular with two of the natives."

"Did you think they might kill you?"

"It is true that I left letters in the station asking anyone who found my body to examine it for spear and bullet wounds. I did not, however, leave the station in fear of my life."

Jackson went on to assert he did not abandon the station at Cape Haven and that all the natives had been fully paid. The promises he made were given with an eye to the future.

"How long have the natives been in the service of Mr. Wrightington?" asked McClure.

"Ten to twenty years."

"Are they still in your service if you've not had a ship at the station for three years?"

"Well, no. They go on their own. If you have no stuff to give the natives the natives will give you nothing."

"Are they entitled to their skins?"

"Yes. But I told them I would do my best to get back."

"You wanted to get back for the skins?"

"I wanted to get back because I don't think white men have acted fairly to the natives."

"You were not a missionary. Can you explain why you promised to give them things?"

"Yes."

"Why?"

"Because I liked them. I have been very nearly back. I told them I would do my very utmost to go back next year, and if I could not get back Mr. Wrightington would send to them. I made no promise on behalf of Mr. Wrightington but on my own behalf."

"What would you promise?" asked Mr. McClure.

"If you had no coat and wanted one and I could spare it, I would give it to you. I do not mean anything personal."

"Did the Esquimaux give you their own coats?"

"No."

"Then what relevance is in your illustration?"

"I would like to give it to them."

"Was it out of pure philanthropy?"

"Pure and simple."

"Was it for services to be rendered?"

"There might be something in that."

"Was it a promise in order that they would give you services?"

"Yes. There is something in that. The assurance they gave me was they would come and work for me if I came back. If they could get the skins they would." Jackson then added sanctimoniously, "I did not bother myself about skins. I told them to keep themselves alive."

"Was the promise you made for past or future?"

"None past. All for the future. I wanted them to come round when I came back."

"If it was for services how can you represent it as philanthropy?"

"I do not. You said it was philanthropy."

"You said it was for mere kindness on your part?"

"Yes. But I had an eye to business. Do you think I would tell a lie?"

"Yes."

McClure answered so bluntly, promptly and effectively that the whole court burst out laughing, including Captain Jackson.

"Have you fulfilled the promise you made?" McClure continued once order was restored.

"I did not make any."

"I thought you said you promised them all sorts of things."

"I promised them that I would try to come back this year and that if I did I would give all these things but I did not get there and that makes the promise null and void." (More laughter in court.)

McClure continued to bore in upon him. He was attempting to demonstrate that the hides and other produce at Signuia had, in fact, never been legitimately purchased from the natives, that all they had received for them, until the advent of Osbert Forsythe-Grant, was a promise or two. Jackson argued that such a suggestion was absurd because the natives would not allow furs unpaid for to be stored in the house.

"Natives don't give credit. Unless you pay them on the nail they won't give you the stuff," he insisted.

Questioned further, Jackson denied that he went out with the *Snowdrop* with the firm intention of looting. He maintained that it was Grant whose object was looting and actually said, "He would rather earn sixpence by looting than two shillings by honest labour."

"Would you ascribe that to an unbalanced mind?" queried Lord Salvesen.

"That was one of the things that made me leave."

"When you found that Grant had given up the idea of going to Cape York why did you not go back to the ship and go to Signuia?"

"All the crew would have tumbled back to the ship."

"Why should they not?"

"Because we would then have gone to Cape York and we would have been dead and there would have been no trial here."

The Court, already amused at Jackson's evidence, laughed loudly at this remark.

"Was it fear of your own safety that prevented you going?"

"I do not know what fear is."

On this note of more than dubious honesty the Court adjourned for that day.

In actual fact, of course, one of the main reasons for the partial mutiny of the crew and Jackson against the owner of the ship was the fact that Grant's original plan was to go right up the west coast of Greenland as far north as Cape York, a hazardous voyage for a small ship like the *Snowdrop*. They would likely have been beset by ice constantly and quite probably frozen in for the winter. Jackson seems to have had a deathly fear of ice. It seems more than probable that Grant is right when he asserts, "Jackson and other members of the crew deliberately encouraged the Danes to pronounce the boat unseaworthy. They wanted no part of a voyage as far north as Cape York."

On the basis of Jackson's evidence things did not look too bad for Grant. It seems as if everyone recognized his unreliability as a witness and his cowardice. It was patently obvious that he feared the natives, Grant, and any sea trip that might be regarded as dangerous. Jackson did not make it at all clear that the trading practices he had engaged in were entirely above board. If the store he went to was denuded he would be completely unable to obtain furs and yet, according to him, large quantities of fur were at the station. Somewhere along the line he was not telling the truth.

Grant's position was further helped by the evidence of Peter Dugal Warrender who went to Blacklead Island in 1904 as a cooper in the employ of Mr. Noble of Aberdeen. He said that in 1905, Jackson, who had come to Blacklead Island, told him that the natives of Signuia were starving and that they were treating him badly.

"He even showed me a bullet hole in the tail of a sealskin coat and said that it was intentionally done."

"Did he lead you to understand that he had his clothes on when the shot was fired?" asked Lord Salvesen.

When the Court had subsided after this question Warrender answered, "Yes."

"Assuming that Jackson when he left the station promised to come back next year and did not come would the natives be entitled to barter the goods at the station to someone else?"

"I think so."

"If they had proposed to barter skins to you would you have hesitated in dealing with them?"

"Not at all. I would have bought them over in a moment."

This evidence doubtless helped Grant but he was sadly let down by a member of his crew — one of the few who stayed with him.

It seems from reading an account of the trial that the witness wanted to protect Grant but signally failed. Under cross-examination he made admissions that served to finish the game for Mr. Grant.

He explained to the Court that the *Snowdrop* had not anchored at the Signuia station because of ice but that boats had been sent into the post. These boats had brought back the produce of the station which he thought was perfectly in order because he knew Mr. Grant had given the natives a good supply of ammunition.

"Was your practice to nail whatever you could get hold of?"

"Yes."

"Is it on that footing that you trade in the Arctic? In all your experience can you point to a station which has been plundered as this one was?"

"We did not know who the stuff belonged to."

"Did you know that the natives were attached to Signuia Station and that the boat loads of produce brought by them had been brought from Signuia Station?"

"I did not know where it was coming from when it was put on board the ship."

"But you knew when they went for it that they were bringing it from the station?"

"Yes."

"Did you know perfectly well that the produce they were bartering was the produce that had belonged to the station?"

"No."

"But you know it was."

"I may have thought it was but I did not know it was."

This answer amused everyone in court except Grant and the Counsel for the Defence.

"Were you present when Mr. Grant received a letter from the natives written by Captain Jackson and left with them?"

"Yes."

"Why was Mr. Grant being given such a letter?"

"I don't know."

"Do you mean to say that you and Mr. Grant never discussed where the produce came from?"

"I had no idea of it. When I went to shoot hares Mr. Grant went aboard the ship. I had told him I was going ashore hunting at Signuia. After I came back to the *Snowdrop* I told him I'd been at Signuia. I tried to get into the house but the door was locked."

"You were going to the station to make sure everything had been removed?"

"Yes."

"Did you not tell Captain Stephen of the *Queen Bess*, in Dundee, that you were at the station and that the natives had brought off the produce of it?"

"I told him the *Snowdrop* was one or two miles from the

station."

"Did you tell the natives Captain Jackson would not be coming back?"

"Yes."

"Did you say that in order to induce them to give you the produce?"

"I don't know."

"What was your object in making the statement?"

"I don't know."

Many others gave evidence and of course Forsythe-Grant and Kinnes took the stand but no one managed to hold the Court's attention or cause such amusement as the unfortunate Captain Jackson.

The trial dragged on for weeks and not until Friday, May 17th, 1907 was a decision handed down. Judgment was given against Osbert C. Forsythe-Grant. The contention of Mr. R. Kinnes that the defender knew the goods were station goods was accepted.

"What actually took place is perfectly straight-forward," said Mr. Hunter, a witness for the pursuer (plaintiff), "Grant told the natives Jackson would not be back next summer and deliberately implied to them that he was there to pick up the goods for him. He doubtless told them Jackson had been in command of the ship at the outset of the trip but that he would not now be back and that the goods could be safely handed over to him. The price paid by Grant to the natives was not for goods but for services."

That is the story the Court believed and it cost Osbert Clare Forsythe-Grant something in excess of 3,000 pounds, an amount that at today's prices would be well over $50,000.

13
Loss of the Snowdrop

The loss of the legal battle with R. Kinnes was a serious blow for O. Forsythe-Grant but although angered by it he was not overcome by it. His determination to remain in the Arctic was firmer than ever. No lost lawsuit was going to keep him out, nor were any of the Dundee whalers or American traders. Forsythe-Grant was irresistibly drawn to Canada's northland. He had to go back. The less charitable of his critics asserted that he simply enjoyed the easy going morality of native ways and the distance such places were from the long arm of the law. Such a judgment is scarcely fair. O. Forsythe-Grant made no pretence of being a saint. In fact he seems to have hated pretenders. Grant liked men to be men. For him manliness was strength of body and mind, the ability to be courageous in the face of danger, the ability to face death calmly and the willingness to endure hardships without complaining. He despised the timid, the squeamish and the indecisive. It seems, for example, as if he thought missionaries might well be a little too ladylike to live in the demanding environment of the Arctic. He was always polite to them but was not above putting them to the test. Archibald Lang Fleming, who later became Bishop of the Arctic was the subject of Osbert C. Forsythe-Grant's tests. He relates the story graphically in his book, *Archibald the Arctic*.

On Saturday he invited me to travel with him along the coast towards Lady Franklin Island where an Eskimo had reported that he had seen tracks of a bear in the snow. We left the house soon after breakfast, discovered no signs of the bear and returned to the post after dark. Having had nothing to eat for eight hours I looked forward to a fine meal of roast caribou. Instead, when we sat down at the table Grant's Eskimo woman brought in heads of two caribou that had been boiled in water. One was placed in front of me and one in front of Grant. These were ghastly looking objects for while they had been skinned the heavy lips had much hair on them and the eyes were bleached and staring. Seeing the shocked look on my face Grant asked me if I did not like haggis. Then, before I could answer the question he added, "Caribou brains are much better!" I noticed that the half cooked brains were oozing through a crack in the skull onto my plate. My host dug his fork into the skull and extracted some of the brains and began to eat. I followed suit. Only with the greatest possible difficulty did I succeed in swallowing a small portion and then I quickly asked to be excused from the table. Outside I was soon relieved and would have liked to remain in the fresh air because I had developed a violent headache but the intense cold forced me to return. Grant made no reference to my absence but there was a flicker of a smile on his lips as he suggested that I should have a cup of tea and a pilot biscuit with English jam. I went to bed wondering what further treatment I should have. Two days later Grant apologized . . . .

In 1908, the year after the trial, Grant was off to Baffin Island again in the *Snowdrop*. He took with him Captain James Brown and eight men as a crew. One of the crew members was Alexander Ritchie, the man with the "evil influence".

This particular voyage was a very successful one until September 20th. On that day the *Snowdrop* was on the point of returning home with a full cargo when it was overtaken by a violent storm. The ship was helpless. The auxiliary steam power was totally inadequate. Both Brown and Grant knew the end was near. To add to the seriousness of the plight there were on board a large number of Eskimos whom they were taking south. Emergency boats were insufficient and launching them next to impossible. Only with the greatest difficulty did they escape with their lives. They were stranded on an exposed section of coast in the vicinity of Frobisher Bay. Before the ship broke up they managed to rescue only a very few supplies. The small stock of biscuits became so precious that they had to be doled out in the most sparing fashion.

Grant took charge. As rapidly as possible, primitive shelters were built. A lookout was posted and careful watch kept. There was a slim chance that a ship would come in sight before the end of the season. No such luck was theirs.

Flurries of snow came almost daily. Nights grew colder and the coastline rim of ice stretched further and further towards the sea. Snow piled up and winter's iron hand held them fast. Now, the Eskimos who had been an additional hazard and responsibility became an asset. These men and women knew how to handle themselves. Snow houses were built and a tiny community of igloos grew up. But things were bad. The hunting was poor. Supplies from the ship were rapidly exhausted although they were on minimum ration.

By good fortune this small community of shipwrecked people was happened upon by an Eskimo who took them to his village but even there provisions were desperately short. It was a starvation winter. The new addition to the population increased the strain on resources. The white men were, for the most part, not such skilled hunters as the Eskimos. The hunters just had to make larger and more frequent kills. With patience and ability the Eskimos stuck to their task and did their best to provide for everyone. Things were barely endurable when the camp was struck by a blizzard. It howled, moaned, bellowed and hissed for twenty days. No one could live in it. The world was blanketed white. Visibility was down to zero. Travel became impossible. No one dared venture more than a few feet from their snow house. It was a mad eruption of icy fury and it almost spelled their doom. Everyone was reduced to eating boiled seaweed and blubber.

When the wind died down and the snow ceased they were living in a land of fantastic shapes, a land of sweeping curves, dune-like drifts and wind-carved figures.

It was a beautiful land that belied its menace. Was there anything they could do to ensure their rations? Was there a trading post they could reach or a wintering whaling ship they could get to? Endlessly the conversations went round and round until it was finally decided that two of them would go in search of a whaling ship that was believed to be in the vicinity of Lake Harbour.

Ritchie and John Morrison wanted to go and they volunteered for the job. They made what meagre preparations were necessary and set out. It must have been well on into the old year before they started their journey. The route they would travel lay along the north shore of Frobisher Bay, across the western end and then down to Lake Harbour, a distance of well over 200 miles. The country they had to travel through was extremely rugged. Rock hills were riven by frozen rivers, windswept and dangerous. Eskimos had made the journey many times before but it had never been made by a white man. When the small party set out it was in poor shape. Lack of food had taken its toll of physical strength. It was a gamble with death. The two Eskimos who accompanied Ritchie and Morrison suffered less than the white men. These men had never travelled in the Canadian north during winter, had never walked behind a dog team before. They were being blooded in a vicious way.

Day after day they moved slowly on. Progress was real though negligible. Eventually they reached a cut in the south end of the Grinnell Glacier and then changed their general direction to the south. They now aimed, not for Lake Harbour, but for the Saddleback Islands where there was a small Eskimo community and where there was a chance of succour from a wintering ship.

After a very slow trip the four men reached the island, but Morrison was ill. Both of his feet were badly frostbitten and one was gangrenous. In some way or another Morrison had either been careless or had had a minor accident. Ritchie examined his friend's feet.

"I don't like the look of them, John."

"What shall I do?"

"I think gangrene has set in. Do you know what that means?"

John nodded. Both of them knew that the only adequate way to deal with it was to amputate. They had little medication and no tools for such an operation.

Ritchie conveyed to the Eskimos the condition of John's feet. They knew of the frost bite but looked grave when they heard of the infection.

The village talked about it. Finally, some of the Eskimo women agreed to perform an operation. With crude tools, no anaesthetic and little skill they hacked off one of his feet at the ankle. Remarkably, Morrison survived this ghastly ordeal only to be faced with the necessity of having the second foot amputated. Once more the Eskimo women played surgeon and removed his second foot. Morrison must have had an incredible will to live for the second operation also failed to kill him. With great kindness and remarkable tenderness the Eskimos looked after Morrison. At one time it seemed as if he might survive. Then infection began to spread up his leg and further amputations became necessary. These were performed but John Morrison died.

Ritchie stayed on at the Saddleback Islands until summer approached and then went to Lake Harbour. He was at Lake Harbour in 1909 when the whaler *Active* arrived but he could not obtain passage on it. This may well have been because Ritchie was one of Grant's men and the *Active* was one of R. Kinnes' boats. Anyway, Ritchie was still at Lake Harbour when the Reverend Mr. A.L. Fleming arrived with the Reverend Bilby. They were amazed at his story which Fleming understates as "one of considerable hardship". Fleming agreed to give him a passage on the *Lorna Doone* and he and Bilby supplied Ritchie with some clothing.

While all this was taking place, a remarkable series of events had been unleashed by the wreck of the *Snowdrop*. In the summer of 1909, the *Jantina Agatha* was sent out specifically to search for the *Snowdrop,* as was the *Paradox* under the command of no less a person than Captain W.J. Jackson. Both of these ships were wrecked. The *Paradox* was nipped in the ice and crushed (It seems that for once Captain Jackson dared to venture a little too close to the ice.) The entire crew was rescued, taken aboard the steamer, *Adventure,* and quickly brought home. Not so fortunate was the crew of the *Jantina Agatha.* This boat came to grief in Cumberland Sound on the 25th of September. After several days of serious privation and exposure the entire crew managed to reach Blacklead Island where Reverend Mr. Greenshields was maintaining a small mission station. Mr. Greenshields had to perform the almost impossible feat of feeding ten mouths for a year when there were on hand provisions for only one. It may not compare with the feeding of the five thousand but it was still a tough undertaking. Only a matter of weeks before the crew of the *Jantina Agatha* was wrecked, Forsythe-Grant and his small group of men were picked up by Peary's ship, *Jeanie,* and taken to Indian Harbour on the coast of Labrador. It was from there that the first news of the sufferings of the *Snowdrop's* crew was made known to the world.

Those years towards the end of the first decade of the twentieth century were crowded with wrecks and near wrecks. Forsythe-Grant seems to have been in peril of his life every year. It would seem that he sought such peril and found in it the real stuff of life. For a few short years he brought a new colour to the tradition of whalers. Like many before him and many since he could not rest easy outside the vast solitude of the Canadian north. In spite of his defeat in the courts and the destruction of his ship, the *Snowdrop,* he returned to the eastern Arctic. During the September of 1911 Forsythe-Grant was sailing towards Nottingham Island on board the Scottish whaler *Seduisante.* The captain was looking for harbour because a stiff breeze was freshening into a gale. As the ship approached the island a lookout spotted a huge herd of walrus.

"Walrus on port bow!" he called out.

They were quite close. Grant tried to spot them with a telescope. Their black bodies were being washed with spray. Foam covered the rocks and the ship rolled in the swell.

"What a herd!" ejaculated Grant. "Just look at them."

Everybody had their eyes on the animals. It was an exciting sight for the hunters. While everybody's attention was on the herd of walrus the ship ran aground. It was not far from shore.

"Lower the boats," the skipper commanded. "We must make the ship as light as possible. All cargo must be got ashore. Quickly!"

Speed was essential. With a gathering sense of urgency, captain, owner and crew turned themselves to the work. On board were some 60 Eskimos and these too were pressed into service. The wind did not moderate. Wave after wave struck the ship now held fast on the rock.

"I think we'd better send the natives ashore, Mr. Grant," said the captain.

"I agree."

The captain and crew stayed on board in the belief that the ship would float free. The tide was coming in. The boat had been considerably lightened. If things got no worse by early morning the ship would be afloat.

Before the full fury of the storm swept down upon them a few hardy Eskimos managed to get out to the *Seduisante* and beg the captain, owner and crew to come ashore.

"We'll ride it out," insisted Grant. "We'll stay with the ship till morning."

The Eskimos seemed to sense the terrible danger they were in because they renewed their pleas with Grant to come ashore. Grant was adamant, however. Ever a man of mettle he was not going to be bent to an act of cowardice, by wind, sea or Eskimo. Like many a brave man before him and many a brave man since, he preferred to establish his heroism rather than his reason.

It was a wild night. Pitch black but for the phosphorescent glimmer of the storm lashed foam; a night of howling winds and mountainous seas. The noise was awesome. Groaning, heaving, creaking, the boat wrestled with the rock and was broken by it. Water rushed in and the pumps were helpless. The ship was doomed.

When the first grey light of morning came the Eskimos watched from the shore. Frantically the crew signaled for help. No one could do anything. A ship's boat was lowered into the boiling cauldron of swirling water, vicious current and waiting rocks. No boat could live in such a sea. A towering wave caught it and in moments it was dashed to pieces. Then it began to snow, snow thick with rain, watery, blinding sleet, a blanket that blotted out the world. No eyes would see the ship or the living men again. The snowstorm ceased. Everything had disappeared. Slowly the natives moved along the shore looking for bodies. Two were found; the bodies of the captain and chief engineer. These the natives took and buried under a large pile of stones not far from the shore. Grant's body was never recovered. He perished in the icy waters of Hudson Strait. So ended, in the words of his nephew presently living in Scotland, "his rather strange but exciting life".

14
Mica

R. Kinnes, Grant's opponent in law and opposition in trade, was interested in Canada's northland. In fact he had a considerable amount of money invested in ventures on Baffin Island, around its coast and in Hudson Bay. Operating out of Dundee, Scotland, he made a living out of whales, seals, walrus, bears and mica. His prime interest was whaling and mica mining.

A short, irascible Scotsman, Mr. Kinnes proved to be a driving employer and formidable opponent. It was under his direction that the mica mine near Lake Harbour was developed. Mica had been discovered near there towards the end of the nineteenth century but nothing serious was done about it until Kinnes began his mining operation. In 1898 his ship, the *Active*, began regular runs to Hudson Bay in order to catch whales, trade with the Eskimos and collect quantities of mica the Eskimos had mined during the year.

Kinnes, a thorough-going and exacting businessman, was particularly interested in the possibilities of the mica mine and did his best to create an efficient money making operation. In order to set things in motion and to make from the start a worthwhile operation, he sent his eldest son to manage the mine and on one occasion he visited it himself.

While he was on his only trip of inspection and participation he kept a fairly full diary. It is not hard to see from his diary that he hated inefficiency and lack of drive. He notes on August 15th, 1900, "As I anticipated the opportunity given us last night to get up to the higher anchorage has been lost and in consequence, another day lost as well." The entry for August 19th is even more exasperated, "After breakfast the captain went ashore to have a look for the boat. I did not go on shore, preferred nursing my cold as there is no knowing when one may get back again from the boating excursion and as I observed the captain had taken his shotgun with him, will be more intent on getting a shot at something than in getting back to the ship again. He seems very much inclined to waste time with such pastimes as shooting deer or hares than in giving his attention to the object of the voyage which is to secure a cargo as soon as possible but we must now certainly wait the return of the boat." R. Kinnes observes, almost with a note of disappointment, "Contrary to expectation the captain came aboard at 12 o'clock."

It almost seems as if he had it in for Captain Murray because on the very next day he is after him again, this time over the water supply. "Captain and I disputed about the quality of the water. They were busy watering the vessel at the time. We went ashore to see the pond to satisfy him that it was not salt water they were taking. He had to give in he was wrong. It is wonderful how many men agreed with him the water was salt on tasting it."

Kinnes was a man who knew his own mind, who made his own judgments and did not suffer fools gladly. During the voyage the crew engaged in several walrus hunts which were only partially successful. On August 22nd a large herd of walrus was spotted. In no time flat the hunt was on. Robert Kinnes did not share in this particular hunt. He watched. Later that day he noted, "As usual bad generalship was shown by the mate. He took all the gunners round to the leeward side of the island with the result that when they began to fire there were so many walrus that the steam from their droppings completely hid the brutes from the men, only four being shot on the island out of hundreds. An extraordinary number were to be seen in the water after the stampede."

The trip became an endless series of frustrations. No whales were sighted or caught. The closest they came to whales was to hear stories about them. An American whaler had the products of three whales on board and the captain spoke of having sighted others but the *Active* saw never a one. "Too late getting here," maintained Kinnes. And he was probably right. With whales remaining uncaught and virtually untraceable, mica became the chief preoccupation of Mr. Kinnes. The previous year the carpenter had brought home some interesting samples of mica from an area where there was no mine. Kinnes was anxious to look at the source of these deposits to see if there was anything of commercial value there. On several occasions he, the carpenter and a few other men made excursions to different islands looking for the spot. Amongst the islands, however, the carpenter became increasingly confused and Mr. Kinnes increasingly exasperated. The charts they had were hopelessly inaccurate and the memories of the men just as unreliable. Although Mr. Kinnes could appreciate the problems confronting them he could not help wondering at their stupidity. "I thought, at least," he writes in his diary, "the captain and the other men would have recognized the place where they buried the cook last year."

On the 14th of August he went ashore at 6:30 p.m. to look at Beacon Island. He found indifferent seams of mica, useless for commercial purposes. The same day he observes in his diary, "I'm beginning to doubt if the carpenter knows where he picked up the specimens." Three days later they went out to search seriously once more for the missing mica mine. It was a terribly difficult area for such a search. The previous day Kinnes had walked to the top of the hill on one of the islands. He describes what he saw, " . . . As far as you can see there is nothing but islands in every direction, hundreds of them, bare, bleak, very suitable for walrus . . . . "

Into that maze of islands the men sailed and rowed. Past island after island they moved. Nobody could tell one from the other. Kinnes tried hard to get the carpenter to fix on one but the poor man was lost. At last after a three hour pull the carpenter took them to an island but they found nothing there. Shortly after that he pointed to another island that he thought was the one but was wrong again. It was evident that the man was completely confused. Kinnes says in his diary, "I came to the conclusion that if it was so difficult to find it was not worth while looking further for it."

Not many days after this abortive excursion Kinnes made up his mind to waste no more time doing nothing but to proceed at once to where the natives reported the presence of sizeable mica deposits. By the morning of the 25th the *Active* was steaming along in sight of the cairn on Big Island. By 12 noon they had reached the north channel of Ashe Inlet. There they picked up natives, boats, kayaks and tupiks and then went round to the mainland to see the deposits. On the morning of the 27th, an Eskimo, Shutapan, and his son came to the ship with about forty pounds of mica. It was poor quality and badly damaged. Kinnes was assured, however, that there was a lot of much better quality.

"I'll come with you, myself, tomorrow," said Kinnes. "I'm not at all sure that you're going to the right place. I think the mica deposits have been worked in the past and the ones I want to continue working on, are further away."

Shutapan said that these deposits were the only ones he knew about although another Eskimo, a crippled man, said that there was another mica deposit quite a bit further away but not so far that they could not make the journey in one day. At 3:00 o'clock in the morning Kinnes roused the others and by 4:00 o'clock they were on their way to the mica deposit. It only took them an hour to get there. There were three mounds of mica pieces near an outcrop from which passing natives had lifted small fragments of mica. For the most part the outcrop yielded very irregular pieces. Kinnes and his men on that day were seriously handicapped in their endeavors to get the mica because all they had to work with was a primitively fashioned bone spade. After some trouble they managed to dig out one piece right down to the rock. This piece was about a foot thick but unfortunately it was split across the middle. Kinnes notes, "I have no doubt if the place were properly worked good deposits would be found underneath as at every point we tried we could always get mica in quantity, small and indifferent pieces to start with but improving as you went in. As the distance was too far away to carry we did not continue operations but contented ourselves by looking all around the mounds and going to the high hills without seeing any indications on these of mica." By 10:00 o'clock that morning they were back on the ship drinking coffee.

During the next two days Kinnes set things up for future

mica mining operations. He sent ashore sufficient wood to build a warehouse for the storage of mica the Eskimos recovered. This warehouse was to be built near the head of the fiord. Once all this was set in motion he took the names of all those who were willing to work and noted what return they wanted for their labour. Mr. Kinnes made it clear that he wanted all the boxes filled with good mica. Only in that way would they merit their wages. On August 29th he paid off all those who had been helping him up until then. Their equipment was offloaded from the *Active* and they parted on good terms. Kinnes writes, "Gave them a supply of bread, coffee and molasses to keep them going for a week or two before they can get reindeer meat for themselves. They feel highly pleased and gratified with themselves."

By the time September 3rd came round Robert Kinnes had had enough of shipboard life and was looking forward to getting back to Scotland: "Am heartily tired of the confinement," he wrote on that day.

Kinnes' mica mine was not a roaring success in spite of the fact that A.P. Low says in the Government Report *The Cruise of the Neptune*, "A valuable mica mine is being worked at a profit on the north shore of Hudson Strait."

Kinnes did not get large enough quantities nor good enough quality. In those days some of the world's best mica was coming from Canada. A large portion of the world's supply was being mined in Ontario. There had been mica mines elsewhere in Canada and two of these had been in the Territories. As early as the seventeenth century mica had been mined by the Hudson's Bay Company at Eastmain, a small settlement on the east coast of James Bay, but after a very few years this was abandoned as unprofitable. In 1876 an American took a large load of mica out of the Cumberland Sound area. According to an article on mineral resources and mining activity in the Canadian eastern Arctic printed in the *Canadian Geographical Journal*, this shipment was worth $120,000. This mine is mentioned by Low in *The Cruise of the Neptune* when he states that it was situated on the west coast of Cumberland Gulf. It seems that the world demand for mica at that time must have been strong enough to encourage men like R. Kinnes to give the business a try. Mica was being used in electrical appliances and in heat resistant construction. Doubtless the growing use of electricity was a prime cause for the increased demand for mica. For R. Kinnes, mica, whales and fur all proved difficult products to obtain. By the early days of the 1900's the halcyon days of the whaler were past and mica mining with native employees in a distant place without adequate machinery was a precarious undertaking. Mr. Kinnes almost lost his shirt in the enterprise.

In order to make operations more efficient the Kinnes company had established posts at Repulse Bay and on Southampton Island. These posts were permanently manned and were reasonably well equipped. They were designed to prosecute whale fishing and fur trading so that when the *Active* made its annual call it just had to pick up a cargo and get on its way again. These outposts did not always have much to show for their year's endeavors but nonetheless it was sound business sense to have men and boats available for whaling the moment the season opened.

Kinnes did the same thing with his mining operations. At least two men were left there all winter so that work was able to begin as soon as enough frost was out of the ground. When the 1903 shipment came back Kinnes was so disappointed at the unsatisfactory quality of it all that he sent his son out to act as manager. On the outbound and homeward bound voyages the son, Walter Kinnes, worked on board as the purser. They left Dundee on the 20th of June, taking a squad of seven quarrymen, and returned on October 20th.

When he arrived at the mine he found that the two quarrymen left there had already extracted about three tons of mica and put it in from 45 to 50 cases. Walter Kinnes immediately put all the men to work on a better quality showing than the one they had been working.

The mica he directed them to extract was amber mica. By the end of the season the men had some 17 tons of mica ready for shipment. It was still in the crude state and would need splitting and dressing in Scotland. The cargo was carried partly in cases and partly loose in tanks. When this was discharged at Dundee the mica in wooden cases was sent straight to the warehouse while the mica in the tanks was put into bags by hand. These bags were taken up to the warehouse and the contents emptied out on the floor. There was quite a pile on the warehouse floor by the time all the bags were turned out.

Once the mica was in Scotland Mr. Kinnes wanted to sell it. He contacted R. & F. Baxter, the only mica importer in Scotland, and in conjunction with this firm the mica was sold to Messrs. Attwater and Sons of Preston, Lancashire. Usually it was sold ready trimmed, not in the rough state. By the time the mica was sold it had been sorted but was still in the crude state. Walter and another man had lifted out the blocks that measured more than four by six inches. It was sent by rail to Preston and there the work of processing began. Soon it became apparent to Mr. Attwater that the mica was not as good as he had hoped, so he tried to back out of the contract. Kinnes would have none of that and the matter wound up in court. Attwater maintained that he had been misled and, not to mince matters, cheated. He complained in court about the poor lighting in the warehouse where he had examined the mica. He also maintained that Mr. Kinnes had encouraged him to believe the mica this year was much better than the previous year's consignment, some of which Mr. Attwater had seen. To emphasize this, Mr. Kinnes is said to have pointed out that his son was sent to the Arctic expressly to ensure that no worthless mica was shipped. Mr. Attwater says, "I attached importance to these statements."

When cross-examined in court Robert Kinnes stated that he had never tried to mislead Mr. Attwater and that Mr. Attwater saw what he was buying and took a chance on the quality. The lawyer for Attwater tried to infer that Kinnes charged too much for the mica. He asked, "Comparing the two prices offered 3/6d for large slabs of trimmed mica and 2/3d for the crude, doesn't the price of crude seem a pretty full one to your mind?"

"No."

"There will be a loss of 50% in trimming mica for market. Wasn't he offering you for the crude stuff a good deal more than 50% of what he was offering you for trimmed?"

"I don't consider in that light he was. I do not consider he was offering enough in either case."

Nobody managed to get the better of R. Kinnes. When Attwater first tried to back out of the deal Kinnes wrote firmly to him. In a letter dated 21st of January, 1904 we read: "Dear

Sirs: Messrs. Baxter have handed me your letter on the twentieth. I positively refuse to enter into any of the side issues you are now trying to raise and it is very annoying to find you doing so after the very explicit understanding we arrived at when negotiating the contract. The conditions were of your own making and you had perfect liberty to safeguard the interests of your firm in selecting and packing before delivery. But after that I told you I would refuse to recognize any claim.

"You entered into contract with as full a knowledge of the condition and quality of the mica as I had. We did not represent it as 'good, selected mica' as your letter indicates. The contract sets this at rest. The bulk was inspected by you and you examined the good as well as the bad and took all the risks, and why you should now try to raise false issues on a contract which you yourselves forced us into is somewhat beyond my comprehension. We have nothing to do with the condition of the mica as it may turn out on breaking the blocks. Their mixed condition was well known to you when you made the contract. Your main stipulation was to keep nothing back and as my part of the contract has been fulfilled I expect you to fulfill yours without anymore trouble and annoyance. Be kind enough, therefore, to understand that I am not to enter into any fresh stipulation on a contract that has now been completed so far as I am concerned and demand an immediate settlement."

He demanded it but he did not get it. The case was processed through the courts until it reached the final Court of Appeal, the House of Lords, itself. It was just a few tons of mica from Baffin Island but had R. Kinnes lost the case it would have finished him. His grandson said, "Grandfather had to win that case. To have lost would have meant financial ruin."

Kinnes was not a loser. He managed to make some profit out of nearly all his endeavors, whether it was the fur business, whaling or mining for mica. Some of his ventures may have been gambles but they were not fruitless. It was men like this who began to exploit the mineral wealth of the Territories, a wealth still barely touched. He gave to the Eskimos a new kind of employment and was thus in the forefront of civilizing ventures. A man of drive, determination and business ambition, R. Kinnes was very different from those who went to the Arctic in search of adventure.

Unlike Forsythe-Grant, Kinnes concentrated all his attention upon making his business successful and avoided unnecessarily hazardous exploits. He drove hard bargains but kept his end of contracts. When he arrived among the Eskimos they met the typical hard-working, hard-driving businessman, a man very different than the usual whalers, hunters, traders and explorers who had made Baffin Island their territory.

Shortly after the mica mine was operating and Kinnes' interest increasing, the Government of Canada decided to do something about the north. It sent Captain J.E. Bernier into its northern waters to intercept whalers and demand that they purchase licences and to call at trading posts to collect custom duty. The end of the Arctic free-for-all was in sight.

15

An Exercise in Sovereignty

Captain J.E. Bernier, the hard-working teetotaler who was skipper of the C.G.S. *Arctic*, wrote to the Department of Marine and Fisheries in a letter dated January 20th, 1908:

" . . . Also I beg to advise you that not having met Mr. Noble of Kekerton, Cumberland Gulf, I was unable to collect from him the whaling licence for whale fishing. So far as I have learned no whales were taken by Mr. Noble this last two summers. We were also unable to collect dues for the Custom's House Department, because we found the gentleman at Kekerton dead.

"I sent him a letter on my arrival here claiming the licence dues and have no reply yet. If I have one I shall forward it to you.

"I shall need from you the necessary instructions with regard to our limit in Northern Waters so that I shall make no mistake when I start in the spring."

For years and years there had been no attempt to assert Canadian sovereignty in the Arctic but now action had begun with such enthusiasm that not even the dead were going to be let off.

In 1907 the Honourable Pascal Poirier moved: "That it be resolved that the Senate is of the opinion that the time has come for Canada to make a formal declaration of possession of the lands and islands situated in the north of the Dominion and extending to the North Pole."

He contended: "It is somewhat — I do not know if I may call it jarring to read occasionally in the United States papers such paragraphs as this — 'The Captain of the whaler so and so has hoisted the United States flag on a certain island, or that some United States navigator in the Arctic waters has planted the United States flag on another island and taken possession of it, when by referring to our atlas we find that these islands and lands are situated in the Canadian waters. Reflecting on what these acts of possession might have on Canadian ownership and considering that they may be merely of sportive character or matters of amusement, still they have serious consequences for the future especially when we remember the importance our friends to the south have attached to the small acts of possession as these in the settlement of disputes with them. In 1783, for example, and later on in the matter of the Ashburton Treaty and still later in the settlement with them of our Alaska boundary."

Previous to this merited outburst there had been secret correspondence between England's Prime Minister and the Governor-General of Canada. The gist of this correspondence was a shared concern to establish without any doubt British sovereignty in Canada's northern territories. One particularly important matter was to make sure that the Hudson Bay was Canadian territorial water. On 24th of July, 1906 Lord Elgin sent a secret telegram to Governor General Earl Grey: " . . . We have Lord Minto's confidential despatch of 23rd June, 1904 by your Ministers. Have no doubt since that date made further investigations into various aspects, geographically, historically and legally, of question of the status of the Bay and Straits and with the Act I shall be glad to have a report embodying any detail on the grounds on which your Ministers now relate to establish the British status of the Bay in order that we may be in a position to return an early and authoritative answer to the representations which United States Government in view of the long period during which their vessels have whaled in the Bay with impunity, may be expected to make."

The fears that a number of government officials had about the attitude of other nations towards Canada's assertion of sovereignty were not groundless. When the time came to collect licence fees for whale fishing in territorial waters and to exact custom dues there were those who thought such actions were unwarranted. These people failed to realize that on the 31st of

July, 1880 an Order-In-Council was passed by which all the "territories, islands, inland seas and waters lying north and west of Robeson Channel, Kennedy Channel, Smith Sound, Baffin Bay and Davis Strait as far as the 141st meridian of West Long- ditude were included in the Dominion of Canada." Certainly for a number of years the Canadian Government did nothing about it but come the turn of the century there was a little twitching in Ottawa and things began to happen. Pressure mounted on the Government because of the number of foreign scientific parties who were penetrating the Arctic and the increasing possibility of their authority being contested. Not only were there scienti- fic expeditions, there was also a tremendous rush to reach the Pole. These expeditions, although scientific, were motivated more by the desire for national glory than anything else. But it is only a short step from being discoverer to being owner. Even though the routes these men planned to travel were largely through Canadian territory there was no Canadian expedition.

That was certainly through no fault of Captain Bernier who tried, with a measure of desperation, to get the Government to underwrite a serious attempt to reach the North Pole. He wrote letters. He pleaded in person. He laid plans. He organized committees. But he never headed an expedition. The Govern- ment offered him the princely sum of $6,000 towards the cost of purchasing a vessel.

In early 1901 a newspaper carried large headlines: WILL CANADA WIN? A GIGANTIC INTERNATIONAL RACE. EVERY NATION REPRESENTED. THE MOST REMARK- ABLE CONTEST IN THE HISTORY OF MAN. The article under these enthusiastic headlines says:

" . . . No less than seven expeditions are being fitted out and will sail from as many ports. Practically unlimited means have been placed at the disposal of Admiral Makaroff. William Ziegler, a millionaire of New York is willing to spend $1,500,000 to enable Evelyn B. Baldwin to plant the stars and stripes at the Pole. The Duke of Abruzzi who spent $500,000 on his first expedition is prepared to spend twice as much if necessary to accomplish this purpose.

"Undoubtedly the greatest factor in the world's race for the Pole is the expedition of Captain J.E. Bernier of Quebec,

Canadian by birth, who offered his services to his King and Canada gratuitously."

With this kind of publicity Bernier's spirits perked up. It looked as if his cherished expedition might become an actuality. Even though the Government was only willing to make a trifling contribution Bernier thought it likely that he could rouse enough public interest to get Canada to the Pole first. Captain Bernier wrote to Major Levasseur, the president of the Quebec Geographical Society, telling him of some of his plans and hopes. "I have distributed over 30,000 circulars throughout the Dominion and every bank in Canada has a subscription list at the disposal of the public. The subscriptions are coming in fairly well. We trust in God and we will have to do all we can to encourage the public to take an interest in the matter and subscribe, as it is rather hard to do so without the government taking the initiative. We, however, have the sympathy of the people at large and with due perseverance we shall be successful in the end."

Three years after this letter was written Captain Bernier is again writing to Major Levasseur. "I am extremely obliged for the congratulations of Chev. Baillairge and Mr. Rouillard and yourself, but the North Pole Expedition has not yet begun, the ship has not even been purchased."

It is very readily apparent that Captain Bernier was by this date fed up with the whole affair. He was genuinely concerned to ensure Canada's sovereignty in the Arctic and was quick to see the significance of the conquest of the Pole, a conquest that would add prestige to Canada and give her international prominence. Captain Bernier wanted some of the prominence too. He sounds almost churlish in one of his letters. The letter is again addressed to Mr. Levasseur and concerns a voyage to the Hudson Bay to take provisions to A.P. Low who had wintered there in the ship *Neptune*. Bernier wants to do more than his terms of reference at that date permit him, "I have not yet accepted command of this coming expedition and will do so only on the condition that more latitude be granted . . . . When I leave here to take provisions to make Mr. Low succeed in his undertaking it may be my name may never be mentioned in the matter. What is the use after so many hard years of work and endeavors to interest the people in their northern heritage if I cannot now begin to act after a quarter of a century of assiduity. Time has fully matured and I must now strike."

Bernier certainly wanted glory for Canada and glory for himself too. In retrospect it seems as if the Canadian Government missed a bet when it failed to give Bernier the backing he deserved. Bernier was unique, a man peculiarly fitted to lead expeditions, particularly by sea and into the Arctic wastes.

Captain Joseph Elzear Bernier was born at L'Islet, Quebec, on January 1st, 1852. His father and grandfather were both sea captains. The service of his family and relatives at sea totalled more than 794 years. When Joe Bernier was only a year old he went to sea with his parents. In 1855 he was at the bombardment of Sebastopol. He sailed with his parents until he was seven years old, at which age he was sent to school. Soon after his twelfth birthday he went to sea again. This time he served as a boy on his father's ship. The following year he became a sailor. At that time the first mate was Tyrrell, a man who later became Captain Tyrrell and he it was who taught the young Bernier to navigate. It was also during these years that he learned to speak English. In 1869, when he was only seventeen years old, he had command of the barkentine *St. Joseph*. He took command of her at Quebec and sailed her to Devonshire, England. On the return trip Bernier's second in command met with an accident so Bernier had complete responsibility for bringing the ship back. It is said that he is the only man to have had command of a ship at seventeen years of age. Bernier crossed the Atlantic 178 times, commanded 46 different vessels, sailed around the world several times and visited Arctic regions. He possessed a letter of commendation from the owner of every ship he commanded. Upon returning from the sea he became dock master at Levis, Quebec. Retirement did not suit him for long. He was soon back at sea working for his former employer, J.G. Ross. In 1903 he retired again and became Governor of the Quebec Gaol. This again did not last long. Bernier hankered for the sea and before the first decade of this century was passed he had sailed under the aegis of the Canadian Government into the Canadian Northern Territorial waters on several occasions. When Bernier went north for Canada it was not to lead an expedition to the Pole but to engage in the interception of whalers, to collect duty and annex land he might encounter that was not already possessed. In fact his duties were really a copy of the duties that had been undertaken by the expedition in 1903 under the command of A.P. Low.

Bernier was certainly the man for the job, a man who would brook no nonsense and who was afraid of no one. Alfred Tremblay, who accompanied Bernier on a number of occasions, can only recall Bernier being afraid once and even then Bernier rapidly recovered himself. As a matter of fact, he was really responsible for Bernier's moment of fear. Tremblay had left the ship at Pond Inlet to explore and prospect. At the outset, J.J. Wilson accompanied him but, between Pond Inlet and Arctic Bay, Wilson took sick and returned to the boat. Wilson was supposed to bring supplies to Tremblay at Arctic Bay but due to a fierce snowstorm Wilson was never able to get fresh supplies for Tremblay to use. With his Eskimo guide Tremblay travelled on that trip just over 4000 miles and was away 359 days. He was away so long that Bernier's crew and the Eskimos of the settlement had given him up for dead. It was August when he got back and he just made it on time. He only had two rounds of ammunition left and no matches. For months he and his guide had been living on raw fish, seal and caribou meat. "The sun was still shining," Tremblay recalls, "when we got back to Pond Inlet although it was two o'clock in the morning. The Eskimos heard us coming and crowded out of their tents to meet us. 'It just can't be you. You're dead,' they kept saying. They thought I was a ghost coming back and even Bernier was a little bit afraid."

Captain Bernier may have been momentarily shocked at the unexpected arrival of a man he had presumed dead but he certainly was not the kind of man to be easily frightened.

When speaking to a journalist in 1908, prior to another trip north, he stated that there were a number of whalers, principally Danish, who were fishing in our northern waters without licences. "These," he said, "I will overtake and force them to take out a licence or make them quit fishing." That is strong language. Captain Bernier also made it clear that he would make the whalers pay duty on their trade goods that they used for

barter with the natives. On his initial trip north for these purposes Captain Bernier managed to collect some $1,500, which,
in those days, was no mean sum.

Certainly, Captain Bernier pursued his task diligently but in
spite of his conscientious attempts to apprehend all the viola-
tors of Canadian sovereignty some managed to give him the slip.

One small steamer, the *Kite*, took off when it saw the *C.G.S.
Arctic* and, being faster than Bernier's ship, got away. It is likely
that the owners of the vessel were traced and that eventually
the necessary fees had to be paid. One thing is not open to
doubt and that is Captain Bernier's anger at the master of the
ship. Although in an interview with a journalist Captain Bernier
speaks specifically of Danish whalers, not a little trouble was
given to the Canadian Government by American ships. American whalers were extremely busy in the Hudson Bay during the
last 50 years of the 19th century and came and went without
let or hindrance of any kind. Towards the end of the century
things began to come to a head. Mr. Robert J. Gilker helped to
stir the Canadian Government into action. On December 31st,
1898, he wrote from Shirley, Massachusetts, to Mr. L.P.
Brodeur (Minister of Marine and Fisheries) with whom he had
had some previous correspondence, " . . . I beg to inform you
that the whalers sail from New Bedford, U.S.A. about June 1st
and proceed to Hudson Bay. They go as far north as Repulse
Bay and winter there. They fish for whales until the ice prevents
them. Then the vessel is taken to winter quarters until they
resume their work in the spring. They winter at Marble Island,
Cape Fullerton and Repulse Bay. There is an American whaler
at Cape Fullerton now. She will leave there for New Bedford
about the last of August, 1899. I beg to inform you I am a
Canadian myself and it would interest me to know if Americans
have the privilege to kill and destroy seals, walrus, and whales in
these waters."

The letter was answered, stating that the rights of American
whalers in the Bay would receive consideration. To this letter
Robert Gilker replied:

"I would ask you the favour to go to Hudson Bay on the
cutter if one is sent up there to investigate as I am able to talk
the native language of Repulse and may be of service to you. I

will beg to inform you that the *Eric* is wintering at Cape Fullerton. The captain sent home eight heads of bone last October to
New Bedford but his vessel has the oil on board yet. I would
also beg to inform you that vessels going up there from year to
year make a practice of trading with the natives for their wives
or squaws and live and sleep with them on the vessel while in
British or Canadian waters. Perhaps you may have heard of this
before as being the way the American whalers act on Hudson
Bay. I remain your obedient servant. J.R.J. Gilker."

Obviously Gilker did not like what was going on. Nor in fact
did the Canadian Government. Slowly things changed. In the
October of 1903 the *Neptune* headed out of Halifax for a two
year voyage to the Arctic. She was under the command of
Captain Bartlett but the expedition, sponsored by the Canadian
Government for purposes of establishing Canadian sovereignty
and enforcing Canadian laws, was led by A.P. Low. This expedition was to patrol the Hudson Bay, set up a police post and
then move towards the far north and the Arctic Islands. In spite
of this trip and subsequent ones made at the behest of the
Canadian Government the question of Canadian sovereignty in
the Hudson Bay was not clearly established. When Canada
decided to impose a licence fee for the privilege of whale fishing
in the Hudson Bay strong reaction was expected from the
United States of America. In a report to the Governor-General
of Canada L.P. Brodeur, Minister of Marine and Fisheries,
writes, "His Lordship . . . expresses a desire for a report embodying in detail the grounds upon which it now relies to
establish British status in the Hudson Bay in order to reply to
representations which may be expected from the United States
Government. In view of the long standing period during which
their vessels have hunted whales in the Hudson Bay without
interference."

British sovereignty in the Hudson Bay and over the northern
archipelago was recognized by the United States of America in
the Treaty of 1818 and transferred to Canada by the Imperial
Orders-in-Council of 1870 and 1880. The Convention of 1818,
after securing to citizens of the United States of America
common rights of fishing within certain limits in the Gulf of St.
Lawrence continued these limits "to and through the Strait of

Belle Isle and thence northward indefinitely along the coast". Even if this vague description could be tortured into embracing the waters of Hudson Bay the specific reservation "without prejudice, however, to any exclusive rights of the Hudson's Bay Company" effectually closed these waters to them. Insofar as the Dominion of Canada acquired the right to the Hudson's Bay Company in their entirety it follows that the exclusion of the United States citizens from these waters had never been tempered by conventional arrangement. Canada's claim to Hudson Bay was only impaired to the extent that apathetic aquiescence and non-interference with the early and continuous operation of the American sea hunters and whalers there might be argued as indicating territorial disinterest.

In 1905 Captain Comer of the United States of America made application to the Canadian Government for a licence to exploit Hudson Bay. This set the cat among the pigeons. A memorandum to L.P. Brodeur notes, "Any present action of a specific nature must, to a great extent, affect the ultimate position which Canada may desire to assume in regard to these waters." Matters were not helped by the knowledge that the Canadian Government had of interchanges between Captain Comer and his own government. Comer made it abundantly plain that he had a communication from his own government to the effect that he would be protected outside the three mile limit in the Hudson Bay. It seems certain that the United States was going to regard the Hudson Bay as international waters. In a carefully prepared report submitted to the Governor-General of Canada L.P. Brodeur adequately argued Canada's position and he wound it up in the following manner. "In the light of conditions and circumstances it would be idle to dwell upon the implied recognition of any contention by the United States Government simply because Great Britain or Canada had abstained, up to the present time, from active interference with desultory exploitation by foreigners. No such significance can be imputed to Canada's want of equipment in the past for the remedy of which she is now providing means."

It has to be remembered that in the early part of the twentieth century this remote region had only recently come into existence as organized districts and the resources and demands of government did not tend towards any immediate development of these outlying territories. Formally authorized government expeditions preparatory to and for purposes of organization for the enforcement of laws were conducted in 1884, 1885 and 1886 by Captain Gordon and in 1897 by Captain Wakeham. These were followed in this century by A.P. Low, Captain Bernier and Major Moodie.

16
Pond Inlet

The expedition under A.P. Low was the first one to establish any permanent posts in the Arctic for the purpose of administering the laws of Canada. Previous to the establishment of these government outposts there had been a few permanent establishments in the Arctic. Whalers from Scotland had set up posts at Pond Inlet, Kekerton and Blacklead Island, Lake Harbour, Repulse Bay and Southampton Island. In addition to these there were a few posts in the Hudson Bay area at which American whalers wintered. Then, of course, there were the Hudson's Bay Company's trading posts in the more southern reaches of the Bay. Some of the men who went north as whalers started to live with the Eskimos and eventually went native.

One such man was William Duval, a man of German extraction, who sailed north in an American whaling ship and eventually made his home in Pangnirtung Fiord. By the middle of the thirties Duval was known all over Baffin Island and has now made his mark on the map of the country, for the mountain just behind the settlement of Pangnirtung has been named Mount Duval. According to a story current in the north, Duval was at one time engaged to the daughter of a Baptist minister in the United States. She jilted him and in despair he signed on with an American whaling ship and never went south again. Even though he did not make it back to civilization it is certain that on occasions he wanted to. In 1907 he was in the Pond Inlet area and he wrote to Captain Bernier.

I take the opportunity of the C.G.S. *Arctic* in Albert Harbour, Pond Inlet to solicit the favour of a passage on the steamer for my family from here to Blacklead or any

other place on Cumberland Sound and the same favour for myself to the terminus of the C.G.S. *Arctic* voyage.
(Evidently, he wanted to dump his family in the Cumberland Sound area and then go on by himself to Quebec.)

I apply to you Commander, with confidence as I would to the Canadian Government whose official representative you are here. My family belongs to the Innuit tribe of Cumberland Sound. It is to improve the existence of my poor young children I wish to take them back to their native land with their mother, so bringing them nearer to their relatives and friends. More than that there are some schools down there with a Christian Mission at Blacklead. My children being old enough to take benefit of civilization it would be unfortunate to deprive them of such a good thing. Here and no other place except Blacklead are there any schools or missions so it is the only place convenient to the education of my poor young chaps. Concerning myself I am German born. However, as I have lived in Canada for twenty-five years and intending to live the rest of my life there I have already made an offer to take my oath of allegiance to become a British subject, which oath you declined to accept. However, I call on you, Commander, to protect me as you would do any Canadian citizen. I am confident that it would be possible and easy for the official representative of the Dominion Government to grant the favour I am soliciting. It might be that you have no possible power to take me down free of charge. Then please let me know what it would be necessary for me to pay and if I can I will do it. So much I will do for the happiness of my young children. It is true we might be very poor and humble subjects of the Crown but we are not less faithful and devoted to the British flag and the country who has just come and took us under its protection and given us the honourable title of Canadian citizens. Now, Honourable Commander, I long for the favour to take passage on the C.G.S. *Arctic* for my family to Cumberland Sound and to Quebec and any terminus harbour for me. I dare to sign, with utmost respect, William Duval.

This wheedling letter left Captain Bernier unmoved. He was not going to encourage a husband in the desertion of his family.

When the C.G.S. *Arctic* sailed, it sailed without Duval.

This was not the last that Captain Bernier saw of Duval. They met again in 1923, this time at a court trial, the trial of the murderers of Robert S. Janes. There is no record of any interchange between Captain Bernier and William Duval but it is certain that by then Duval was so much a part of the Arctic landscape that he would never really have belonged anywhere else.

On the expedition following the one William Duval tried unsuccessfully to join, Captain Bernier had along with him as second officer, Robert Janes. Janes was a native of Newfoundland and a competent sailor and adventurer. He became so enamored with the north and the opportunities for trading in the north that he managed to scrape up enough financial support to set up a trading post at Patricia River on Eclipse Sound in the year 1916. His attempt at trading proved disastrous. The financial backers in Newfoundland let him down and his condition rapidly deteriorated. For the last year and a half of his life his circumstances were unbelievably miserable. Like William Duval he tried to obtain passage outside but his attempts were frustrated. That was in 1919. Janes realized how desperate his situation was and decided to journey down to Chesterfield Inlet on the west coast of the Hudson Bay. The journey envisaged was a long, difficult and dangerous one. He had only travelled as far as Cape Crawford, about one hundred and fifty miles as the crow flies from the settlement of Pond Inlet, when he ran into trouble. At Cape Crawford was a fairly large collection of Eskimos, among whom was Nukallak. For some time Janes and Nukallak had been at variance and shortly after Janes' arrival Nukallak and two other Eskimos decided to kill him. Exactly what transpired between Janes and the natives it is not possible to determine. It seems certain that Janes had been acting in a high-handed manner and had not always dealt fairly with them. One story told about him is that he used to break a file in half when trading. The story may well be true but the reason for only trading half a file at the time may simply have been an intolerable shortage of trading goods. Janes apparently made one fatal mistake at Cape Crawford. He lost his temper. What triggered his outburst no one seems to know but while he was raging he threatened to shoot the Eskimos' dogs and shoot some of the Eskimos too. This was enough for the natives. Any angry man is dangerous. A man unable to control himself must be destroyed.

"We must do something about him," said Nukallak.

"We must talk."

They talked. It was almost a formal court sitting to try an absent man. Janes was discussed carefully and sentenced to death. Nukallak, Uguyungnak and Ahteetah plotted his murder.

Uguyungnak went up to Janes' igloo, stooped down and entered. Once inside he said, "A friend of mine outside has some furs to sell."

Janes, always eager to buy pelts, immediately went out to see this man. As he came out he was shot. The bullet went into the mid section of his body. Dazed, he just stood there staring and uncertain. Ahteetah walked up to him and pushed him down and Nukallak put a bullet through his head.

The deed was now done. The execution had been planned carefully and it was regarded by the Eskimos as a just end for a dangerous man. Nukallak was rewarded by others of the community. They brought a number of furs to him as gifts. The Eskimos did not dispose of Janes' body in their usual manner but endeavored to give him a proper burial. Staff Sergeant Joy, who was in charge of the investigation into Janes' murder, speaks of the interment as "an admirable and Christianlike act". The Eskimos usually expose their dead but these men, knowing the practice among white men was different, went to considerable trouble to inter him.

The wheels of the law grind slowly anywhere and with extraordinarily glacial-like fashion in the north. Not until 1923 was a court held at Pond Inlet and the three men tried for murder. The Court made its way north in no less a ship than the C.G.S. *Arctic*, the very ship in which Janes had sailed as first officer. The *Arctic* is a ship that merits mention. It was quite an old tub.

In the report of the Eastern Arctic Patrol for that year there are a number of unkind things said about this boat:

It is hoped that before many years are past, development in the north will justify the Government in putting on the work a steamship of suitable size, worthy in every way of the country and Government it represents. It is rather humiliating sometimes to meet foreigners as at Godhaven or H.B. Co. officials as at Pond Inlet in 1922 and Pangnirtung in '23 and be obliged to apologize for the *Arctic* and her appearance even though all concerned are thoroughly aware of her staunchness and her peculiar suitability for ice work.

Originally rigged as a barentine she was a credit to the Navy and was a good sailing ship with auxiliary steam power for use in calm weather or emergencies and without steam at all, being able to take care of herself in any ordinary weather if necessary. As she is now, having been rigged in the interests of economy with three "pole" masts and fore and aft sails she is dependent on steam power practically at all times, the sails helping appreciably only when the wind is fair. Without steam the ship is helpless in any kind of breeze and the constant menace of being caught on a lee shore with the engines out of commission as they are apt to be when they are most needed gives Captain Bernier many an anxious hour. Under present conditions this ranks easily with the danger of being forced ashore or on the reef by the ice as the greatest hazards of the work in the north.

The Government, having committed itself to a policy of renewed interest in the north, should have a ship that would be a credit to all concerned, if only to impress strangers, company officers and natives alike. They should all realize that the Government is the biggest thing in the north and that all others are subservient thereto. This, of course, is not the case when the Government is represented by the *Arctic*, and the Hudson's Bay Company can send in a splendid ship like the *Nascopie*, twice the size of the *Arctic* and a real steamship in every sense of the word and absolutely independent of the winds that blow.

In spite of the *Arctic's* inadequacies there was never a disaster during the Eastern Arctic Patrol. The Government, however, did see the merit of the numerous criticisms of the *Arctic* and managed to arrive at an agreement with the Hudson's Bay Company whereby the patrol travelled on the *Nascopie* in succeeding years.

The C.G.S. *Arctic* arrived in Pond Inlet on August 24th, 1923. On board was the Stipendiary Magistrate, Mr. L. Rivet, K.C., of Montreal and Messrs. Adrian Falardeau and L. Tellier, counsel for the Crown and Defence respectively.

At the trial, which began on August 25th, the paths of three men, Janes, Duval and Bernier crossed for the last time. Bernier was the captain of the ship bringing the Court. Janes was the subject of the enquiry. Duval was the interpreter. According to a report made to the Department of the Interior the proceedings opened with all the proper ceremonial accompaniments. The Magistrate, lawyers, Clerk of the Court and jury selected from among the ship's officers and crew, the Inspector of the R.C.M.P. with a corporal and a guard and the three prisoners went ashore in the launch in the midst of a snow storm and proceeded at once to the police building. After the jury had been sworn in, the judge, lawyers and other officials fully gowned as they would have been in civilization, the police on duty in full uniform, with a corporal as the judge's personal attendant, all took their proper places. The opening of the Court was attended by practically all the members of the ship's personnel and by as many Eskimos as could be crowded into the building. The formal opening of the trial was preceded by a few remarks by the presiding magistrate and addressed particularly to the natives and translated into Eskimo by Mr. Duval. He informed the natives that the purpose of the trial assured them of justice and fair play, explained that the proceedings were exactly in accordance with the customs of civilization and stated that had a white man killed an Eskimo the proceedings would have been exactly the same . . . . The prisoners, however, did not seem to realize the gravity of the situation. The examination of the witnesses proceeded rather slowly, partly on account of the fact that everything had to be done through the interpreter and partly because an Eskimo, when questioned, is more likely to give the kind of answer he thinks is expected than to analyze his own thoughts on the subject or express what he really thinks. As a result of the

repeated attempts to elicit detailed information from the witnesses, Mr. Duval had a very trying day. He seemed to think
that the witnesses were not as stupid as they appeared to be but
were purposely pretending ignorance of the purport of
questions put to them. Things were finally sorted out and
verdicts were required from the jury. Nukallak was found guilty
of manslaughter with a recommendation of mercy on account
of extenuating circumstances. Ahteetah was acquitted.
Uguyungnak was found guilty of aiding and abetting and
sentenced to two years close confinement at Pond Inlet. The
sentence passed on Nukallak was ten years in Stoney Mountain
Penitentiary and he was escorted to the outside by Corporal
Jakeman and two constables.

A report concludes, "Before embarking Mr. Rivet impressed
on the natives the gravity of the offence for which Nukallak
was being taken to prison and the manner in which such an
offence was punished in white man's country. He also laid stress
on the Government's intention to have the law respected by
both white men and natives. It is felt that the holding of the
Court among the Eskimos will have a salutary effect and should
result in the greater respect for the value of human life by the
aborigines of the far north."

Before the missionaries went there the long arm of the law
had reached for the far north. The absence of the church meant
that Robert Janes was denied a proper burial. As it turned out
he was buried three times. Staff Sergeant Joy, who made the
critical initial investigation into the murder, had found Janes
partially buried. He remarked on the fact that the Eskimos had
gone to considerable trouble to inter the white man for they
knew the custom of white men was different from their own.
Joy had to disinter him, of course, and examine the body. After
this careful examination Janes was more satisfactorily buried in
the region of Pond Inlet. For a number of years Janes was
allowed to rest in peace. However, he had been buried where
the land was gradually washing away and in the course of time
Janes was almost on the surface of the earth. At the time when
Janes' grave became almost uncovered Kidlapik was a special
constable working for the R.C.M.P. at Pond Inlet. He was given
the task of relocating Janes. He and an Eskimo friend, Kullu,

set to work and dug up Mr. Janes. His caribou clothing was still in fine shape and he did not look bad either. Kidlapik and Kullu noticed his shiny gold teeth and a gold ring on his finger. He had not been robbed. They dug a grave some fifteen or sixteen feet away and laid him, this time, permanently to rest.

Twelve years after the trial, in 1935, Uguyungnak was still hanging around the R.C.M.P. post at Pond Inlet. He seemed to have formed an attachment for the police. He was so closely attached to the post that John Doyle, the policeman there at the time was under the impression that he was still a prisoner. Uguyungnak was a particularly tough old man. During his life he knew some terrible hardships. On one occasion he was travelling between Cape Crawford and Pond Inlet when he ran into slush ice. His feet were rapidly frozen. He built a tiny igloo and waited for conditions to improve. By the time the weather had improved his feet were in a terrible state, gangrene had set in and his condition was getting desperate. Using a jacknife Uguyungnak cut off his toes and sewed up the stubs with deer sinew. When Jack Doyle arrived, there, Uguyungnak's wounds were healed and the ulcerated sores on his heels were responding to the treatment Constable Gray was giving them. It was in that same year that Uguyungnak left the R.C.M.P. post.

By this time, 1935, Canada's hold on the Arctic was firm and her sovereignty becoming more and more assured. Captain Bernier, irascible and determined, had done much for Canada as had, in their own way, men like Janes and Duval. These men were the vanguard of our civilization, representatives of a different way of life and subservient to laws the Eskimos had yet to hear about. In an odd way these three men crossed each other's paths, Bernier, the sea captain, Janes, the trader and Duval, the white native. Bernier held the kind of position that ensures his place in history. Not so the other two of more humble station.

Captain Bernier on most counts was a man to remember. The Eskimos remembered him for years. One who knew him and was in Pond Inlet in 1935 tells a story about Captain Bernier that sounds very different from the usual stories heard of this hard working teetotaler. Tom Kullu, who used to work for

Captain Bernier when he went into harbour in a little bay just east of Pond Inlet, liked to tell this story: "Oh, that Captain Bernier. He fine man. He fine man. Every morning I come with wife. I say, 'All right, Captain Bernier, what I do today? Go hunting?' 'Oh Tom, have a drink of rum.' I say 'O.K.' I have drink of rum. Oh, good rum. My wife she have drink of rum. Then Bernier says, 'Well Tom, maybe you have another drink of rum.' And I say, 'O.K.' and I have another drink of rum. Then Bernier says, 'Tom, maybe you have another drink of rum.' By and by I fall asleep. Every day I never go hunting."

"What happened to your wife?" is the question then asked of him.

"I guess she worked for Captain Bernier."

Unlike Janes and Duval, Bernier was just a visitor to the Arctic, not a resident. Bernier died outside in Quebec on December 26th, 1934. Janes was murdered and buried in the Arctic wastes and William Duval died and was buried there too.

At the time of his death Duval had become an important man among the Eskimos. His shack in the camp on Cumberland Sound was the most impressive tupik of them all. Built out of canvas, driftwood, stones and whatever else he could lay his hands on, he had the only mansion there. At this camp Duval still retained some semblance of his more civilized past for he had built for his own use an outside toilet. This was his way of tipping his hat to the civilized society he had left behind. It was at this camp that Duval died. His death was quite an event. The Eskimos wanted to do it justice so instead of burying him under stones they endeavored to give him what they understood to be a Christian burial. The only structure they had in camp that could possibly be used as a coffin was the outhouse so William Duval was buried in his toilet.

17
James Killibuk

There are a few men still living in the eastern Arctic who remember well the last days of whaling and the early days of government activity. They can talk with vigour and excitement of Forsythe-Grant, William Duval and Captain Bernier. They remember the boats, the *Snowdrop*, the *Seduisante*, the *Active*, the *Era*, the *Albert* and many more. For these old men of the Arctic the memories of those days are nostalgic indeed.

Killibuk of Pangnirtung is one such man. James Killibuk was born on Blacklead Island. The exact date of his birth is not known but he must now be well on in his seventies. He has been retired from the Hudson's Bay Company for a decade or more although he still assists around the store at Pangnirtung. All the policemen, Hudson's Bay Company men and missionaries who have worked in and around Pangnirtung know James Killibuk. Hugh Margetts summed up the attitude of all of them when he said, "Killibuk? What do I think of him? Why, he's a damn good man in every way."

It is Eskimos like Killibuk who have, through their own peculiar skill, created the myth that all Eskimos are naturally great mechanics. Some of them are. Many of them are not. James Killibuk, however, is exceptional with machinery.

"He could copy anything," says John Wickware, a Hudson's Bay Company man who spent nine years at Pangnirtung.

"I remember, on one occasion, my wife was putting a blanket through the wringer of our gasoline powered washing machine (This was some time after the Second World War). All of a sudden the whole thing flew apart. My wife called me and I took a look at it. The thing was a mess. The crown gear on top of the drive shaft from the motor had smashed. This gear drove the axle which operated the rollers. While I examined the mess Killibuk watched.

"'I'm afraid there's nothing I can do about that. It's smashed but good. Beyond repair. I'll have to order a new part.'

"Killibuk took a step closer, examined everything carefully and then said, 'I'll fix it.'

"He took the broken gear and squared shaft and went away. Two or three days later he came back with a new part. Quickly and efficiently he reassembled the machine, started the motor and my wife was able to do her laundry again. Believe me I was both surprised and interested. I asked him what he had done and how he had done it. 'I used the crank shaft from a marine engine,' he explained. 'I made the gear out of a chunk of metal from the same engine. I cut it all to shape with files and hack-saws.'

"It was a beautiful job. You could hardly tell that it was not machine made. There were thirteen teeth in that gear and each one was exactly right in depth, pitch and everything.''

Years earlier, Alan Scott had observed the same skill. Alan, who was not a mechanic, decided that he needed to know how the engine in one of the Hudson's Bay Company's boats work-ed. With infinite care he completely dismantled the engine, marking every part as he went along. While he worked Killibuk watched him. Alan was a little dismayed when he stepped away from the chaos he had caused but, with patience and determin-ation, he eventually got the engine back together and, to his delight and surprise, it started right away. His only reason for stripping the motor down was for his own information. Now, feeling himself an expert mechanic he took a look at the large Thornycroft engine used in the big boat. This engine had never worked properly and time after time had let them down. It was now so hopeless that the smaller engine Alan had just reassem-bled would have to be used.

For quite a while Alan looked thoughtfully at the Thorny-croft engine.

"I wonder if I should," he said, half to himself and half to Killibuk who was standing nearby. He paced up and down for a few moments and then said, "No. I don't think I'm going to push my luck. That engine can stay as it is — useless."

"Let me have a try," said Killibuk, "I'll take it apart."

Very painstakingly, Killibuk stripped the engine right down. He took it completely apart. He had the rods off, the bearings off and the pistons out. Finally, he found the trouble. A ring on one of the pistons was broken. This did not beat Killibuk. He searched around the camp and eventually came across a piece of sheet metal made of steel that was the right gauge for making a piston ring. He worked and worked at it and eventually managed to cut a ring that was exactly the right size.

"Goodness knows how many times he came to the store," says Alan Scott. "He used up pretty near all the hacksaw blades I had. He must have worn out dozens."

With infinite care, Killibuk notched the ring and worked it into place on the piston. He reassembled the motor. Then came the acid test. Would the engine start? Killibuk tried it a few times and it fired into life.

"We were glad of it," Alan Scott recalls, "because when the boat went into the fiord there were a lot of pretty rough tides to handle and tricky currents. The big engine was a tremendous asset, especially when towing whaleboats."

Killibuk was interested in machines and attracted by them. He never disguised this fascination. He wanted to know how machinery worked and was prepared to take the time to find out. The attitude of some other Eskimos was a little different. They all regarded the inventions of white men with curiosity but were not interested in the mechanical technicalities. They were not so impressed with the wonders of modern science that they wanted to spend a lot of time studying them.

Johnny Wickware observed this sort of attitude in the early fifties when the first DC 3 ever to land at Pangnirtung arrived.

"Many of the Eskimos had never seen such a big aircraft," he says. "It was huge. The whole settlement was down to look at it. One Eskimo paid a little more attention than the rest. He tapped the fuselage, looked under the wings, walked around the tail, felt the rudder and the skis. He acted just like a man examining a new car. If there'd been a door handy he'd have slammed it."

After a few minutes the examination was over and he stood

away from the aeroplane and gave it one more all-embracing glance and turned away.

"What do you think of it?" asked Johnny, who had watched the whole episode.

"Huh," he grunted, "if the Eskimos had needed one they would have built one."

It was not Killibuk who said this but he certainly had many of the skills that an early aeroplane builder would have needed. Killibuk did not learn this skill from aeroplanes, however. It is almost certain that he was introduced to engines by the whalers and men like Duval. William Duval had an old boat powered by steam. It is said by some that on occasion the only fuel he had to use in the thing was seal oil and the smoke and stench from it would have given even the mildest member of a pollution control committee unbearable nightmares.

Killibuk was a leader in the Pangnirtung community for years and has, in comparison to others, been an affluent member of that society. There was, perhaps, only one person who had superior wealth during his earlier days and that was Mrs. Duval. James Killibuk's daughter, Mrs. Rose Okpik, says of Mrs. Duval, "She was rich, very rich, being married to that German fellow she had all sorts of things. Her home was the best one. She had a lamp and kitchenware. Yes, Mrs. Duval was rich."

She was not only a rich woman but she was also a domineering woman and many of her contemporaries did not think too highly of her.

In later years, after her husband's death, Mrs. Duval was as blind as a badger. In spite of her incapacity she still retained importance in the settlement and was a leader among the women. Something dreadful happened when she died, however, and the Eskimos think it was some sort of retribution for her behaviour to them. After her death there was a funeral and her body was buried in some sort of makeshift coffin. The influence of the Anglican Mission in Pangnirtung assured that the bodies were not simply put under piles of stones. In spite of the grave and the coffin, a pack of loose dogs managed to dig up the grave, get at the body, dismember and eat it. This was a horrifying thing to happen and unquestioningly, in the eyes of the Eskimos, a mark of judgment against her.

The presence of the Anglican Mission in Pangnirtung in 1930 had not removed from the native people all of their old convictions. Most of them became Christians by baptism and other outward forms of allegiance to the Church but, deep down, the superstitions, beliefs and allegiances of earlier years still clung. This is not to belittle the work of men like Fleming, Bilby, Peck and the Turners. They, too, knew how tenaciously the Eskimos held to the beliefs of their forefathers. In spite of this commitment, however, the Eskimos gladly received the news brought to them by the missionaries. In many places they came to regard the priests, both Roman Catholic and Anglican, with great affection. In Pangnirtung, for many years, a brother of Canon John Turner worked with great effect.

Arthur Turner was loved by the Eskimos. Killibuk knew him well and the daughters of the two men were great friends. The two men respected each other. Killibuk still lives but Turner is dead. All Pangnirtung mourned when Turner died.

John Wickware was the manager of the Hudson's Bay Company post when Turner passed away. He recalls the event vividly. "I think the saddest thing that ever happened to me in Pangnirtung was when the Reverend Mr. Arthur Turner passed away. He was a legend with the people and it was an awful blow to them all when he died. There were no fancy funeral arrangements. We made his coffin out of what lumber we could. Held the service to the best of our ability. There was one strange thing about that service I cannot forget. The natives had built the casket open at the top. The head and shoulders of Mr. Turner were open to view until the time of interment. I don't know why it was made this way. Unfortunately, when it came time to close the casket it was discovered there were no holes made for the screw nails to be put in. I can remember standing in the church watching Jonasee pound four inch spikes into the casket. Every ring of the hammer sounded like thunder in my ears. I'll never forget it as long as I live."

The Turners made a lasting contribution to the changing pattern of Eskimo life and will not be forgotten for many years.

It was people like the Turners who formed the backdrop of Killibuk's life. Even as a boy he witnessed the activities of white men and knew the strange blond giants from across the sea. He heard the rich deep brogue of the Scots and, as a lad, learned his first few words of English. It was an exciting time for him when the whalers came. There were huge boats for him to board, strange musical instruments to listen to and great things to be had for fur. Then 1914 came and whaling ceased. The world was enmeshed in war. Whalers sought bigger game. The great days of the sailing ship died forever.

Killibuk remembers one isolated trader left at a whaling station for more than three years during the 1914-18 period. Not a ship was to be seen and not a message came. Every day, come summertime, James Killibuk recalls this man climbing to the highest point near to his station and gazing out to sea through a telescope. The Eskimos called him "the man who is always waiting".

There was another white man in Baffin Island for whom the Eskimos had a similar name, Hector Pitchforth. He was called "the man who is always going". Pitchforth had a small trading post in the Home Bay area and for years he stayed there but seems to have insisted constantly that his term was soon to be up. At least that is how the Eskimos understood it although this fact is not borne out by the assistant who was sent out from England in 1924 for he said, "Mr. Pitchforth . . . expressed himself as quite happy in the life he was leading and more than once said to me that he had no wish to go back to England. The only indication I remember that he still had any interest in the world of civilization which he had left behind was that he asked me what government was then in power. I shall always remember him as a very fine character."

It is not known whether the man who was always waiting ever lived to see a welcome smudge of smoke on the horizon but it is known that Pitchforth died on Baffin Island. Killibuk doubtless knows the story. Occasionally Eskimos from Pangnirtung would make their way over the long trail from the fiord to Home Bay. Alan Scott heard of Pitchforth from Killibuk and decided to go see him, not realizing at the time that he was already dead. The previous year the newly arrived doctor in Pangnirtung had tried to see him but because of terrible weather the small party had had to turn back. In fact, when the doctor got back to Pangnirtung, his sled was in splinters, the dogs near to death and he, himself, in dreadful shape. Alan Scott listened to his story and thought to himself, "I'll show him when I get the chance."

His chance came. He set off with a couple of Eskimo guides and left Killibuk in charge of the store. It was nice and warm when they started. Deep into the valley of the fiord the sun shone and the men enjoyed its warmth. Up on the height of land at the end of the fiord, however, it was cold. By the time they were really up into the mountains it was very, very cold. They made camp at the foot of a glacier. Before turning in they set a few traps nearby because they had noticed a great number of very tame white foxes in the area. In fact, the foxes were so tame that they came almost right up to the men. All three of the men were glad when the chores were done and they could creep into the snow house and get out of the wind. They made themselves comfortable, ate, crawled into their sleeping robes and slept. During the night there was a terrible upheaval. Alan did not know what was happening. There was an enormous noise, a sound different from anything he had ever heard before, and then with inexplicable suddenness the top of the snow house was completely sheared off. Apparently the glacier had started to move and a large piece had broken from it. The three men scrambled out of the igloo and ran pell-mell for their lives in all directions. Huge chunks of ice crashed around them. Like bombarded soldiers they sought shelter from the thundering, bursting bombs of ice. It was a frightful few minutes for them all but they survived. When everything had settled down they returned to their snow house which was now completely crushed. Carefully they gathered together as many of their possessions as they could find and then counselled among themselves as to what to do. Alan was all for going on.

"We're not too badly off," he pointed out. "None of our dogs are killed and we all escaped scot free. Let's keep going."

The Eskimos eyed each other undecidedly.

"While you're thinking about it I'll go and pick up the traps," said Alan.

There was no fur in any of the traps. Quite obviously a lot of foxes had been caught but it was equally obvious that wolverines had got to them first.

"Too bad," muttered Alan, "luck doesn't seem to be with us."

When Alan got back everything was ready for moving again. It was decided to continue on the trip toward Home Bay. By nightfall they were a little closer to Hector Pitchforth but travel had not been easy. A strong wind had begun to blow. There was no suitable snow for an igloo so they set up a tent Alan had brought, wedging it firmly into the ice. During the night the wind became a howling gale and ripped the tent to shreds. Scott relates: "By this time I had had enough of it. I decided to return to Pang." The return trip was no picnic but they made it. That was the closest Alan ever came to seeing "the man who was always going".

Pitchforth became the sort of man the Eskimos talked about. Eccentric to begin with, he became increasingly odd. Gradually the natives began to fear him. The supply ship that was supposed to come never arrived and Pitchforth became entirely dependent upon the charity of the Eskimos. He was uneasy with them. He believed they were plotting his murder and they believed him to be bewitched. In his horrible hovel of packing cases and cardboard, Hector Pitchforth lived out the closing years of his life in a frenzy of suspicion. The time came when no one would go near him. His cries for help were unheeded and his needs unmet. The finger of death was upon Mr. Pitchforth. In his lonely madness he struggled to live but the finger moved, the hand gripped, and Pitchforth died. He died calling for help that never came. Months passed before his body was found. No Eskimo would approach his shack and not until a patrolling policeman was in the area was Pitchforth's death confirmed. It was the constable from Pond Inlet who found him. He was told by the Eskimos that they thought Pitchforth was dead in his cabin. The constable discovered Pitchforth lying hunched up on his bed, his hands doubled up and stiff. He had been that way for months.

Constable Murray thought that the best thing to do was to take Hector back to Pond Inlet with him so he loaded him on his komatik and headed back. Once back in Pond Inlet Hector was put in the police warehouse. The warehouse was not heated so he was all right there. Hector sat in that storeroom, all hunched up, for a very long time. If there were any Eskimos around anytime the constable went in he would say in a pleasantly cheery voice, "Good morning, Hector." The Eskimos did not like this cavalier attitude towards a corpse. Finally, Hector Pitchfork was buried at Pond Inlet, but not until after the summer had come and he was thawed out.

18
The Storm-built Tomb

A year or so after Pitchforth died, Jack Doyle went north. One of Doyle's earliest duties on Baffin Island was to travel down to Home Bay to check on all the effects Pitchforth had left.

"The poor guy hadn't left much," says Doyle. "There were a few rusty pots and pans and a few rifles that looked like Franklin relics. The Eskimos hadn't been near the place. They were scared of old Aoudla. According to the Eskimos I met down there, Pitchforth used to go into all kinds of rages and curse and swear. Fact is, it's a wonder they didn't kill him."

By the time Doyle returned from this trip he felt much less of a greenhorn and settled in rapidly to life as a northern policeman. He liked the north from the very start and proved an ideal policeman for that part of the world.

The isolation appealed to him. The close camaraderie he was able to enjoy with the other white men in the small settlement appealed to him. The police, Hudson's Bay Company employees and the Roman Catholic Missionaries spent quite a lot of time in each other's company and invariably had a get together on Friday evenings. Quite often the R.C.M.P. would do the entertaining and when they did there was always a good spread. Lobster sandwiches and the like were the order of the day.

"In fact," says Doyle, "we had more lobster than we knew what to do with. I got quite sick of lobster."

In addition to canned treats, Jack Doyle always made a cake. He regarded himself as something of a specialist and, according to his own unverified testimony, they were usually pretty good. One day things went wrong.

"On this particular day," says Doyle, "I was making an extra special cake. I forget what you call it. It's named after some city in the States, Washington, maybe, or was it Boston? Anyway, it was to be a layer cake with frosting and jam and all kinds of things lashed on it. I was just about to put salt in the cake when the spout came off the container and about a cupful of salt went into the batter. For a moment or two I stood there dismayed."

"Throw it out," said Bob Gray, who had seen what happened.

Jack was just about to toss it out when he thought he would have some fun with the boys.

"I'm not going to pitch it out," he said to Bob. "I'm going to cook it up and feed it to them."

He put an extra large helping of baking powder in it so that it would rise and it came up looking pretty good. As soon as it had cooled off, he covered the whole thing, top and sides, with a thick layer of lusciously rich frosting.

"Doesn't look bad," said Bob, seeing the finished article.

"Looks real tasty, I think," said Jack, well satisfied.

He had not long finished the job when the missionaries began to arrive. It was just the Roman Catholic Missionaries. The Anglicans did not join them on these parties. There were three missionaries, Father Cochard, Father Danielo and Brother Volant. When the time came for lunch Father Cochard said, "I'm not going to eat many sandwiches. I'm going to have some of that cake. Sure looks good."

It wasn't long before he was ready for a piece so Jack cut him off a really large wedge and, as he handed it to Father Cochard, Father Danielo said, "I'll have the same."

Jack watched. They ate. They ate without comment.

"How about you, Brother?" he asked Brother Volant.

"I'll finish my sandwiches first, thank you. I'm not too fussy about cake."

The priests plodded painfully through their pieces to the last crumb. Try as they would they could not disguise the occasional pained expression. Finally, Volant was ready for a piece. He took one bite and spat it out right away.

"What is this?" he demanded.

"What's the matter, Brother? Don't you like it?" Doyle asked. "That's a Maritime salt cake. We eat it all the time in the Maritimes."

This was a particularly dirty trick because the Roman Catholic Missionaries were unquestionably the poor brethren. Every time it was their turn to entertain they did their utmost to put on just as lavish a spread but their meagre resources had to be stretched to the limit. For weeks Brother Volant nursed a small quantity of butter. With a flourish he'd make its presence known on the table but neither he nor the priests ever touched it. It was a "for guests only" butter dish. Small wonder they viewed with such eagerness the spreads put on by their rich neighbours. A cake that looked like Doyle's was unheard of in the mission.

During the second year that Jack Doyle was stationed at Pond Inlet he had to make a patrol down to Igloolik and into the camps in the Foxe Basin area. On his way down he called at Tom Kullu's camp. It was Tom Kullu who could remember Captain Bernier. When Jack arrived Tom Kullu was away but his son was there. Jack did not think much of the son. He was a strange young man who spent most of his time bumming around the camp at Pond Inlet.

One time in the fall, shortly after the ship had left, Jack Doyle invited this young man to come for a seal and rabbit hunt. It was a nice calm day and more of a picnic than a serious hunting trip. The young fellow was quite willing to go with Jack. He took with him an old .44 that had no sights and was held together rather insecurely with several strands of rusting wire. They pulled the boat into Milne Inlet and started looking for Arctic hare. They didn't have to look far. There were rabbits all over the place. Jack took a couple of shots and the young fellow watched. The noise of the shots had scarcely died away when another rabbit was spotted sitting motionless nearby. Tom Kullu's son saw the rabbit and hollered at it. The rabbit did not move so he picked up a pebble and threw it at the rabbit. As it started to hop away the young fellow grabbed his rifle and shot it on the run. This struck Jack as extraordinary for an Eskimo.

"He wouldn't shoot a sitting rabbit," says Jack, "Anyone

would think he was trying to be an English sportsman."

It was this rather strange young man who entertained Jack at Tom's camp.

Jack may not have been pleased to see him but Kullu junior was certainly glad to see the R.C.M.P. constable because that meant pilot biscuits, jam and other white man's food. The young fellow liked Jack's food but some of the food the Eskimos liked was not to Jack's taste. Very early during his stay in Pond Inlet Jack had run into some Eskimo tastes that were less than appealing to him. It bothered him to see the Eskimo kids rooting around for the biggest lice to crack in their teeth but what Tom Kullu was eating one day bothered him even more.

"What's that you've got, Tom?" Jack asked, as he watched him reach into a little rubber bag, take out some white powdery stuff and nibble at it.

"Partridge shit," said Tom.

"Partridge shit?" ejaculated Jack, "That's terrible."

"Aw Jack, you know nothing, It's good. Try some."

"No thanks," said Jack hastily.

"All shit is good, Jack. Only shit not good is man shit and seal shit."

As Jack settled in to Tom Kullu's igloo he wondered what kind of treatment he was in for. He still had not been long enough in the Arctic to take all the Eskimos' ways in his stride. Kullu's son's wife was there and she was a dirty character. She was spitting around everywhere and making Jack more and more uneasy. It came time to eat. With expert aim and offhanded ease she spat into the frying pan and wiped it out. Jack would not have minded so much only it was his frying pan.

"Here, give that to me," he demanded.

Surprised, she handed it over and Jack gave it a thorough cleaning.

"Don't do that again. I don't like it," he growled at her.

"Gee, she's a dirty character," he said to her husband.

"She's all right. She's just young," he replied.

"She's old enough to know better," muttered Jack. "She's a mother."

He had hardly said this when the baby on her back began to squirm and she pulled it out fast. She had recognized the wriggle and knew the baby was having a bowel movement. Quickly, she put her hand under the kid and caught it all. She then went over to the lard pail they used for refuse and wiped off her fingers and finished the job by licking them clean. Jack had just finished his supper.

"Tell her that's a filthy thing to do," Jack said to young Kullu. "It just isn't proper."

When the message was transmitted to her she answered via her husband, "It's only milk."

There is no doubt about it. Some of the Eskimo ways were more than trying for men brought up with very different standards of cleanliness and behaviour but as a rule these things, so immediately obvious, did not preclude the men of the north from loving it there. They grew very fond of and dependent upon the Eskimo people and learned a respect for them that has never been lost. This is true of Doyle.

The year 1939 marked the commencement of Jack's second term at Pond Inlet, a term that proved even more eventful than the first one. By the time he had been back there a year he was able to speak a fair amount of Eskimo and was now able to handle the customs of the natives with confidence and poise.

In the spring of 1941 Jack Doyle set off on what proved to be the longest patrol he ever made, longest in terms of distance and time. The patrol started as a routine jaunt to Igloolik and back. This was an annual venture for the Pond Inlet Detachment. Doyle set out with two Eskimos, Kumanapik, the Special Constable, and Iitukukshuk, who was hauling dog feed for them. They set out overland and managed to get almost through Cockburn Land when it turned cold, desperately cold.

"We can't travel today," said Kumanapik after having poked his head out of the igloo. "It's too cold."

The air was crackling with frost. It was beautiful but deadly.

All three of them stayed in the little igloo that day. Jack spent most of his time reading.

The next morning it was the same. It was snapping with cold.

"We're out of oil," said Jack to Kumanapik. "Go out and fill the primus stove."

Kumanapik went out but was back in a minute.

"Oil won't pour. It's frozen."

And frozen it was. They had to haul the oil drum into the igloo and light a seal fat fire under it until the oil was warm enough to flow again. The oil had jelled.

For four days and nights the men were stuck there with little to read and nothing to do. In order to help pass the time they had competitions to see who could find the most lice in their underwear. They were better off doing that than attempting to travel, for movement in such cold weather would have been almost suicidal.

Finally, the weather eased a little and they set off again. Only a day or two later they ran out of dog food. During that bitter cold weather they had had to keep the dogs well fed and now they had run out of food. But luck was with them. The day their supply was exhausted they spotted caribou.

"Look!" said Kumanapik, "Tuktu."

On the side of the hill Jack could see a cloud of steam but no animals.

"There's caribou there," Kumanapik explained, "Caribou for sure."

They stopped the team and started up the long side of the hill. Iitukukshuk did not join them in the hunt. Kumanapik put his rifle over his left shoulder and Jack put his over his right shoulder and they walked right in among the caribou. The rifles looked like antlers and as they moved Kumanapik made noises like caribou grunting and puffing. They got so close that they could see the animals' eyes blinking.

"Now," said Kumanapik, dropping to his knees and beginning to fire.

They both shot many times. Deer were falling all around them. It was easy. In no time they had a more than adequate supply of fresh meat. All the best parts they cut up, piled on the sledges and then moved on. By the time they reached Foxe Basin, however, the dogs had become pretty thin. Dogs do not do well on a diet of caribou flesh alone. Kumanapik, Iitukukshuk and Jack were just beginning to get a little worried about this when they ran into a small band of Eskimos who had a large supply of walrus meat so they traded venison for walrus. This soon put the dogs back into shape and without any further incident the patrol reached Igloolik.

The settlement of Igloolik is on an island of the same name, just off the northeast coast of Melville Peninsula. The island is low lying and flat, the highest elevation being about 500 feet. It is clear that the land has slowly risen in the area for old beach lines are visible and the presence of sea mammal bones at the highest elevation tells the same story.

When Doyle and his team arrived at Igloolik they were coming to a community that has proved of immense value and interest to the archaeologist. In *Settlements of the Northwest Territories*, a series of volumes produced for the Advisory Commission on the Development of Government in the Northwest Territories, the writer says, "Among archaeological sites in the Canadian Arctic Igloolik provides a unique record of unbroken habitation. Since the end of the last glaciation the land in northern Foxe Basin has been rising continually due to the isostatic caused by the removal of the weight of the ice sheet. Shortly after the row of points, which now comprises the highest elevation of Igloolik Island, emerged from the sea, the first human settlements were established there. The time at which this occurred has been fixed by radio carbon dating at approximately 2,000 B.C. Since that time the local people have kept shifting their dwelling places closer to the shore every two or three generations as the land steadily rose. Because the density of the population never increased and because in the absence of agriculture the people depended almost completely on sea mammals, there never was any reason to go back inland. All the previous habitation sites were left quite undisturbed."

It was from a site on Igloolik Island that the oldest bow to be found in North America was discovered. The bow, made out of antler, was radio carbon dated approximately 800 B.C.

The village of Igloolik gradually evolved around the Hudson's Bay Company store and the Roman Catholic Mission. It is situated about two miles from Turton Bay, a very large bay that plunges into the heart of Igloolik Island. For the traditional life of the Eskimos the settlement is poorly placed. The site it occupies is not one which self-supporting Eskimo hunters would have chosen as the best area from which to exploit the local resources. Igloolik Point on the southeastern corner of Igloolik Island is much better suited for that. However, other factors dictated the location of the settlement and the establishment of the Hudson's Bay Company store was undoubtedly the key factor.

Jack Doyle was glad to reach Igloolik and have the chance of sharing a few stories with Jack Stanners, the manager of the local Hudson's Bay store. The trip from Pond had been a long one and a cold one. After a good night's rest at the Company's establishment, Jack went and spent some time with the Roman Catholic Missionaries, Father Bazin and Father Danielo. The priests welcomed him warmly and offered him a drink of a "liqueur" they had manufactured.

"Whatever is this stuff?" Jack asked, tasting it.

"Why? Don't you like it?"

"It not only smells potent it is potent," said Jack, taking another sip of the pinkish stuff. "That must be nearly pure alcohol."

"Actually, we made a little wine", the priest explained, "and it turned sour so we distilled it. What you're drinking is the result of our little experiment."

"It's good," he said, holding up his glass.

"I'm glad you like it," said Father Bazin. "We don't. In fact we'd like to get rid of the batch. You can have the lot, four bottles full."

Jack accepted the offer and packed it with him when he left next day for Ugli, Island. Ugli Island is south of Igloolik and was the site of an Eskimo camp. Jack took a few days to make the return trip to this place and during that time cleaned up the liqueur. The trip was unexceptional and had been merely a routine patrol. Even the liqueur did not serve to make it exceptional. He expected that when he reentered Igloolik he would stay there a day or two and then head back to Pond Inlet. When he got back, however, Jack Stanners had some disturbing news for him.

"Not long ago," Stanners began, "an Eskimo was in here from Boothia Peninsula who says that a whole family has been murdered over in the Creswell Bay area. Have you heard anything about it?"

"No, I haven't," said Doyle. "Did the story sound authentic to you?"

Stanners assured him that it did so Doyle decided to head out towards Creswell Bay, which is in the vicinity of Fort Ross.

The same night that Doyle made the decision to go to Fort Ross, Canon Turner arrived in Igloolik. He stayed the night only and announced his intention to head towards Fort Ross the next morning. Doyle left a day later with his two Eskimo companions and caught up with Turner at the Fury and Hecla Straits. For a while they travelled together and then Turner headed out across the Gulf of Boothia and Doyle continued up the west coast of Brodeur Peninsula.

Turner headed off on his own but neither Doyle nor his companions were prepared to risk their lives among the grinding ice floes of the Gulf. They stayed on or near land until they reached the place where the Eskimos usually cross, a point near the south end of Prince Regent Inlet. Shortly before they set out across the ice they began to run short of dog food but fortunately managed to sight and shoot a polar bear. Very near to where they shot the bear they happened upon two old Eskimo encampments that neither Iitukukshuk nor Kumanapik had ever heard of or seen before. These camps intrigued Jack because they showed signs of being ancient but this was no time for an investigation. They pushed on.

They wound up on the west side of Prince Regent Inlet some miles north of Fury Point on Somerset Island. Near to the shore where they struck land they came across the remnants of an old ship that Doyle believes was abandoned there in the middle of the nineteenth century. There was a large anchor, bits of rope and various items of wreckage. Some small items Jack picked up for souvenirs.

In the vicinity of the wreck they ran into an abundance of game. They killed seven polar bears. It was none too soon either for the dogs had got into their food supply and eaten all the bacon, beans and biscuits.

Once Somerset Island was reached the teams turned south and headed towards Creswell Bay and Fort Ross. A day or so's journey out of Creswell Bay they ran into a few traps and a little later on came upon a lone Eskimo. He was a fine fellow. He introduced himself as Joshie. Fortunately, he had a little bannock along with him and some tobacco. By now Jack was more than tired of a steady diet of bear meat and the Eskimos were missing their smokes.

Joshie accompanied them to Creswell Bay. It was good to have him along for he was able to take them the most direct way to the small Eskimo encampment.

After the excitement of their arrival had died down a little, Jack began to ask questions about the rumoured murders in the area.

"The fellow you're looking for is Joshie," one of the natives said. "The man you came in with. He's your man."

Before questioning him, Jack discovered that Joshie had a bad reputation among the other Eskimos.

"I'm told you deserted your family," Jack began, "and caused their deaths."

"I left them in an igloo," said Joshie. "A storm blew up and buried the snow house. I had built it near the base of a glacier."

"Why wouldn't you tell the people here where the igloo was?" asked Jack. "They say you wouldn't take them back to the site. Is that true?"

Joshie did not answer.

Doyle took him into custody and headed for Fort Ross, still another forty or so miles away. Once at Fort Ross, Doyle heard the whole story from Ernie Lyall, a man well known in the Arctic. He knew these Eskimos particularly well because his wife was one of them.

Little by little the story had come to Lyall and by the time Doyle arrived he knew it all. In January of 1941, Joshie, his family and his brother and his family settled in a couple of igloos built at the base of a glacier in Creswell Bay. Had they realised that the advent of a storm would cause an enormous build-up of snow where they had placed their snow houses it is more than likely that another site would have been chosen.

Farley Mowat, writing an account of what took place at that time, suggests that the reason these people built in such a place can be traced to the fact that they did not understand the nature of the land they were in. These Eskimos, he points out correctly, were not raised in that part of the world but in Cape Dorset and had only moved there because the Hudson's Bay Company prevailed upon them to go. There was good hunting to be had in the Fort Ross area and lots of fur — hence the Company's desire to have good hunters there. Mowat, however, misplaces the site of the tragedy by at least 200 miles and tells a story that is of questionable accuracy in other respects.

Mr. Mowat may well be correct in his assertion that the site chosen was a demonstration of ignorance but he does not account for what Joshie did during the storm. He was not, as Mowat suggests, simply a victim of the barbaric activity of both the Hudson's Bay Company and the police.

The night of the storm was terrible. The wind roared and moaned. Snow eddied around the igloos and began to build up. Joshie and his family huddled securely in their little white tomb. The family slept.

"Joshie! Joshie! Joshie!"

He woke. Someone was calling him.

"Joshie! Wake up! We must move! If we don't hurry we'll be buried in the snow."

It was Joshie's brother from the nearby igloo. He had fought his way through the storm to save Joshie and his family. Once Joshie was awake his brother left to get his family through the storm to a safer location.

Joshie did not call the others. For a moment he glanced at them snuggled together on the sleeping platform. He paused and then turned away. He gathered his personal belongings together, saw to the dogs and then turned his attention to the house. By this time the porch had collapsed. It was terribly difficult to reach the trapped people. He did manage to rescue his adopted son, Eekeedloak, by digging through the drift, making a hole in the porch roof and dragging the boy out. It could well be that by now Joshie was exhausted but his next actions do not really support the view that he desperately wanted to save the rest of the family.

Two days passed before he went to the nearby Eskimo community in Creswell Bay and when he did get there he would not return with rescuers to show them exactly where his igloo was located. In spite of this, several Eskimos went back and tunnelled into the drift for almost 20 feet. It was learned later they only missed the igloo by 5 feet.

Once Doyle was assured of the truth of this story he realized that at the very least he would have to charge Joshie with criminal negligence.

"I guess the first thing to do is to have a look for the bodies," said Doyle to Ernie Lyall. "Can you come with me and give me a hand?"

Lyall agreed to go with Jack and suggested also that Kavavau, his father-in-law, and a couple of other natives should come with them.

"They'll have to be able to show us more or less where the igloo's buried and they'll help us dig, too."

Two days after Doyle arrived in Fort Ross he was on his way back to Creswell Bay. It did not take them long to find the igloo's location and begin digging. It was an awful job. The snow was packed as hard as ice. They dug and dug and could not find the igloo. In the end Jack called it off and told Iitukukshuk and Kumanapik that he was going to have to stay at Fort Ross for the summer and they may as well take the better dogs and one komitik and head back to Pond Inlet. This they did and, eventually, after spending most of the summer at Arctic Bay, they arrived back in Pond Inlet in September just a week before Constable Doyle arrived on the *Nascopie*.

Doyle returned with the others to Fort Ross, waited for a month and then, towards the beginning of June, decided to have another go at exhuming the bodies. This time he returned with a larger team of diggers, and Joshie himself, who pointed out the general location of the igloo. There was at least thirty feet of hard packed snow where he told them to dig. It did not take them as long as they expected to break into the igloo but once inside they could find nothing. They tunnelled out in many directions. In some places the tunnels were twenty feet long and thirty feet under the snow. Progress became very slow and extremely risky. Snow had to be passed back, put on ledges and then shovelled outside from there. The searchers had an eerie feeling as they wormed their way into that snowy tomb.

Finally, Jack said to Ernie, as he came out from the drift, "I'm going to call it off. I think it's too hazardous."

"I agree," said Ernie. "We'll just have to come back again when the snow's gone."

"I suppose it will melt some time this summer."

"Oh yes, a good bit of it will go. You'll probably still have to do some digging but it won't be anything like it is now."

Back to Fort Ross went Jack Doyle again, this time to wait for break-up. Jack passed the time hunting with Allan Thorburn and Ernie Lyall and the natives. He did not hang around the post very much. He preferred to be out. One of the duties he undertook was to scout ice conditions for Inspector H.A. Larsen who was coming through the Northwest Passage in the *St. Roch*. He went up and down Bellot Strait, climbed up the hills and when it was all clear got in touch with Larsen by radio. Allan Thorburn was the radio operator there and managed to get through to Larsen without any trouble. Only a few days before the ice really went out Jack Doyle was faced with another problem, a problem very different from the murder investigation.

A small group of Eskimos from the King William Island area came into camp and they had with them a young boy of 16 or 17 years who was in serious trouble. Jack Doyle describes him as the dirtiest thing he ever saw in his life. He was like an animal. He had the hunted, whipped look of an unwanted cur and when he was spoken to he would just sneer and look up with shifty, unsteady eyes. He could not walk, only crawl. Soon Jack knew the story. The Eskimos had only brought him to Fort Ross because they had heard there was a policeman there. They wanted to hand the boy over.

"We can do nothing with him," they explained to Jack. "He is beyond us."

"What's the matter with him?" Jack questioned. "How is it he's like this?"

"He's possessed," said one of them. "He lives with the dogs and cohabits with the bitches."

Jack, like it or not, was left with this kid. The first thing he did was to clean him up. With a tubfull of warm water and a household scrubbing brush, Jack set to work. In spite of all his endeavors he could not get all the scurf off him. It was a ghastly job. The boy had an internal infection that caused him to screech with pain when he urinated and he was running with matter. When Jack had done the best he knew how he said, "Get up! Walk!" It was like a New Testament command. The boy struggled to a standing position and then took a few shaky steps, all hunched up. But he did walk and it was a beginning. Right until ship time Jack kept after the young lad, making him keep clean and forcing him to walk. It was a busy time for Constable Doyle for he still had to deal with Joshie. Finally, he had to leave the boy for a while in order to carry on further investigations at Creswell Bay.

He took a whaleboat with a few natives, together with Joshie and Ernie Lyall, and rowed the 70 miles up to the bay. Fortunately, they had a little bit of a sail along with them which they were able to use as well so the rowing was not too bad.

They went as near as they could to the locality of the igloos by boat and then set up camp and went to work. There was some snow still around. Digging was started around the igloos and it was not long before Jack dug up a leg. In short order all the bodies were then uncovered. They were found some thirty feet from the igloo. Desperately they had tried to tunnel out. For days they must have waited for Joshie to return and when no one came a belated attempt at escape was made. All of them were terribly emaciated. Leading in the tunnel was the old woman. Then came the wife and the four children were behind her. It was a silently awful moment when all were uncovered and the real enormity of Joshie's indifference revealed.

"Ernie," said Jack, "I don't think it would do too much harm for a good Catholic to read the Anglican burial service. Do you?"

Ernie agreed that it did not matter very much so they buried the six of them right there. One by one the stones were brought and piled on the bodies, a tiny pyramid of rocks. Joshie was a silent and passive witness to it all.

Later that same evening, Ernie, Kavavau and Jack were together in the tent when Ernie said, "Where's Joshie? You'd better watch that guy, Jack. I don't trust him."

"Nor do I, come to think of it," said Jack. "I think we'd better get the rifles from the boat. Joshie might get after them."

"He's a bad one," Ernie went on.

Jack agreed, stood up and went out of the tent. Just as he emerged he saw Joshie going towards the boat.

"Hey!" yelled Jack, "where are you going?"

Joshie stopped and, looking like a child caught in mischief, said, "I was just going for a walk."

Doyle grabbed him and shoved him back in the tent and then went and fetched all the rifles.

"Here Kavavau, you sit on this," he said, handing him his rifle, "and don't let it out of your sight."

Joshie was Kavavau's step-son and unlike him in every way. Kavavau was a big, friendly, reliable man while Joshie was surly, unreliable and dangerous. It is said that Joshie deserted his family in order to take up with another woman. The storm was a convenient executioner.

In September the supply ship, *Nascopie*, arrived at Fort Ross but was unable to stay for more than one day because of bad ice conditions. Joshie appeared before Inspector D.J. Martin for a preliminary hearing, charged with criminal negligence. He was released and ordered to appear for trial in September, 1942, when the ship would call again.

Joshie never did come to trial for that same winter he died. He caught ship's flu and never recovered. The case was closed when Sergeant H.A. Larsen, Master of the R.C.M.P. schooner, *St. Roch*, which was wintering at Kent Bay some 200 miles from Fort Ross, sent a message, short and to the point, "Native Joshie who was on trial at Fort Ross now dead."

Before the *Nascopie* had arrived Jack had had to do something about the young lad who had been left in his charge by the King William Island Eskimos. When the *Nascopie* arrived Inspector Martin would want to know what charge was being laid against the young man. So Jack radioed Ty Bergman, his partner at Pond Inlet, and asked him, "What section of the Criminal Code is buggery?"

Bergman thought Jack was pulling his leg and back came the message via the Hudson's Bay Company posts at Pond Inlet and Fort Ross, "What are you guys up to over there?"

Jack then had to explain the situation to Ty to get a sensible answer out of him. By the time the boat arrived, however, Jack had things neatly organized and laid a charge of buggery against the young fellow. When he came up before Martin he pleaded guilty to the charge and was placed in Jack's custody, and taken to Pond Inlet as his prisoner.

The doctor on board the *Nascopie* diagnosed the lad's sickness and prescribed large quantities of water, sulpha pills and exercise.

Jack kept him active all the following winter. Day after day he had him outside running and walking between the Hudson's Bay store and the R.C.M.P. buildings.

"Come on, run!" Jack would roar at him and the lad would really run.

That winter he improved so much that Jack gave him four or five of the scruff dogs and a young pup and a few traps and he tried his hand at trapping. His sickness cleared up and by the time spring came round he wanted to marry one of the nice young girls in the settlement. Jack thought this was all right but he had better handle the matter cautiously so he went to the parents of the girl and said, "You can take him with you to your camp. He can hunt and help you around the place but he is not to sleep with the girl. Is that clear? He is not to stay with the girl until I give permission."

Things went well for the lad. He worked hard. The people came to like him and he eventually married the girl. The only condition the police insisted on was that the doctor should examine him at ship time.

It can hardly be doubted that this young fellow had been given up by his people. An orphan with poor intelligence, he was a liability his people did not want. Quite possibly he was left to die among the dogs and only because of an exceptional will to live and physical resilience did he manage to survive. Gradually he became like the animals with whom he was raised and but for the fortuitous presence of Constable Doyle at Fort Ross he might well have been destroyed. Only the strongest and the best survive in a primitive Eskimo society and often it is in the heart of Baffin Island that this is made most plain.

19

Strange Screams of Death

Constable Doyle was able to rescue one young man from death, or a life of indescribable misery, but such aid has only been available in Arctic Canada for a few short years. In this century when the rest of Canada has known anaesthetics, surgery as well as welfare and relief programmes, these few people at the top of the continent have been forgotten until the most recent of years. They have been rarely visited and hardly known. They were Canadians without knowing it and Canada claimed them without knowing them. No people of our land have experienced in this century more desperate privation or more constant hardship. Yet they have survived.

In 1903-04, the same year that the government ship, the *Neptune*, sailed north to bring Canadian law to northern settlements, two widely separated spots in the eastern Arctic witnessed a fearful struggle to live. In one case the fight was lost and in the other the fight, at fearful cost, was won.

For a number of years prior to the turn of the century there had been considerable activity by whalers and traders in and around Southampton Island. The whaling ship, *Active*, used to call regularly at a station maintained there by the Cumberland Gulf Trading Co., a Scottish whaling company. Without knowing it, this investment led to the total extinction of a particular group of Eskimos.

At the dawn of the twentieth century there was on Southampton Island a tribe (Sadlirmiut) that numbered about sixty-eight people. By the end of 1904 the group was virtually extinct. Only two people were left and one, a woman, married out of the tribe. The end for the Sadlirmiut came swiftly and completely. No one really knew about it until a few years later and no one really cared anyway.

Every year the whaling ship, *Active*, would pick up a group of Eskimos from Big Island and take them to Southampton Island where they would hunt, work, whale and generally service the needs of the company. The local Sadlirmiut were not used. Contact with them had apparently proved more difficult than contact with those to the north and east at the foot of Baffin Island. It is certain that they were very different in many ways from the other Eskimos. David Damas of the National Museum of Canada writes in *Science, History and Hudson Bay*, "The Sadlirmiut were aberrant from the other groups in their great permanency of settlements and in a number of features of material culture that distinguished them rather sharply from other Canadian Esquimaux cultures."

According to A.P. Low, writing in his report, *The Cruise of the Neptune*, it was the activity of the imported Eskimos that paved the way for the destruction of the Sadlirmiut. These strangers invaded the island with modern weapons and soon slaughtered or frightened away the deer — a prime source of food. The local natives, armed with bows and arrows and spears, could not compete with these invaders and soon they starved. Hand in hand with hunger came disease and finally death overtook them all. Low winds up his brief account of the tragedy, "Some regulation should be made to prevent this unauthorized movement of the natives, or similar wholesale slaughter will occur again."

Therkel Mathiassen does not agree with Low that the prime cause of the destruction of the Southampton Islanders was starvation but blames disease. He still blames the whalers, however, for he says that it was typhus introduced by them that wiped out the tribe. Ladies of the early twentieth century had no idea how many lives the whalebone in their corsets had cost. The prosecution of business by a civilized country amidst a primitive people has always been brutal.

The death of the tribe on Southampton Island was actually witnessed by a few white men who had spent the winter at the Cumberland Gulf Trading Co. station.

It was on the 18th of July, 1903, that the *Active* arrived in

Southampton Island. She had set sail from Dundee on the 12th of June and had had a reasonably satisfactory voyage. Early in July a call had been made at the Lake Harbour mica mine and at Big Island to pick up the summer's crew of helpers. When she reached Southampton Island the first object everyone spotted was the ketch *Ernest William* flying the ensign at half mast. It looked ominous. Captain Murray made immediate enquiries. The news was bad. Six boats, each with an Eskimo crew and a Scotsman in charge, had been caught in a violent storm while engaged on a whaling expedition in the vicinity of the settlement and were driven out to sea. Three of the boats had not returned. Eight days had now passed since their disappearance and the worst was feared. On the afternoon following the *Active's* arrival, two of the missing craft turned up, bringing with them the crew of the third. A Mr. James Brown was in charge of the boat which sank. When the boat went down the Eskimos had managed to scramble onto the ice but Brown had been thrown into the water. Miraculously, he was rescued and lived. He and his crew stayed on the ice twenty-four hours before one of the boats managed to take them off. During that time they were without food, weapons or shelter. It had been a close call for them all.

The Dundee newspaper which reports the incident then goes on to say, "A curious sequel to this adventure — interesting as a proof of the extent to which the Esquimaux are influenced by superstition — fails to be recorded. After the accident the natives absolutely declined to remain at Southampton and in deference to their wishes the station was shifted to Kekerton, a couple of days steam around the coast."

The fact that this happened in 1903 and the fact that this is the date agreed upon by Low and Mathiassen as the year of the Sadlirmiut's end is surely no coincidence.

The year after the extinction of the tribe on Southampton Island there was a second struggle for existence in the Canadian Arctic. The story of this struggle has become one of the eastern Arctic's most famous tales. Knud Rasmussen was the first to record it and since then it has been written a number of times and details of it have been very carefully investigated by Father Guy Marie Rousseliere, O.M.I.

In the winter of 1904-05 there was famine on Baffin Island. During the summer of 1904 a small group of Pond Inlet Eskimos moved deep into the interior of Baffin Island to hunt for caribou. The hunt was unsuccessful. Things began to look bad.

"We are going back to Qilalukan (a camp near Pond Inlet)," said Piuatuk to his wife, "I have decided. And Aksarjuk is coming too."

The two men, accompanied by their wives and children, started on the long trek back towards Pond Inlet. They left behind Qumangapik, Sigluk, Kunuk, and their families. For the few who were left behind the situation grew steadily worse. No caribou were sighted. The lake beside which they camped yielded no fish. They cried out to the spirits to preserve them. Still no caribou came and the stomachs of all were empty.

The first victim of the famine was Ataguttaaluk's baby. It died as she carried it on her back. Ataguttaaluk and her husband, Qumangapik, looked after its burial. By the side of the lake a tiny heap of stones marked her resting place — secure for a while from dogs, bears, foxes and wolves. Qumangapik was very sad. He grieved deeply. Mysteriously, however, the needs of the tiny camp became known in Pond Inlet. Prayers to the spirits were borne upon the wind, carried along valleys and over the mountain passes till they were heard by the shaman at Pond Inlet. Qaumayoq, the shaman, held a seance. Dark was the night and breathless the audience as he listened to the voices no one else could hear.

"I hear," he told the waiting group, "I hear cries coming from the land. I hear lamentations. I hear the sound of sorrow. Sounds come from the south, from inside the land. They come from Qumangapik."

Everybody believed the shaman.

"Apitak," Qaumayoq called, "you must go into the land. You must find Qumangapik. Take your dogs. Take provisions and go."

Apitak lost no time and was soon on his way to the rescue. Not long after he left, Piuatuk, who had been with the group during the summer, decided to go after Apitak and offer his help too. On his way, Piuatuk killed a few caribou, one of which he cached for his return journey. He cached the caribou near the lake where Qumangapik, his wife and others were camped.

When Piuatuk reached the camp Apitak was already there. Both of the men urged Qumangapik to return with them but he refused. Their arrival had buoyed his spirits a little and he began to think they would kill caribou in the region and anyway he was loathe to leave the grave of his child. Apitak, having seen the group was still alive and still had hope, left them and returned to Pond. He took with him one of the women in the group, whose husband had grown disenchanted with her. What was more important to a few of the men still left in the camp, however, was the fact that he also took the caribou Piuatuk had cached.

After a few days, with game conditions remaining as poor as ever, Piuatuk, Sigluk and Iktukusuk set out, following Apitak's trail.

Things went badly from the start. Sigluk froze his feet and became a liability to the other two.

They had started off with no food and when they reached their cache the caribou was gone. The only thing they could do now was return to camp. Slowly, the men, komitik and dogs moved back. Day after day, while their strength remained, the men went hunting — but no game was seen. Soon, the dogs were all eaten. There was not much meat on them when they were butchered but they were better than nothing. Bones were gnawed and sucked. Anything became food.

Winter deepened. Nights grew colder, days shorter and then the sun disappeared. The wind moaned among the hills and swept remorselessly across the lake. Death inched its way towards them all. Sigluk was the first adult to die.

They managed to get Sigluk's body out of the igloo and bury it near the lake shore, but he was the last to be cared for in this way.

Qumangapik said, "I will go towards the sea for seals. Perhaps I can reach it."

"Don't go," pleaded Monica Ataguttaaluk. "The wolves, they will get you. I want you to stay."

Qumangapik stayed.

The children died.

Piuatuk left the camp and walked alone towards the sea. He plodded away pitifully, deliberately.

The seal tent was eaten. Whips were chewed. Clothing was devoured and bones were gnawed but hunger still drove its sword into them. All of them wanted to live, especially Monica Ataguttaaluk. She held more tenaciously to life than any of them. Monica was a remarkable woman. Gifted with a forceful personality and above average intelligence she always made her presence felt. Peter Freuchen, who met her years later in Igloolik, called her "First Lady of Fury and Hecla Strait". Later still, she became commonly known as the "Queen of Igloolik".

Father Rousseliere writes, "If she had been born under other skies she would probably have occupied an important niche in society. At the 70° Latitude North she had to spend her life trimming seal oil lamps, chewing the soles of boots and in short carrying on the many domestic tasks which are the law of women."

Perhaps it was this woman who first suggested that there was flesh to eat in the camp. Nearby, as they crouched, famished and threatened, were the corpses of the children and outside was Sigluk. Dulled by starvation, they were slipping slowly but inexorably into a torpor from which there was no return. Too weak to walk, too weak to hunt, almost too tired to think, they waited for death.

"Their souls have gone," Monica muttered. "It cannot be wrong."

Qumangapik looked questioningly at her. But he knew what was in her mind. He, too, had thought it.

If they were to stay alive there was only one thing left for them to do — eat the corpses.

No one spoke. They pondered. The wills of them all said "Live! Live! Live!" Their bodies ached for food. Their dreams were filled with the sights, sounds and smells of meat — red meat, fresh meat, meat dripping with blood. They were Eskimos, flesh eaters, carnivores. What diet was seal skin tents and caribou droppings!

Monica shrank from the first taste of human flesh. When the thought had first entered her mind she had been filled with revulsion. But that was yesterday. The thought was back with her now and entertained. Her eyes wandered from knife to corpse and then back to the knife again. She could see them both from where she squatted. Even as she pondered her husband spoke.

"My little dear," he said, "when I die you will eat me also, won't you?"

Strange insight. He had penetrated her thinking.

"You will eat me and you will be found when people cross the land."

Monica answered nothing.

That night he died.

The three remaining people tried to get him up onto the platform but failed.

Monica said to Kunuk and Iktukusuk, "He is dead now. He wanted to be eaten. Let us put him on the ground and eat him."

A sudden callousness had taken hold of her. The revulsion was gone. It seemed right to eat.

Kunuk butchered his father. As he sawed off his head he cried. He wailed with horror as he opened up the body but something drove him on and the three survivors feasted. When Qumangapik's body was finished they started on the children and then they hauled in Sigluk. Like vultures they lived, hovering around the corpses. A madness was upon them all. Human flesh now tasted good.

The days were lengthening when Kunuk died. He died shortly after Sigluk's body was devoured. The two women fell upon him and ate without regard for what they were doing.

"It's good, eh?" said Iktukusuk, gnawing on a bone, "It's good."

Monica did not answer.

"Since people die," continued Iktukusuk, "let us eat the dead. Now we have lost the taste for ordinary game."

Such talk put Monica on her guard. Soon, Kunuk's body would be finished. Then, what would there be left to eat? She began to fear for her life.

With a slowness that only the Arctic seems to know, the days began to grow a little warmer. Shadows grew shorter at noon and the land began to stir again. Monica began to believe, with genuine hope, that she would yet live. Soon, Kunuk's body was stripped. Monica kept her husband's pocket knife handy. It was a knife traded to him by the whalers and was equipped with a large awl. She feared Iktukusuk, the one who liked the taste of human flesh.

One day Iktukusuk asked her to look for lice in her hair. They were bothering her. Monica began to peer through the mop of thick black hair and as she looked she recognized this as her chance to kill Iktukusuk. Surreptitiously she worked open the awl in the knife and then, with a sudden firm jab, she drove it in to the exposed ear. Blood trickled from Iktukusuk's nose and she died.

At just about the time that Iktukusuk was being murdered, Padloq, his wife, Tagornaq, and their adopted daughter, Atuat, set out from Igloolik on a trip to Pond Inlet. Padloq was out of ammunition and needed urgently to trade for some. The preceding summer Padloq had spent on the land and had set up a number of food caches which he deemed adequate for his purposes. Before Padloq left, however, the oldest man in the camp at Igloolik said to him, "It has rained in the middle of the winter. Such bad weather is a bad omen. There are somewhere people who are in great trouble."

It was, for Padloq, as though an oracle had spoken and the words were not forgotten. It was a frail looking group that left Igloolik that April of 1904, just two adults, one child and four dogs. Their provisions were meagre too, one male caribou and one seal for the dogs. Often Padloq and his wife had to help move the sledge and little Atuat would ride. It was a slow, long journey; a journey that was filled with portents — omens that filled Padloq with unease. One morning when they were in the interior of Cockburn Land a ptarmigan flew by. Tagornaq threw a walrus tusk at it and missed and then she aimed at it with an axe and missed again.

"Strange things are going to happen, Omaga," she said to her husband, "strange things."

Padloq agreed. "You notice too, how the sledge keeps sticking for no apparent reason on flat land and even when going downhill?"

Tagornaq nodded. Atuat listened.

The nearer they drew to Monica's igloo the more frequent were the signs. Just the night before they came upon her, Padloq dreamed a dream which he later interpreted as being Qumangapik's way of telling him what had happened so that his wife, Monica, might live. The trip became an eerie series of omens, not fully understood but tinged with warnings of sadness.

The day after the dream the little party ran into deep snow which they managed to struggle through slowly. They now had only three dogs, their only female having died on the trail. Gradually they edged their way towards the big lake. As they advanced they heard the strident shout of a human voice. The cry echoed out among the rocks and surrounded them with its sound.

"What is it mother? What is it? Is it a fox? Is it a wolf? Is it a wolverine?"

"Yes." Tagornaq answered vaguely, still listening.

Padloq moved silently on.

Suddenly there was the voice again. The noise hovered in the air, a disembodied shriek, a frightful howl, not human, not animal. They listened. Now the voice again and this time it was clear.

Padloq and Tagornaq exchanged glances.

"It is someone who has eaten human flesh," said Padloq.

By now Monica was mad with loneliness, hunger and fear. She wanted to be rescued but feared her rescuers. She wanted to be found but knew security in her isolation. It was a terrible moment when she spied movement in the distance and knew she was to be discovered. Like a flightless vulture she crouched in the midst of human bones and entrails and waited for her rescuers to enter.

By now Padloq had spotted the shelter, half hidden in a drift, and had begun to move directly towards it. He reached it and looked in. On the floor of the shelter were two human skulls and intestines. There was still a little left to eat. Monica looked up at Padloq. Her eyes were bloodshot with weeping and suffering.

"I have eaten my children and my husband," she said, muttering and moaning.

202 The Howling Arctic

Padloq and his wife could not believe she still lived. She could not walk. She was nothing but skin and bones. She had even eaten some of her own clothing. Padloq was greatly moved by what he saw and greatly moved by what he heard. He could scarcely believe that this living skeleton had once been a young woman.

At last he said to her, "You had the will to live. Therefore you live."

Patiently, kindly and with great forbearance Padloq and his wife cared for Monica. Atuat was afraid of her and lost her appetite. At Monica's insistence they turned from their intention to go to Pond Inlet and went back to Igloolik. Doubtless, Monica did not want to meet the brother of Iktukusuk, whom she had both killed and eaten. On the trail she dreaded meeting other Eskimos and howled and wailed when they came in sight. It was an awful cry that all who heard could never forget.

Once back in Igloolik, Monica gradually became reintegrated into the Eskimo society. At first she was stared at in awe by the children but the weeks, months and years sped by. She married a great hunter, Iktuksarjuaq and together with him became famous in the north. White people named them "The King and Queen of Igloolik". Monica died on July 16th, 1948. Father Guy Marie Rousseliere said the liturgical prayers of the Roman Catholic Church over her body.

20

The Wreck
of the Nascopie

Monica Ataguttaaluk lived long enough to see an astonishing change in the Eastern Arctic, but it was not until towards the end of her life that things really began to happen in Igloolik. Some other settlements in the Arctic developed faster then her community. Not until 1939 did the Hudson's Bay Company open a store there and only two years previously had the Roman Catholics started a permanent mission. Prior to that the natives from Igloolik received Christian instruction and traded for goods at Pond Inlet or Repulse Bay. Whichever settlement they headed for, it was a long trek.

Igloolik was not easily accessible. The first visitor to that general area was Thomas Button. He sailed up Roes Welcome Sound but did not penetrate into Foxe Basin. Captain W.E. Parry spent the winter of 1821-22 on the southeast coast of Melville Peninsula and the following winter went further north to Turton Bay on Igloolik Island. Parry managed to establish friendly relations with the Eskimos from whom he was able to glean a number of facts concerning the geography of the area. In the middle of the 1800's, Dr. John Rae went in to the area during the Franklin search and he was followed a decade later by Captain C.F. Hall. Apart from the occasional whaler who stopped at Igloolik towards the end of the century the settlement remained unvisited.

Not until the Fifth Thule Expedition under Knud Rasmussen, Peter Freuchen and Mathiassen was there any systematic work done in that part of the Arctic. At just about the same time as Rasmussen and his team set to work, the Government of Canada began the annual Eastern Arctic Patrol.

In the years between the voyage of the *Neptune* and the first organized patrol there had been some Canadian activity in the Keewatin, Baffin and the Bay but it was still, largely speaking, a neglected land. Sovereignty had been asserted but much more needed to be done for it to be maintained. The patrol, however, was not merely an exercise in sovereignty but a serious attempt to begin continuous and effective administration of the scattered settlements of the north.

In 1922 the first annual patrol was made. For this patrol, as for all the early patrols, the Government chartered ships. The ships they employed were the C.G.S. *Arctic* and the *Beothic*, neither of which was entirely satisfactory. These boats were old, slow and expensive. They could not always get where the patrols wanted to go. Right from the very start, in fact, the inadequacies of the C.G.S. *Arctic* were apparent. When the boat reached Pond Inlet on the first of the patrols in 1922, a Captain Munn, who was freetrading there, reported to the authorities rumours of murder in the Cumberland Sound area. Sergeant Joy, who was stationed there, supported Munn's stories.

According to the tales brought to Pond, one of the natives around Cumberland Sound had "got religion" to such an extent that the other natives shot him but failed to kill him. These men then, apparently, repented of their action and nursed him back to health. No sooner had he recovered than he ordered one of them to shoot two other Eskimos who would not accept his ascendancy. The man obeyed. Fortunately for everyone concerned, the madman's control was short lived for he, himself, was shot by another Eskimo. His death came just in the nick of time. He was about to smash a woman's skull with a hammer when the bullet hit him. This incredible story needed investigating so Sergeant Joy asked for passage down the coast of Baffin Island to Clyde River. Captain Bernier had to refuse because there was no way that the old tub, the C.G.S. *Arctic*, would be able to handle the ice conditions. Captain Bernier's decision was heartily concurred with by the leader of the Eastern Arctic Patrol, Major D. McKeand. He writes in his report, "I thoroughly agree with Captain Bernier's decision for from even the short experience I have had with this boat in the ice I can say if it were not for Captain Bernier's almost uncanny way of scenting trouble we would have been in many a tight fix before this, even this summer which has been a particularly favourable one from the weather standpoint."

What was required for these patrols was an up to date, powerful, well designed and well equipped icebreaker. But things did not substantially improve until a deal was made with the Hudson's Bay Company for the use of the *Nascopie*. Each year the *Nascopie* went on a supply trip to all the Hudson's Bay Company trading points and it was thought possible that some sort of deal could be made with the Company to accommodate the government administrators. Finally, such an agreement was reached and the Government, for a fixed price, was carried by the Company's ship, the *Nascopie,* into Canada's Arctic each year.

There were distinct advantages for both parties to the contract. The only serious criticism levelled against the arrangement was that it identified the government administration too closely with the Hudson's Bay Company. The Government could not afford its own ship so it used that of a commercial enterprise.

For fifteen years the *Nascopie* plied the Hudson Bay and on up to the Arctic settlements, carrying with it the brass of both the Company and the Government. The boat was the scene of all kinds of incidents, from weddings to funerals and from trials to toothpullings. Year after year it became the vehicle of medicine and missionaries, traders and tourists. The *Nascopie* was the most famous ship of the north.

Major McKeand, for many years, led the patrol for the Government. He was a man with a wide experience and a great fondness for talking about it. It appears that, at one time, he was in South Africa and actually fought in the Boer War. Perhaps that is the origin of the "Major". During combat he was wounded on his backside — a military mark of some merit! At least that was Mr. McKeand's attitude to it. On one occasion he happened to meet Bishop Turquetil in the showers on board the *Nascopie*.

"Oh, did I show you my scar, Reverend?" asked the Major, bending over.

"I see nothing, Major," responded the Bishop after close examination.

The Eskimos had a name for the Major which he thought meant "Great White Father". In actual fact, however, the name referred to his wandering eye. The "squiffy-eyed one" would be a free translation.

While McKeand was in charge of the government end of the operation, the overall command of the ship was, for many years, in the hands of Captain Mack and Captain Smellie. They were both competent seamen who managed to sail safely in dangerous waters for many years. They had a good ship to command and knew how to handle her. The *Nascopie* was designed to take rough treatment and this was fortunate for frequently the propeller on the ship would be so badly damaged that it had to be changed.

In 1934 this fact was strongly emphasized before the Senate by Captain Bernier. The subject under discussion was the Hudson Bay route. Pressure was growing for the shipment of prairie produce via Churchill, Manitoba. When it was pointed out that the Hudson Strait was navigable, Captain Bernier felt bound to be heard.

"Oh well, it is possible to navigate the Hudson Strait — of course it is possible. But if the honourable gentleman would listen to me he would learn that there are tides in the Straits and, as you know, tides ebb and flow four times a day. It is just as well that this house have a little information on the subject."

Captain Bernier went on to give a little lesson about this and to make his point plain he referred to a specific incident. It appears that Captain Mack once had an officer of the Mounted Police on board his ship and his orders were to do what this officer said. Upon reaching the Hudson Strait the R.C.M.P. officer gave the order, "Go ahead. It is clear water." Captain Mack, feeling he must obey orders went in but after he'd been there for two or three weeks he had to come out with the flow of ice. The ship was pushed back into the Atlantic and a second entry had to be made. Time would have been saved if he had waited until the ice had all passed before entering at all.

Bernier went on,

If you leave Montreal on the 6th or 7th of July and get to the mouth of the Straits between the 12th and 15th you can proceed into the Bay with a ship like the *Nascopie* but she is not of ordinary build. My Honourable friend from Saskatchewan (Mr. M. Gillis) is, I suppose, more familiar with prairie schooners than with ocean vessels . . . The *Nascopie* is made saucer shaped. My Honourable friend from Saskatchewan did not seem to know what that meant so I will tell him. The sides are shaped somewhat like a saucer so that if there is a pressure of ice around the sides the ship is bound to lift up. If she did not lift up she would be crushed like an egg and that would be just what would happen to a vessel of ordinary shape.

My Honourable friend from Saskatchewan has referred to the navigability of the Hudson Bay route. Well, if you go down to the Department of Railways and Canals you can see a ship's log that gives some interesting facts. The log is not advertised anymore than the advocates of the seaway talk anymore about the canal being frozen in the winter. The log shows that on the 5th of August the ship was in ice and fog with one blade of its propeller gone and that as it proceeded it continued to lose more and more of its propeller until when it reached Port Nelson on the 19th of August it had left only about half of one blade. Captain Mack, of the *Nascopie*, used to take three propellers with him. When one became broken by the ice he would stand the ship off from shore and spot a place free of boulders. Then at high tide he would back his vessel up there and beach her; and when the tide went out the damaged propeller would be removed and a new one substituted. But can honourable members imagine an ordinary ocean steamer, with plates only 3/8 of an inch thick, being subjected to treatment of that kind? It is preposterous . . . . Captain Bernier made his point.

In view of the nature of the *Nascopie* and the skill of her captains it is all the more surprising to learn that she sank in 1947. At the time of the sinking the skipper was Captain Walters. It only happened a mere 23 years ago so there are still many living witnesses. In spite of this, however, the cause of the wreck is a mystery. Many questions are still left unanswered. It is a puzzle to historians. Certainly the Hudson Bay has become the graveyard of many a fine ship, but not in beautiful weather, on sunlit days, amidst calm seas and on well travelled routes. But, on such a day, in such a place, at such a time, the *Nascopie* met her end.

On July 20th, 1947, Constable J. Decker of the R.C.M.P. reboarded the *Nascopie* at Lake Harbour. He had disembarked there thinking he was going to stay, only to find that his first duty in the north was to travel to the next port of call, Cape Dorset, to register the Eskimos for family allowance. He did not mind. He had made friends with many of the people on board and another day and night would be quite pleasant.

On July 21st Constable Decker was up on deck. It was a rare, glorious day in the Arctic's short summer, a day when the north wore its kindest smile. Jack watched the hills of Baffin Island slowly unwind. The air was light and clear, invigorating. Idly, he let his eyes move from land to water and then ahead to Cape Dorset, some five miles away. They would soon be there. Jack was standing on the starboard side and well forward. He looked at the water ahead of the boat.

"Do you see that?" he asked the fellow standing next to him.

"What?"

"Do you see that ripple? It's right ahead."

"Yes. I do. There's a play on the water right enough."

These comments had hardly been made when there was a bump and the *Nascopie* slid up on a reef. No one was alarmed. The deck sloped from forward to aft at about ten degrees. Everyone was taking it easy and apparently rather enjoying it. There had been many bumps more impressive than this one.

The engines were reversed but the boat held fast. Passengers leaned over the deck rail to watch. Nobody for one moment regarded the ship as doomed. A few hours after the ship struck, Captain Walters ordered everyone but the crew ashore. Come high water he was certain that with a lighter load the boat would float free. It was a fairly simple matter getting everyone safely ashore. No one was worried. It was a great day. Sometime after midnight, at high tide, attempts to free the vessel began. A kedge anchored at the stern was lost when the cable broke under strain from the winches that were attempting to free the boat. In spite of this, however, the ship slowly dragged itself off the reef. As it slid backwards, sharp toothed rocks gouged into her belly and water rushed into some forward areas. Unsteadily, the ship's direction was changed and she began to move forward. Accurate steering was impossible and before anyone knew it the ship was back up on the same reef again but this time the stern of the ship rose high out of the water. The deck sloped so steeply that it was next to impossible to stand on it. Nothing would now release it. No matter how determined the winches were the ship would not budge. Things now looked bad.

During the night a wind had sprung up and the water had grown a little uneasy. With the wind came rain — cold, drizzly, misty, penetrating. It became a nasty, unpleasant night. Shortly after 2:30 a.m., water poured into the stoke hold and the firemen were sent ashore on the scow. Their arrival on shore was the first intimation to the passengers and others that all was not well.

Captain J.G. Wright, who was in charge of the Eastern Arctic Patrol, organized a native crew and a peterhead boat to go out to the ship to give any assistance that might be required. This boat was a few miles out when it met three ship's boats proceeding cautiously towards shore. All the personnel of the ship were on board. Len Adie, the first mate, who was among the men, said that as the last of them left the *Nascopie* a small ice field moved in about her. And their last sight of her in that drizzling dawn was with her stern high in the water, a thirty degree list, steam rising from her furnace fires and the ice about her. In his report, J.G. Wright says, "It seemed a fitting end for the *Nascopie* that she should rest in the Arctic seas she had sailed so long, surrounded by ice which she had fought successfully on so many occasions and which now, in token as it were, claimed her for its own."

But the *Nascopie* did not take one last bow and disappear with dignity beneath the curtain of the Arctic sea. She hung around on the rock like a mouldering corpse bashed by the waves and plundered by men. She hung there ignominiously, five miles from Dorset, where, on a well travelled waterway, in blazing sunshine, on a calm day, she had come to grief. As one man put it, she scratched her bottom and died.

For a while the *Nascopie* was like a bank with all the vaults wide open and no personnel there to guard the treasure. Her cargo became a fair target for the adventurous and there was no shortage of such people. Night after night and day after day the wreck was visited. All kinds of things were brought ashore, especially liquor. Along the south coast of Baffin Island that winter there was more Scotch than ever before, or probably since. There was so much at Lake Harbour, some 300 miles down the coast, that many a time Scotch whiskey was used instead of wood alcohol to prime the primus stoves. It is anyone's guess how it got that far along the coast and anyone who knows the north should be able to guess correctly at the first attempt.

Liquor could have caused a problem at Dorset. The emergency camp was overcrowded and law and order had to be enforced. If the sailors had managed to get into a really large supply of alcohol there could have been trouble for the R.C.M.P. Soon after the various groups had landed and been settled in the different quarters, the officer in command of the patrol assigned Inspector Parsons and three R.C.M.P. constables to law enforcement. To boost the squad, Alex Stevenson of the Hudson's Bay Company was sworn in as a special constable.

Under the noses of the law enforcement officers some liquor was brought to Dorset but was quickly found and confiscated.

During the days immediately following the wreck, a Hudson's Bay Company Canso came in and flew out the captain and other Hudson's Bay Company personnel. Meanwhile all the registered and first class mail was salvaged although some of the paper records were water damaged.

Day after day the wreck was raided. One enterprising Eskimo stripped the captain's cabin of its mahogany veneer and lined his own shack with it. Others, in their enthusiasm, salvaged numerous useless objects like electric light bulbs — all kinds of things of value and use were bypassed in order to get the bulbs.

Salvage work was not without peril. Often it was necessary to crawl deep into the bowels of the ship to places from which escape would be impossible should the boat slide from its perch. J.G. Wright makes special mention of J.G. Hadden, postmaster, Inspector Parsons and Alex Stevenson, " . . . these three men," he says, "descended into the bowels of the wreck which listed at an angle of 30 degrees on the reef in constant danger of slipping off into deep water. They forced open doors with pick axes and invaded flooded cabins to rescue valuable Government records. Due to their efforts it is doubtful if anything irreplace-able has been lost although most of the records are in bad shape from sea water."

For almost two months the whole of the ship remained visi-ble. Then, on September 25th, it broke in two and the forward half slipped into deep water. It was October 15th before the stern half disappeared and the *Nascopie* was gone from sight forever.

The wreck is a simple fact of history but the why of the wreck is far from being obvious. Naturally enough the master of the ship was held responsible. What or who else was there to blame? Who ordered the ship on the course it was taking? Was someone drunk on duty? How could an ordinary constable detect a ripple and not an experienced seaman? So the ques-tions multiply. Round and round the bay circulated these ques-tions and others, and up and down Baffin Island went the queries. The only answers were guesses and the guesses became rumours and the truth remains buried. It was a simple, though expensive, human error says one witness. It was a gigantic conspiracy says another witness. What do you mean — conspiracy?

"Well, it's like this," and the witness pauses to savour the rumour he is about to begin. "The *Nascopie* was old, due for replacement. The Company needed a new boat. When hotels no longer pay, the owners burn them. When mines are going out of business what is better than a convenient fire? But when a ship's old, don't burn it, wreck it. Wreck it nice and gentle. Don't hurt nobody. Just get rid of the boat. Make a report and collect the insurance. See what I mean when I say conspiracy. Someone was paid off to put an end to the *Nascopie*."

Believe it or not that is one of the fantastic rumours that clings to the mysterious wreck of the *Nascopie*.

21
The Haunted Land

James Bell, the great big Hudson's Bay man from Lake Harbour, was delighted with the liquor bonanza caused by the wreck of the *Nascopie*. It is quite likely that he had something to do with its transportation from Dorset to Lake Harbour, for the passenger list shows Jimmy Bell was on board when the ship was wrecked. James loved his liquor and he loved his food. It was he and a fellow named Andre D'Aoust who spent the whole winter of 1947-48 wading their way through this salvaged liquor. It was a glorious winter. Anyone who knew James Bell knows just how glorious it was. Jimmy was a great person to know. Everyone who knew him speaks well of him. He was a Scotsman who came over to Canada between the wars to work for the Hudson's Bay Company. When he arrived in Montreal he was a naive Scottish lad, unused to the ways of the world. He came with another well known man of the north, Jimmy Smith. These two, on disembarkation, were wandering through Montreal when Smith spotted some enormous oranges on display.

"Say, Jimmy, did you ever see oranges like that, my boy?"

"Nay, lad, I never."

"I'm in to buy one of those oranges. What do you say?"

"Aye. I dinna have many dollars but I think I can afford one of those giants."

The fruit was tastefully arranged and was irresistible to these two lads who had been brought up in Scotland on slender fare.

"I can hardly wait," said Jimmy Smith, while walking out of the shop holding the fruit in his hand.

Quickly they ripped the peel off and Jimmy sank his teeth into the fruit.

"Ugh!" he said, spitting it out, "it's sour."

"I'll tell you," said Jimmy Bell, getting ready to eat his, "mine's going to have to be mighty sour for me to spit it out."

James Bell took a bite.

"I agree with you, Jimmy. It's horrible."

Both of them threw the remains into a nearby garbage can in quick succession. Neither had ever seen a grapefruit before!

It would not have been so bad for them if they had had money to spare but they were fairly short and they still had to have their hair cut. Coming to a new country, starting a new job, working among new people, they felt it necessary to look their best. So they went to a barber shop after their introduction to grapefruit. The visit was a minor disaster. Like the couple of greenhorns they were, they let the barber talk them into a shave, face massage, singe, and hair treatment, as well as the ordinary haircut. The bill was phenomenal, something like $2.00, and their funds almost exhausted by the time they escaped the barber's clutches. They both looked sharp and smelled delicious. But they were broke. It was in this fashion that James Bell was introduced to Canada in general and Montreal in particular.

James Bell came to love Montreal. He made plans to retire there. It is even rumoured that he set up business there, illicit business. A story is told, the truth of which no one can vouch for, that at one time he and another Hudson's Bay Company man saved enough money to purchase a fully equipped "cat house" in Montreal. Those who knew James Bell best say that such a purchase was a possibility.

Jimmy was always a big man but once in the north he became huge. He had an enormous appetite and at one sitting could eat eight to ten pounds of seal meat. It disappeared into him just as if he was a polar bear. According to Peter Murdoch, who stayed with him at Lake Harbour, he weighed about three hundred and fifty pounds and on one occasion had to be lifted into a peterhead with a block and tackle.

The year after the wreck of the *Nascopie*, Jimmy Bell was transferred from Lake Harbour to Cape Dorset. It did not matter much to him where he went in that part of the world. He knew it all and loved it well. At Cape Dorset he replaced R.

Cruikshank who had served the Company on the Belcher Islands prior to the famous murders. Peter Murdoch, who had been with Jimmy Bell at Lake Harbour, rejoined him at Cape Dorset. When Peter arrived there, Jimmy Bell came out to meet him. Peter did not recognize him. What he saw was a skinny-looking fellow wearing baggy clothes, his face lined and his eyes a sickly yellow.

"Jimmy," said Peter, clasping his hand, "what's the matter?"

"I dinna know, but I'm plain right off my food."

Murdoch could scarcely believe his eyes or his ears. This was not the Jimmy Bell of a year ago. This was but a shadow of the man. It upset Peter to see him like this for he had a special affection for this old Scotsman. It was Jimmy Bell, in a way, who had come to Peter's rescue when Peter had initially gone north. In his early days as a Hudson's Bay Company clerk he had not hit it off too well with Johnny Wickware at Pangnirtung and Johnny had packed him off to Lake Harbour with a dog team and told him not to come back. Murdoch admits he was a little bit of a problem and thinks it likely that Johnny Wickware asked Jimmy Bell to try to do something with him. Jimmy succeeded. Bell was the kind of man who commanded respect and was regarded by all the men whom he liked as a jewel, but by all others as an enemy to be feared.

"Can I fix you something to eat?" Peter asked Jimmy, later that first evening.

"No, not a thing. I canna even stand the smell of cooking. I dinna want a thing. In fact I dinna even want the smell." He paused. "Maybe you could see your way to eating elsewhere, huh?"

"Sure," said Peter, "if that's what you want."

So Peter began to eat all his meals with the Eskimos. It bothered Murdoch that Jimmy would not eat a thing, nor drink anything but a little water. Peter soon realized that Jimmy was seriously ill and that if he failed to persuade him to eat something he would simply starve to death.

"Wouldn't you like just a taste or two of seal ribs?" Peter queried one day.

"Uh, uh," Jimmy grunted and shook his head.

"Jimmy, you've just got to have something. You'll starve,

man. I'll fix a little for you."

Poor Jimmy could no longer stand the smell of tea but he finally succumbed to Peter's persuasion and allowed him to prepare a few seal ribs. When they were served he gazed at them for a few minutes, fighting wave after wave of nausea, and then, with a surge of determination and desperation, ate them. But it was no good. In a very short time he was writhing in pain and with a rush he spewed it all out.

"Peter," he said, "dig out the book and see if you can find out what's wrong with me."

They were sitting in the living room and the bookshelves were nearby. Rapidly, Peter found the huge medical book and thumbed through its pages.

"Jimmy," said Peter, after perusing the book for a while, "you've got cancer. You've got cancer of the stomach. That's what it says in this book."

It was a brutal diagnosis and a brutal declaration, but it was honest.

"Let me look."

Carefully the pages were read, turned and reread.

Jimmy sighed.

"If I have cancer I want to die in the north. I want my spirit to stay in the north. When I die my spirit is going back to Arctic Bay. That's the place I really love most — Arctic Bay."

Peter was silent. Jimmy got up and walked out of the house. In the days following this diagnosis, a diagnosis that both Peter and Jimmy felt sure was absolutely correct, Jimmy very rapidly deteriorated. Each day he stayed in bed but then at night he would go for a walk. When ever he went for a walk Peter followed him. He felt responsible for him. On one occasion they had just returned from this nocturnal stroll when Jimmy, sitting on the edge of the bed, began to vomit violently. Often he had vomited before but never quite like this. Blood, rich, dark and forbidding, poured out. It splashed into the small can he was holding with such force that it splattered onto the walls, floor and even ceiling. When the attack passed Jimmy lay down on his bed, exhausted, frightened, and at least for the moment, beaten.

Peter made him as comfortable as he could and then cleaned

the place up. He washed the walls, floor and ceiling, an unpleasant task for a man who was watching another man die.

"I've got to do something," thought Peter. "This is now a number one emergency."

Almost fiercely, he grabbed the key to the radio transmitter and tapped out a telegram to the Hudson's Bay Company headquarters. He described Jimmy's symptoms and, without Jimmy knowing it, signed Jimmy's name. He had just finished when he heard heavy breathing behind him and suddenly realized that Jimmy Bell was looking over his shoulder.

"What do you mean by that?" he roared, almost like the old Jimmy.

Without more ado he took after Peter verbally and physically. In spite of the fact that he was desperately ill, he summoned enough energy from somewhere to slap Peter around until it hurt.

"Take it easy, Jimmy," Peter said, fending off the blows. "You know as well as I do you need help."

Finally, Jimmy heeded what Peter was saying and gradually calmed down.

"You'd better get back to bed, Jimmy," urged Peter, propelling him in that direction. "I'll rub you down and give you another enema."

That sounds strange but that is exactly what Peter had to do. The only thing that gave Jimmy any relief at all was to have his back rubbed and to have an enema. Often Peter gave him as many as three in a day.

The moment Peter's telegram was received in Winnipeg, the Hudson's Bay Company acted. A Canso was sent in and Jimmy was flown to Winnipeg where he died some six weeks later. The diagnosis made with the help of the medical guide had been accurate. Jimmy Bell had died of cancer.

But he did not die where he wanted to die. He had wanted his grave to be a northern one and his funeral to be in a land to which he had given so many years of his life. Instead, he was buried amidst the flat monotony of southern Manitoba. Bell, however, was not beaten by that. Jimmy Bell was not going to be fettered by such conventional things as graves. He said, before he died, that he wanted his spirit to continue to inhabit the Arctic and, according to some, it does.

The Hudson's Bay post at Arctic Bay was haunted. Footsteps were heard in the storeroom and no one was there. Dishes rattled in the sink and no visible hand disturbed them. Doors opened when no hand was on the latch. Shadows, barely visible, flitted from room to room.

"It is the ghost of Jimmy Bell," said the credulous.

"It is imagination," said the scoffers.

"It's weird," said the frightened.

No one seems to know the real truth, but many know of the strange occurrences at Arctic Bay. On one occasion the dishes were being banged around in the sink by an unseen hand when the Hudson's Bay Company manager there said, "Leave the goddamed dishes alone, Bell, and get to hell out of here!"

This reaction was met with even more violent activity. It seemed as if the spirit of Bell was enraged by such treatment. The dishes were bounced around with destructive vigour.

The bangings, knocks and other mysterious noises became so frequent that an R.C.M.P. investigation was called for. The force, famous for getting its man, could not, apparently, get Jimmy's ghost. The hauntings continued. In fact, manifestations were so persistent that finally the old post was evacuated and a new one erected.

For the Eskimos there would probably be little difficulty in believing that the spirit of Jimmy Bell was stalking about the store as they readily believed in the presence and movement of spirits and ghosts. The world of the Eskimo is crowded with spirits, spirits that may be dangerous or benign. Such spirits may appear, or may simply be as powerful and unseen as the wind. Seances, such as the one Qaumayoq had when he heard voices coming out of the heart of Baffin Island, were not unusual. For the Eskimos the spirit world is close. They move freely and swiftly over the tundra moss and mountain height. They are confined by neither space nor time, darkness nor light. When the wind howls and all is still they come. As a man, a bear, a dog, a wolf, a fox, a bird, a fish, a shadow or a noise, they come. The Territories are crowded with unfettered spirits, thick with ghosts whose eyes, ears and intelligence follow the affairs of men. The Eskimos knew of the disturbances at Arctic

Bay and, with a touch of fear, agreed it was a ghost, perhaps the uneasy spirit of Bell.

In spite of the Christianizing of the Eskimos by Roman Catholic priests and Anglicans, many of the old superstitions cling. During the 1950's when J.C. Barr was stationed at Craig Harbour, he was witness to an interesting survival of a superstition. At that time, he and his special constable, an Eskimo, were on patrol. It was a routine patrol check on the location, condition and size of muskox herds in the area. Crossing over to the north part of Devon Island they ran into a large herd of muskox and decided to camp there. They tied all the dogs, made tea and then settled in for the night. During the night, Barr and his companion were both wakened by the furious barking of the dogs. They both thought muskox had come around the camp so they grabbed their rifles and looked out. There were no muskox in sight but there were two wolves, a male and a female. The female seemed to be trying to entice the dogs to take an interest in her while the male sat silently watching, some fifty yards away. The Special promptly upped his rifle and managed to nail the male wolf. It was a good shot. They both were pleased. As Cliff Barr watched the Special walk over to the carcass of the wolf, he thought of a conversation they had had earlier that very day. They had discussed the old religion and superstitions of the Eskimos and one of the stories the Eskimo had told concerned the wolf.

"We used to believe," he said, "that when a good hunter died he became a wolf."

"What happened when a wolf was killed, then?" asked Barr. "Perhaps the hunter had killed his own brother or father or uncle."

"Ah," said the Special, "in the old days the hunter had to skin the wolf and then cut off the head to release the spirit of the person inside. But that was in the old days. I don't believe that now. I'm a Christian. That was before we were Christians."

After the wolf was killed and while the Special was busy with the skinning, Barr lit the primus stove and began to prepare a cup of tea. He crouched in the tent over the primus and looked through the tent flap at the Eskimo. It did not take the man long. He soon had the pelt off. As he finished the job he straightened up, turned around, took a quick look at the tent, and then, with a sudden move, lopped off the wolf's head. This done he walked back to the tent.

"You may be a Christian," said Barr laughing, "but you sure as hell aren't taking any chances, are you?"

Not only did the Eskimos believe in reincarnation and the existence of the spirits, they believed too that the spirits could be angered, placated and contacted. This was made abundantly plain to Dr. Kaj Birkett-Smith in 1923. Dr. Birkett-Smith was, at the time, a member of the Fifth Thule Expedition which was under the leadership of Knud Rasmussen. Inadvertently he became the subject of the shaman's seance.

Igluyuk, a shaman on the west coast of Hudson Bay, held a seance because mysterious people had been seen. Members of the camp, in which Birkett-Smith was a guest, had seen, over to the west, people where they knew there could be no people. The story grew amongst the Eskimos and they began to be afraid.

"Who were these men? What were they doing? Why were they there?" they asked.

The only satisfactory explanation was that these figures were not men but spirits and they seemed to be threatening spirits.

"Evil spirits are upon us," they said to each other and the shadow of fear grew dark in their minds.

"We must have a seance," said Igluyuk.

And so the preparations were made — for when Igluyuk spoke the people listened. Igluyuk was a powerful man and his words had to be obeyed. Igluyuk had a reputation that made him feared. As a young man he had coveted the wife of another and in order to obtain her had killed her husband and the rest of her family. Dr. Birkett-Smith says that when the R.C.M.P. investigated the killings during the early twenties they actually engaged Igluyuk as their special constable. The murders were not brought plainly to light and Igluyuk was left behind as the representative of Canadian law enforcement.

Dr. Birkett-Smith was aware of the seance that Igluyuk was going to hold but he had no idea of the reason for it. He was interested in what took place but was not invited to share in any of the ritual. When the seance was over and the necessary revelations received, Igluyuk came to Birkett-Smith and said, "The evil spirits are around our camp because of you and the other members of your party."

Birkett-Smith was puzzled but said nothing.

"You are the cause of the threat. The spirits are disturbed because you have been wearing sealskin boots inland and such boots must not be used inland. In order to protect yourself you must take your sealskin boots back to your own country when you go and give them to your mother and she is to pin them on her dress at the nape of her neck in order to ward off evil spirits which would otherwise attack her from behind."

Dr. Birkett-Smith assured Igluyuk that he would do as instructed and this put to rest the fears of the community.

For Eskimos, who could so easily believe in the frequent intervention of the spirit world and the proximity of the departed dead, the events at Arctic Bay, though possibly frightening, were not surprising. Anything out of the ordinary was immediately attributed to the activity of the supernatural.

As late as the 1950's Corporal David R. Van Norman, who was stationed at Frobisher Bay, had to investigate the death of a man who had gone polar bear hunting some 30 miles out of Cape Dorset. Nuviayyuk had mysteriously died when about to shoot a polar bear. With inexplicable suddenness, life literally fled from him. The Eskimos began to talk about his death and they even suggested that the bear's spirits had killed him. Other rumours grew as well. Murder was even hinted at. These various stories became so insistent that Van Norman was sent over from Frobisher, as coroner, to conduct an enquiry. He flew in the police plane to Dorset and then picked up an Eskimo guide and headed out to the grave. There was a howling blizzard blowing when they exhumed Nuviayyuk. They took the rocks off the body, stripped the clothes from it and made sure he had not been stabbed, clubbed or shot. Everything looked in order. It seems that the excitement of the hunt had proved too much for him and he had died of a heart attack.

Heart attack — maybe. But it is much more mysterious and in keeping with the Arctic wastes to think in terms of the spirits of the bear than of a cardiac embolism. It is somehow more satisfying to think of James Bell disturbing the peace at Arctic Bay, rather than lying coldly silent in a Winnipeg cemetery.

22
The White Flood

A few years after the death of James Bell the traditional north died too. Defence experts in sunnier climes decided to protect their possessions with a radar curtain across the top of the world, so the Distant Early Warning Line was built. It was an enormous undertaking, expensive, extravagant and, according to some, virtually obsolete by the time it was finished.

Never in all its history had the north witnessed an invasion like that of the mid fifties. It was phenomenal. Buildings sprang up, aircraft buzzed and men flooded in. The whole operation was far more vast than the installation of a few airstrips during the Second World War and that had been a big enough venture. In fact, it was in those earlier days that the present community of Frobisher was born. A site further down the bay on Pugh Island was abandoned by the United States Air Force in 1942 in favour of a site on the Sylvia Grinnell River.

Frobisher Bay has the longest history of any place in the eastern Arctic as far as the influence of white men in concerned. In the tradition of the Eskimos, the story is still told of the five white men who were captured from among Martin Frobisher's crew in 1576. Events as startling as this invasion from another world, by men who spoke strangely and acted oddly, were not to be forgotten. Frobisher's advent is held firm in the collective memory of the Eskimos.

Martin Frobisher thought to exploit the area for minerals and for this purpose he organized a fleet of vessels with a large complement of men to go there and begin mining operations. The fleet came to grief in a storm and what ore was brought back turned out to be valueless. It was not due to mining that Frobisher flourished, but because of war and the needs of aircraft. A large airstrip was built on the present site in the early forties to serve as a refuelling and servicing depot for aircraft flying the northern route to Europe. Other airstrips were built at Churchill, Chimo, Southampton Island and Thule in Greenland. The construction of the air base facilities eventually caused the Hudson's Bay Company to move from Ward Inlet into the same area. In 1955, work on the DEW Line caused a major flurry of activity in the Frobisher Bay area and the settlement grew by leaps and bounds. It was an ideal centre from which supplies could be sent to the different DEW Line stations gradually erupting across Baffin Island and further west.

Right in the middle of much of this activity was David Van Norman who could speak Eskimo, write well and handle responsibility effectively. It was he who was chosen to assist the United States officials locate the various sites for the radar stations in the eastern Arctic. In order to do this he was transfered from the R.C.M.P. to the Department of Northern Affairs. By the time Van Norman was asked to work in this capacity he had been in the north for the best part of seven years and had had an interesting variety of experiences. It gave him a background that fitted him well for the multiple tasks the DEW Line operation thrust upon him. He managed to get along well with both the Eskimos and the white men. He was known to the Eskimos as "The Tall One".

Unlike many men who have lived in different and unusual places as soldiers or policemen, Van Norman took a great interest in the native people and took the trouble to keep notes of many of the events he witnessed. He listened to their tales with the attentive care of an interested listener and heard, from some of the old Eskimos, strange tales, tales that had no real ending, tales that seemed to wind out of the mist of memory into a mist of uncertainty. He heard such tales from an old woman at Frobisher, Ua Pausian. She would act out stories of the great black ravens, and she told him one story particularly tinged with mystery.

"When I was a little girl," she began, "it must be 75 years ago now, I remember going out in a big boat with several others. There were women in the boat. I do not remember men. Yes — there were women. It was a women's boat. As we drifted with the wind and tide we saw another boat. It was a small boat. Gradually we moved toward it. We could see people in it. We shouted. There was no answer. The boats touched. Inside we saw two men, dead. They were white men. Quickly we pushed away. Everyone was afraid. I remember that — the fear. No one wanted to go near it again. No one wanted to look again. That was a little boat of death. I saw it. I looked at it as it drifted away. That memory is vivid in my mind."

Ua fascinated Van Norman. Her life embraced so much change and her memory was still so vital.

"If only her stories had endings," says Van Norman, "but, like the boat with the two dead men in it, often there is little but an isolated fact or two."

It was Ua who offered a little girl to Van Norman for a future wife. One night at about 11:00 p.m. a message was brought to the R.C.M.P. post telling Van Norman that a young woman, Pitsulak, was in desperate straits in childbirth. It was not often that men were invited to do anything at a time like that. As a rule such matters were for the women alone. Van Norman was not expected to deliver the child but it was thought he might be able to get medical help from the United States forces. He tried but there was no doctor or medical orderly in camp. Having checked this out Van Norman made his way to the tumble down heap of boards, canvas and tin that was Kavavau's and Pitsulak's home. It was dark and smelly in the shack. The place seemed crowded with Eskimo women. When Van Norman's eyes became accustomed to the gloom he could see Pitsulak, who had been in labour for nine or ten hours, squatting on a bed and obviously in great pain. There was one woman behind her with her arms around her middle, pushing and squeezing and there were two women on each side also pushing and squeezing.

"Hold on," said Van, interrupting the operation, "let her rest a while. Now then," said Van Norman kindly to the woman, "relax. Unclasp your fingers and rest, calm and quiet."

He put cold cloths on her head. Things seemed to be going a little steadier and some of the tension eased. But the pains still kept coming and the baby, although on its way, seemed unwilling to be born.

"Here," said Kimatii, one of the women who had been sharing in the proceedings, "I know what to do. Pass me that margarine."

Van's eyes went over to the corner of the shack where there was a case of margarine. It was a familiar sight in those days. He was not surprised to see it. Earlier that year the government authorities in Quebec had seized tons and tons of margarine because it was illegal to sell it there at that time. After it had all been seized no one knew what to do with it until someone had a bright idea and suggested it should all be given to the Eskimos. This was done. The Department of Natural Resources sent it up by the ton. Everyone had margarine. The dogs were eating it. The kids were eating it. Dog teams from other settlements came for loads of it. There was margarine everywhere and there was some in Pitsulak's shack.

"Come on, give me some margarine," Kimatii repeated.

She took a large packet, whipped it out of the wrappings and smeared it all over her dirty, unwashed hands and arms. She plastered the stuff on, right up to her elbows.

"Now then," she said, "stand aside."

This was addressed to Van Norman in particular and to everyone in general.

Pitsulak was lying on the bed nearly naked. Kimatii spread her legs and then plunged her hand in. With obstetrician's skill she aided the birth of the child and in a matter of mere minutes the child was out and gasping for air.

When the cord was cut, Ua grabbed the child, a baby girl, and, wiping her with a piece of dirty cotton batting, said to Van Norman, "When she gets big enough she can be your wife."

It was in Frobisher that Van Norman met old Noah. Noah had been on the *Seduisante* when it was wrecked off Nottingham Island. He remembers well the winter they spent there, away from the usual camps. They had no dogs with them and hardly any ammunition for the rifles they carried. The situation was grim, but they survived. In order to stay alive they had to revert to the most primitive ways of hunting and fishing — although at the start a few supplies from the wrecked ship helped to supplement their diet. The men and women, with typical Eskimo hardihood and determination, set to work and fashioned stone-tipped weapons and, with a combination of skill and luck, managed to last the winter. It was almost a year after the wreck that they succeeded in getting back to Lake Harbour. The boat in which they had gone ashore was their means of transportation through the tricky water and dangerous seas.

Tales like these intrigued Van Norman and because of this interest his Eskimo improved and his understanding of the people enlarged. But not all his time was spent with the native people. A good part of his time was spent with United States servicemen working at the Air Base and personnel belonging to the Canadian Department of Northern Affairs. This was before the construction of the DEW Line site, and he gained a first hand knowledge of the service personnel who would be greatly involved in the work on these radar sites. Van Norman became an ideal middle man.

One of Van's specialties was cards. He was a great poker player. He says, "In a moment of inspiration or lunacy I bet $1,200 on a card. I think it was inspiration because I had a sure hand. I knew I had the low hand and no one else could have it. I wanted to scare a bunch of people out by making this large bet but it didn't work because three of them stayed in. It was twenty minutes before the next guy made his move. That was poker, real poker. By the time the game ended there was $6,000 in the pot. I shared it with one other fellow who went high."

In 1955 and 56 Frobisher Bay began to resemble, in some respects, a gold rush town. The trinity that seems to be present in all such places was present there — gambling, liquor and ladies. All three were a problem. In one report, submitted by the police, particular mention was made of liquor and prostitution. Liquor is a problem wherever it goes and too much was consumed too often in Frobisher Bay. Prostitution, however, was something new for that part of the world. The police had two cases drawn to their attention involving Eskimo women and military men. The women had accepted money for services rendered and whether they realized it or not they were acting as prostitutes. The report that was sent in to Ottawa eventually found its way to the desk of the Deputy Minister of Northern Affairs, Gordon Robertson. He promptly wrote a letter to Miss

Phyllis Harrison of the Welfare Department at Frobisher. Mr. Robertson expressed his concern about the reported cases of prostitution and asked Miss Harrison to put an end to it immediately. The letter maddened Phyllis.

"Hang it all," she complained to Van Norman, "What can I do about it? Does he think I can solve a problem that's plagued the world for thousands of years?"

Miss Harrison was getting angrier by the minute so Van Norman suggested she outline her thinking to Mr. Robertson. This she did. It was a good letter. She pointed out that prostitution was the world's oldest profession. She explained the fact that better brains than hers had tried to solve the problem. She indicated, too, that the United Nations itself was working on the problem and so on. When she had got all this off her chest she assured the Deputy Minister she would try to do something about it.

"Be sure of this," she exhorted the Deputy Minister, "if I come up with a solution it should be patented because the world has been awaiting such a cure for thousands of years."

Liquor was the cause of real uproar towards the end of the fifties when Corporal Van Norman and a Constable boarded a Liberian ship to search it. According to information that had come to the police, officers and men from the *C.D. Howe*, the annual patrol ship that was docked at Frobisher, were going over to the Liberian ship, which was waiting there, and buying rum. Two laws, at least, were thus being violated. The Liberian ship coming into port was supposed to have its holds completely sealed and secondly any liquor brought directly from it was contraband.

When Van Norman went aboard he virtually seized the ship. This caused quite a commotion. The boat was held for about a week, when it was finally released upon payment of a modest fine.

After the Liberian ship was boarded, Van Norman and assistants boarded the *C.D. Howe* and told the captain that they were going to search it. This startled the captain.

"I have no need of a search warrant," Van Norman assured the captain who was beginning to object, "I have full authority to proceed."

In a very matter of fact way it was made clear by Van Norman that there was to be no nonsense from anyone. This kind of action was unprecedented in the north and took everyone by surprise. The police found rum from the Liberian craft in every corner of the ship. The only place they did not search was the captain's cabin.

"I don't really believe you have any in there, sir," said Van Norman. "There's no point in wasting our time searching your cabin."

By the time the search was over they had a considerable haul of confiscated rum.

"Now, then," Van Norman said to the twenty men involved, "we're going to lay charges against you. We're not going to arrest you but you will be expected to appear in the Magistrate's Court on Monday at 10:00 o'clock in the morning. If, however, the ship is out of the Northwest Territories by that time then you are out of our jurisdiction."

Whether the ship was due to leave or not, the *C.D. Howe* was gone long before 10:00 a.m., Monday. That is probably the only time in its history that the ship did not receive a really free, happy, easy-going and enthusiastic welcome and farewell on its northern patrols.

Police involvment with liquor in the Northwest Territories was, of course, not limited to one incident. During the hubbub of DEW Line construction days, the Company policy forbade alcoholic beverages. Such restrictions seemed made only to be challenged. Liquor found its way into the camps in all sorts of ways. Aeroplanes would offload it at the end of a runway and then taxi to the legitimate unloading area. Sometimes it was disguised in soft drink cans. The cans would be punctured, the soft drink drained out and replaced with liquor. The hole would then be quickly fixed with a drop of solder.

Liquor was consumed not only by white men but found its way to the Eskimos too. Recently it has become legal for Eskimos to drink alcoholic beverages and without a doubt it is becoming the single most desperate problem of the north. The introduction of alcohol has been a terrible disservice to the native people. In 1968 the Government Alcohol Education Officer was talking with Simonee, the Eskimo elected representative to the Northwest Territories Council from Frobisher Bay, and they were both drinking.

"You come to us," said Simonee, "asking us how to solve the problem of drinking among the Eskimo people. What nerve! You brought the problem, now you solve it."

On a continent where alcohol addiction and its attendant problems are rampant it is sometimes hard to laugh at what liquor occasionally causes but a sense of humour must not be lost. In the north it often lay at the root of some of the funnier occurrences.

Van Norman tells a story about three men who were, for a time, together at Coral Harbour on Southampton Island. They were Constable Freddie Oxham, Dr. Bob Ewart and Charlie Henderson, the manager of the local office of the Canada Foundation Company. Quite frequently, aeroplanes would come in from the south to Coral Harbour and on one of these the three men managed to bum a ride back to Churchill. Once in Churchill they went on a spree and drank rather too much. Charlie passed out downstairs in the hotel bar so Bob and Freddie carried him to his room and made him comfortable. While he was lying there unconcerned and peaceful one of them had a brainwave. For the next little while they had a lot of fun. When Charlie woke up he had a plaster cast on one leg right up to his hip.

"It's too bad, Charlie," one of them said to him, "You fell down the steps of the hotel last night and broke your leg."

Charlie believed him. Once back at Coral Harbour Bob Ewart let the site superintendent in on the joke and waited to see what Charlie would tell him. (Neither Charlie nor the other men were supposed to have gone to Churchill.)

"What happened to your leg?" asked the super.

"We were unloading a plane last night and a heavy box slipped and fell on me," said Charlie.

For the next few days fellows kept asking Charlie how his leg was.

"It's not bad," he'd reply. "It's just a little uncomfortable."

After the best part of a week Bob Ewart told him to come to his office.

"I think we should take a look at that leg, Charlie," said

Ewart as he took a pair of heavy scissors and cut the cast right off.

"Stand up and try walking a bit."

Charlie looked at him incredulously.

"Go on, try walking."

Charlie took a few hesitant steps and then Dr. Ewart let him in on the joke.

It was a fairly harmless practical joke that helped to alleviate the boredom of routine, a boredom that was sometimes terribly oppressive in those isolated communities.

A year or so prior to this event and before construction began on the DEW Line sites, Van Norman flew north to help select sites for the radar stations. One of the most interesting places he landed was at Kivituk, a tiny Eskimo settlement on the east coast of Baffin Island. There he met old Nyukty, the unofficial camp leader. Nyukty was a man of great experience and was greatly respected. As a small boy he had gone to Scotland with Captain Peterson on one of the whaling ships. This experience, coupled with the fact that he was the camp patriarch, made him a memorable man.

The Kivituk people, to whom he belonged, had lived in that area of Baffin Island for many generations and they loved this piece of land they called their own. On the hillside, rising above the camp, were many rock mounds where grandparents, fathers, mothers and others were buried. This land was the land where the Kivituk people had lived, hunted and died. In the summer it was a good place to be but oftentimes the winter brought hungry days, weeks and months and sometimes starvation.

It was a history-making event when the plane landed near to the settlement at Kivituk and the first overtures were made that would lead to the establishment of a DEW Line site on their land.

As the only Eskimo-speaking member of the party, Van Norman introduced the little group to the Eskimos and explained to them why they had come. He addressed his remarks to Nyukty in particular. He tried to explain to him what was being planned and told him that it would make a lot of difference to his people.

"It will mean opportunities for work for all of you," said

Van Norman.

Nyukty nodded.

"Many aeroplanes will be coming in."

Nyukty nodded.

"Buildings are being constructed right across the north to where the sun sets."

Nyukty nodded.

"We will not rush you. Talk about it with your people. Find out what they think. When we return tell us how you feel about our coming here."

"I understand," said Nyukty. "We will talk about it and we will tell you what we think when you come back to our land."

It is highly probable that this meeting with the Eskimos was little more than a diplomatic manoeuvre. The requirements of the DEW Line were top-line priority and it is highly unlikely that any objections of a few Eskimos would cause serious changes in plans. Let it be said, however, the diplomatic confrontation was much to be preferred to arbitrary action that did not so much as tip the hat respectfully to the people whose land it was by tradition. The task of the administration was difficult. They were trying to rush the Eskimos into an electronic age overnight.

A short time later Van Norman and the others returned to the selected site at Kivituk and asked Nyukty for his views and the views of his people.

"We have talked about it," said Nyukty, "and we are glad you are coming. We want you to come. We think it will be good for us."

Wherever possible this kind of assurance was sought from the native people. No one was blind to the fact that in order for the DEW Line to be created something had to die. In some places in the Canadian Arctic it altered completely the whole way of life for a settlement. A huge step towards white men's ways was made and the step back never taken.

Nyukty lived to see the changes in his little settlement but he did not live long after the radar site was built. He died far from his little home, out on the hunting trail.

Van Norman recalls the story of his death in this way. "Four men went out hunting on the ice floe — Nyukty among them.

As they hunted, a strong wind blew up and separated the ice floe from the shore, blowing it far out to sea. Eventually, the vagaries of wind, current and tide pushed the floating ice back to land many miles south of the settlement. The four men were still alive but their condition was serious. All of them were soaking wet, the temperature was in the low forties below zero and they had lost all their equipment but one sleeping bag. Two of them decided to try to walk back and the other two, one of them Nyukty, crept into the sleeping bag. Those who set out to walk were some way along when one of them passed out and froze to death. The other, feeling he couldn't make it back to camp, returned to where the two were huddled in the sleeping bag. While he was away Nyukty had died and the other fellow's condition had deteriorated seriously. By now all the dogs had come ashore and, in ravenous mood, had circled the sleeping bag and attacked it. They had ripped open the bottom and started to eat Nyukty. The one who had done the walking saw Nyukty's body half out of the sleeping bag, surrounded by dogs. He attacked them instantly but, try as he would, he could not keep them away. He, alone, was not strong enough to do anything and he was rapidly losing the fight to stay alive himself. Nyukty's companion was no help to him and was soon dead in the sleeping bag too. Now only one man was alive. He was still alive when spotted by a police search plane and it was from him I heard the story."

Even with aircraft handy and a radar site nearby the Arctic could still bare its fangs and eliminate the careless and the weak.

A few of the service personnel who went north in those days endeavored to do a few things Eskimo style. Wing Commander Frank Campbell Rogers was one such person. He asked Van Norman if he could join him on one of his patrols and Corporal Van Norman readily agreed. He told his special constable that Frank C. Rogers would accompany them and told him, too, that they would give him a hard time.

"You're low man on the totem pole, Frank," Van Norman told the Wing Commander. "So I think you'll have the skivvy jobs to do when we're out on the trail."

"That's o.k. I don't mind," agreed Rogers.

"It's a good job he didn't," says Van Norman. "We had him

feeding the dogs, chopping the ice and cleaning up the whole trip. He was a good sport about it and really pitched in. He was quite persuaded that such jobs always fell to the greenhorn."

On another occasion Wing Commander Rogers asked Van Norman if he could find a way to make a patrol to Oudjuak Lake.

"I'd especially like to go there," said the Wing Commander. "I understand a very unusual fish is to be caught in that lake."

"Yes. I know about them," said Van Norman. "In fact I've been to the lake several times."

"The fish there are some kind of cod, aren't they?"

"Yes. I call them a cannibalistic cod. They feed on each other. The lake has been landlocked for thousands and thousands of years and this form of cod has evolved."

"Can you catch them easily enough?"

"Oh sure, no problem at all. All you need to do is cut a hole in the ice and jig for them."

"Do you think you can arrange a trip?"

"That won't be a problem. In fact I'm ready for the trail anyway."

Not long after this conversation the two men set out with two Eskimo guides. It did not take many days to reach the lake.

With the rapidity born of much practice the Eskimos built a snowhouse by the lake and the two white men set to work cutting a hole in the ice. Once the hole was cut they started to jig. All they used for a lure was a piece of yarn tied to a hook. It was all they needed. The fish went crazy for the bait. Fish after fish was caught and in no time at all they had a heap of some 90 fish on the ice.

"Good fishing, eh?" said Van Norman to the Wing Commander when they were sitting in the igloo with a mug of tea in their hands.

"Uh, huh," said Rogers, taking a swig of tea. "That's quite a pile of fish we've caught. They sure look ugly though, don't they?" and he pointed to a small heap that had been brought inside the snowhouse.

Van Norman agreed with him and picked one up and looked at it more closely. As he looked it over he had an idea.

"Let's play a trick on the Wing Commander," he said to the

Eskimo guides.

He explained his scheme to them as he reached in his pocket for a knife and began flicking the eyes out of the fish. Soon he had a tidy little pile by his side. Campbell Rogers watched.

Van picked them up in cupped-hands and offered them to the natives. Each Eskimo took a dozen or so. He then offered some to the Wing Commander.

"No, thank you."

"Come on now," urged Van Norman, "you'll just have to take some."

"Really?"

"Yes. You must. The Eskimos will be put out if you refuse."

"O.K.," said Rogers reluctantly and he gingerly took one between finger and thumb.

Van Norman kept the rest. There was silence in the igloo. Campbell Rogers looked at the Eskimos, then at Van Norman and they all looked back at him.

"What are you waiting for?" he asked.

"You," said Van Norman monosyllabically. "As the guest of honour you are expected to eat the first one."

Rogers eyed the eye. He hesitated and then quickly popped it into his mouth, scrunched and swallowed. Nobody else moved.

"What about you fellows? When are you going to eat yours?"

In perfectly plain English one of the Eskimos answered firmly, "Oh, Eskimos never eat those."

Campbell Rogers took the joke in good part and appreciated the gusto of the natives' laughter. He knew they now had a story to tell their friends.

They did not stay long at the lake. In a couple of days they were on their way back to Frobisher. Several hours out on the trail they met a small party travelling in the opposite direction. They stopped and talked.

"We're going to Lake Oudjuak to catch a few specimens of the unusual cod fish trapped in that land-locked lake." explained a member of the party to Van Norman. "It's a very unusual fish."

"So I understand," said Van.

"I believe," went on the ichthyologist, for that is what he turned out to be, "that there are only 200 such fish in the lake."

"I don't think that figure is correct," said Van Norman.

"You don't? I'm sure that's the figure I was given — and on excellent authority."

"Well, I'm afraid that figure's a little out of date."

"Really?"

"Yes. I think there are now only 110 fish in the Lake."

"Oh?"

"You see, we caught 90 the other day."

The scientist was very upset about this but they parted without anything worse than a few hard words. Campbell Rogers was glad of the chance to enjoy a joke that was not at his expense.

It was an interesting encounter on a snowbound trail — a scientist, a serviceman and a policeman, each one a representative of the people who have forced such changes in the Eskimos way of life.

These changes were thrust upon the Eskimos of the east because of the demands of military tacticians and the threat of war. Until the incredible advance of science and the threat of war coincided, the Eskimos remained virtually untouched. Unlike the west, the east has never been the centre of a great gold or uranium boom.

23
Gold

"Gold Rush", the words are mesmeric. They conjure up a vision of struggling, fighting men, vast wealth, pretty women and an inescapable madness. In the latter half of the nineteenth century, from California to the Yukon, men followed the yellow metal. They canoed down dangerous rivers, waded through swamps, crossed mountains, fought flies, Indians and each other. Some of the wildest, maddest moments in our history were sparked by gold. It has been sought in the farthest flung corners of this huge country.

In 1911, Alfred Tremblay, the little prospector who travelled with captain Bernier on the *Minnie Maude*, was invited to join in a search for gold in the Northwest Territories.

"I'd like you to join me," wrote Captain W.A. Munn from Revelstoke, British Columbia. "I and associates are planning an expedition to North Baffin Island to prospect for gold."

Captain Munn assured Tremblay that this venture was a sure thing. He, Tremblay, had no need to worry about anything. The ship would be well outfitted and gold and glory would be there for all. Munn wanted Tremblay because he was a man with northern experience and also some knowledge of geology. In spite of Munn's very persuasive manner and lengthy correspondence Alfred decided against going with him. It was a wise decision.

The *Algerine*, the ship chartered for the expedition, was completely wrecked soon after it entered Pond Inlet. All the persons on board were rescued and, according to Mr. Tremblay, taken on board the *Neptune* that was in the vicinity. The *Algerine* was a wooden sealing steamer, owned by Bowring

Brothers Limited of St. John's, Newfoundland, and had first supplied the Newfoundland Sealfishery in 1893. From 1893 to 1912, inclusive, she brought in a total of 206,720 seals. She was lost on July 16th, 1912, four miles off Cape Weed, Pond Inlet. On Munn's return from Baffin, a journalist interviewed him about his expedition to Pond Inlet. Captain Munn, who previous to the expedition had talked loquaciously of "gold and glory", now told the reporter that both the gold and the glory could go to hell.

This may have been how Captain Munn felt when the ship sank beneath him but he did not feel like that for very long. Soon after the abortive visit to Pond Inlet in the *Algerine* he began making plans for another venture. As far as Munn was concerned there was gold in the Arctic and he meant to have a large share of it. He returned to England and floated a company, the Arctic Gold Exploration Syndicate Limited. He held the largest share in the company and was its managing director. Under his guidance the syndicate purchased the whaling ketch, *Albert*, a famous little whaler that had plied her trade for many years in Arctic waters. The ketch cost £800 initially and then had to be refitted, a costly undertaking. She was equipped from keel to masthead for the expedition. Part of the refit was the installation of a new engine, a 120 h.p. internal combustion Bolinda.

The *Albert* was originally built by H. Fellowes & Sons yard at Yarmouth in 1899 and brought to Dundee in 1903. She was a sturdy little vessel of 97 tons, well constructed with strong and sound timbers. Until purchased by the gold-bedazzled syndicate she had served her time well in northern Canadian waters as a whaler.

On June 7th, 1914, she set sail for Baffin Island. The ship was skippered by Captain W.J. Milne. The first mate was Adams. These two and the crew took care of the sailing while Captain Munn, the expedition leader, took care of the prospects for gold. He talked to his companions, Mumford and Cummings-Taylor, about his exploits and the possibilities of riches that were theirs. He outlined to them his theories and his dreams. The talk went round and round and, in the middle of it all, was gold.

"I've got a hunch," said Munn for the thousandth time, "that there's gold, gold, lots of gold in Baffin Island."

"Uh, huh," said Mumford and Taylor, waiting for what they knew to be the rest of the conversation.

"You see, lots of gold has been found in the Yukon. Now, if you look at a map and follow the lines of latitude you will see Baffin Island is in the same latitude. I think there's gold ore stretching across the north. There's got to be."

Hunch is the kindest word to use for such a theory but it is no more ridiculous than the gambling man who goes out to play cards because he feels like winning.

Munn felt like winning and he involved the good ship *Albert* in a wild, romantic voyage for wealth.

"As soon as we land," he told Mr. Cummings-Taylor, a Dundee whaler who was going to be left on Baffin Island with Munn, "we'll set up a trading post. It won't take us long. The sections are well built and we'll have it together in a trice."

(Before setting sail, a Peterhead builder had made a wooden house in sections and also a corrugated shed for stores.)

The *Albert* reached Pond Inlet safely and the expedition for gold was well under way. Munn and Taylor were soon in business trading and fairly comfortable in their new home. Mumford, the other companion of Captain Munn, was not going to be staying in the north with them. On September 28th, 1914, Munn and Cummings-Taylor were left on Baffin Island to pursue their fortune and the fortune of the Arctic Gold Exploration Syndicate Ltd.

It was a forlorn adventure. No gold was found. A world, plunged into war, lost sight of the two lonely adventurers and the Arctic Exploration Syndicate Ltd. folded. Information about Captain Munn is sketchy. In earlier days he had written at considerable length of his adventures in the Canadian northland, both in the east and west. According to his critics, however, his writing is unreliable and he is not an accurate reporter. Although he spent many years pursuing wealth and adventure in the Arctic he died as a beachcomber on the Seychelle Islands in the middle of the Indian Ocean. As for Mr. Cummings-Taylor, the information is sketchier yet. It seems, however, that Mr. Colin Brand of Glasgow, remembers him and recalls correctly that he died back in Scotland as recently as 1958.

There is a fascinating postscript to this romantic story of the search for gold in northern Baffin Island and it concerns the ketch *Albert*. According to one story she is still being sailed and according to another story she sank in 1923.

On the 9th of June, 1964 in the *Aberdeenshire Advertiser* there was a story headed: "Has There Been a Hush, Hush Gold Rush in Baffin Land?" In this article the reporter links rumours of gold in Baffin Island to the activities of the *Albert*. The reporter says that in 1959 it had been brought to the newspaper's attention that the *Albert* was still plying the trade routes. He goes on, "Five years may seem a long time to be waiting for a story to break but patience brings its own reward and so it came about that on the last trip home from the Faroe fishing grounds skipper James Bruce of the Peterhead boat, *Daisy II*, sailed in with two snapshots. These are reproduced here. The photographs were taken at Transjisuaaj in the southmost of the Faroe Islands. They are in fact of the *Albert* leaving from that port for Greenland the last week of May, 1964."

If this report is correct then the little ketch has survived an extraordinary number of Arctic winters and is a museum piece of some value.

It was the *Albert* that picked up the crew of the *Easonian*, the very last of the Dundee whalers to go to Cumberland Sound. This happened in 1923. The *Easonian* had left Dundee with high hopes and a large amount of money invested in her. Newspapers spoke sanguinely of the rebirth of the great whaling days and encouraged the entrepreneurs responsible for the venture. Everything came to nought, however, when the ship burned. It was the good old *Albert*, trading in the area, that rescued the shipwrecked sailors.

In that same year, 1923, William Duval went to Scotland in the *Albert*. Mr. Brand, who was on the ship and is still living, recalls it clearly.

"He came back with us," he says, "from Cumberland Gulf to Peterhead and landed there in full Eskimo regalia — quite a sight!"

During the course of her lifetime the *Albert* has been skippered by many interesting captains, has carried many fascinating passengers, has been involved in numerous exciting enterprises and, if the newspaper is right, has a story to tell that now spans two world wars and a revolution in seafaring practices. In spite of her long life, however, for sheer romance and mystery, her pursuit of gold with Captain Munn can hardly be topped.

Since those days others have searched the vast plains and mountain ranges of Baffin Island for gold and other precious metals. The gold has still to be found but other discoveries have been made that may well prove of greater value to their owners, to Canada and to the world than another gold mine. Only a few years ago Mr. Murray Watts was instrumental in the discovery of huge deposits of iron in the Marie River district. For many years he has travelled the Northwest Territories and for many years he has been making interesting finds but it is more than possible that this will be his biggest and his best. Mr. Watts has made such a large personal contribution to northern Canada that he was recently given the Vincent Massey Award, an award given annually to the person making a particularly significant contribution to the development of northern Canada.

When Mr. Watts first made his way north, the expeditions he accompanied were far more primitive than those launched today. The maps he used were often hopelessly inadequate. Coastlines were often only vaguely sketched and sometimes bays and rivers were entirely missing. It took him weeks to reach the area he wanted to examine. Once there the transportation inadequacies confined that area to quite small proportions. In those days transportation by aircraft seemed inconceivable and yet in a matter of a few short years Dominion Explorers, N.A.M.E. (Northern Aerial Mineral Exploration) and Consolidated Mining Company were all using aircraft. In fact it was actually while flying across Baffin Island that Murray Watts first spotted the area now famous in mining circles as one of the largest potential iron ore zones in the world.

With the advent of aircraft even the inaccessible eastern area of the Northwest Territories began to be probed more regularly. The Barren Lands were entered, the Arctic coast was visited and the Arctic Islands were crossed. In those early days trails made by aircraft crossing the north would show on the map as slender, widely separated lines. Even the aircraft seemed to cling to coastlines where navigation was more straight forward and the country better known. It took men like Punch Dickins to slash across the country from east to west.

The *Canadian Geographical Journal* of August, 1944, notes:

"In the 1928 season, investigation was limited chiefly to the coast with exploratory flights inland . . . During the winter N.A.M.E. maintained their base at Baker Lake while the Dominion Explorers party stayed at Tavani, the latter group made a difficult flight to Baker Lake but abandoned further attempts at winter flying. They also tried to move freight by tractor north from Churchill over sea ice along the coast.

Early in the spring of 1929 men and planes gathered at Churchill and started an early season of reconnaissance. Spring mists hung over the land most of May, hindering ski plane observations, and then in late June flying was suspended until the ice on the lakes broke up. Ground parties could do little more prospecting until the end of June when the surface was free from snow.

The Nipissing and Knight companies confined their summer activities chiefly to proving and developing their claims on Term Island and on the north shore of Rankin Inlet.

According to Mr. I.H. Smith, now an 80 year old man living at Churchill, the ore the company found there was immensely rich.

"It went," he says incredulously, "$58,000 to the ton! Now then, $58,000 a ton and that, mind you, when gold was $26 or $27 an ounce."

Certainly the ore was good but it is hard to believe it was that good. Don Cameron, just a young prospector in those days, was the man who talked to Mr. Smith about what had happened on Term Island. He had gone in there with a number of students to work on the claims where some gold had been discovered the previous year. They found a vein that was rich and promising so they set to work. Using a bar and a hammer they dug a trench, some six feet deep by thirty feet long, following the gold. Unfortunately the vein pinched out. It was like a voluptuous but reluctant woman, full of promise and very exciting but not really satisfying. In all, the Cameron party recovered about

1100 pounds of well picked over ore that they intended to take outside. On the trip south, the aircraft, with Don Cameron on board, ran into a slight storm and put down for shelter at Eskimo Point. When it came time to take off, the aeroplane just could not make it so the load had to be lightened. Don Cameron kicked some of the samples off the plane into the bay at Eskimo Point.

"There is," says Mr. Smith, "about $8,000 worth of gold lying in the bottom of the bay at Eskimo Point right now."

When the aeroplane landed at Churchill the ore was taken for storage at the Hudson's Bay Company and sent from there by train. Mr. Smith recalls the event vividly.

"I saw the clerk of the Hudson's Bay when he took those samples to the train. He carried a gun but the gun was superfluous in those days."

Although the initial venture at Term Island came to nothing the exploration around there continued. Don Cameron found gold on the Wilson River and other locations nearby, but to this day, although the search continues, no gold mine has come into being.

One of the strangest stories that comes from that part of the world and a story that is surrounded with the magic of gold has yet to be fully told. The events are recent and the end of it all is still unknown.

A few years ago three men from the University of Illinois arrived in Churchill ostensibly to watch birds. This provoked no surprise among the local inhabitants. Churchill is a place especially loved by ornithologists. One day these men went to see I.H. Smith.

"Have you ever seen the giant goose, the blue goose?"

"Oh yes, many times."

"Have you any idea where their nesting grounds are?"

"Sure enough. I know where they nest."

Mr. Smith could not help noticing how eager they seemed to be to hear his answer. He was used to ornithologists. His own wife took an interest in birds. These fellows were different.

"About latitude 61 degrees, 30' lies Eskimo Point and due west from there is a large sand lake and sand hills and that's where you'll find the blue goose nesting."

"Is that a fact!" they said and one of them blurted out, "When we find that spot we've found a gold mine."

Now Mr. Smith was really puzzled and showed it. One moment they were talking about birds and now they were talking about gold mines. Insofar as Mr. Smith was an old man the Americans did not mind explaining themselves.

"We are," said one of them, "interested in birds but we are interested too in gold. A blue goose came into our possession and when we were examining it we discovered traces of gold in its feathers. We think the gold came from where it nests. The bird, fluffing itself up on the sand, fluffed gold onto its feathers."

Mr. Smith could scarcely believe his ears. He had lived long enough to hear some tall, tall stories but this was the best.

"Will you come with us?" one of them asked. "We're going to charter a plane as soon as possible."

"I'm too busy now," said Mr. Smith, begging off, "but anyway I told you where to look. You don't need me now."

The three men left Mr. Smith's home and he has never seen them since.

Did the goose with the golden feathers nest on a gold mine?

24
Nickel

No gold mine has ever evolved on the west coast of the Hudson Bay but a nickel mine has. Land originally investigated and reported on in 1929 became the site of Canada's only Arctic producing mine of the present era. Early in the 1950's work in the Rankin Inlet area proceeded apace and by 1955 the North Rankin Nickel Mine Company was able to announce that it had outlined an estimated 460,000 tons of nickel-copper ore with a grade of 3.3% nickel and 0.81% copper. It was sufficient for the company to implement plans to bring a mine into operation. In 1956 a nickel concentrator reached the property and the process of ore recovery began in earnest. A government publication comments, "The Rankin Inlet Mine was the first truly Arctic mine to operate in Canada as distinguished from the sub-Arctic environment of the Yukon or the Mackenzie district. It provided a testing ground not only for mining and milling techniques in an Arctic environment, but it also provided an opportunity to test the adaptability of Eskimos to modern industrial employment on a relatively large scale."

Less than eighteen months after the mine had started production there were more Eskimos being employed than white men. For some work the Eskimos were superior to the white man. Dr. Weber, in a written report on the use of Eskimo labour, says, "The native Eskimo following, in some instances, only a short period of training has supplanted the white worker returning to civilization after a tour of contract." Dr. Weber cites particular examples of this and indicates the following instances, "Miners underground, cage tenders, deckmen, mechanic's helpers, crushermen, ball mill operators, filter and dryer plant operators and bagging plant operators."

In spite of the fact that this native help was often superior to white, the Eskimos were paid miserable wages. Father Eugene Farfard, the Roman Catholic priest at Rankin Inlet in those days, was incensed by the striking contrast between the living conditions of the Eskimos and those enjoyed by the white employees at the mine. Farfard complained to a reporter for an Ontario newspaper who visited Rankin Inlet, "When employed by the North Rankin Nickel Mines they (the Eskimos) are paid 63¢ an hour in food store cheques, exchangeable through the Hudson's Bay Company. They exist in this land of plenty in the primitive conditions of stone age man . . . ."

The reporter describes Father Farfard as "an unforgettable personality" and writes quite lengthily about him. In the article he recounted some of his experiences with the priest.

Two days after my interview Father Farfard allowed me to accompany him on two sick calls and later that same day he invited me to his own little Eskimo tent. On entering this excuse for a dwelling I was shocked to find . . . the frightful condition under which Father Farfard somehow exists. He has no bed and sleeps (or rather I imagine he tries to) in a sleeping bag on the bare stones on which his tent is pitched. He has no chairs or table and practically no food. On the occasion of this visit he had no bread or butter and all he could offer me was a cup of tea without milk or sugar, served in his one solitary handleless cup . . . . Yet Father Farfard does not in the minutest degree pity himself. With his bright jovial personality, lightning wit and hearty laugh he personifies anything but an ascetic. With merry twinkling eyes set in a well chiselled and unwrinkled face he would look younger than his 55 years if he shaved off his beard . . . .

As well as the spiritual destiny of his particular flock . . . his burning passion is directed towards the preservation of the entire Eskimo race. He realizes, as do most of the intelligent Eskimos themselves, that the days of the famed Eskimo hunter of the wide open spaces is now rapidly coming to a close. He sees the ugly spectacle of doom hovering over his beloved people as evidenced by the alarming spread of tuberculosis among them. He also realizes fully with his 37 years of Eskimo brotherhood behind him that the Eskimo must now adapt himself in all haste to an ever changing world or perish from the face of the earth.

For the sake of survival he knows, and has told me, that adjustments to the white man's indescribably better living conditions is an urgent necessity for them. The white man's skills and crafts must be rapidly learned but in the process (and this is important) the Eskimos must exercise great care to avoid the real danger of moral contamination by the impact. If only "Big Brother White Chief" could be induced, convinced or even forced to pay the Eskimos the same wages as the average white Canadian receives for the same work instead of the long standing malpractice of remuneration with cheap goods and store cheques . . . a tremendous victory would be achieved in the emancipation of the long suffering Eskimos. He could then handle his own money, purchase the vital necessities of life, live in a properly equipped civilized habitation and quit for ever his stone age existence. It would be possible for him to settle down normally and with his sterling honesty together with other outstanding qualities and talents he could become a useful asset to Canadian community life. Thus would Father Farfard's dream come true and the noble Eskimo race be freed from the threats of extinction.

Although there were inequities, the management attempted to be fair and on the whole tackled a tricky job effectively. At first the Eskimos did not like working in the mine but slowly adapted to it. Air drills and dynamite frightened them and routine work was foreign to them. They were used to the leisurely tempo imposed upon them by the changing seasons, not the shrieking demands of a mine whistle or siren. In spite of this, however, eventually they were employed in all branches of the mine.

North Rankin Mine did not only have to contend with tricky labour problems but was faced with serious difficulties relative to communication and transportation.

Only for a few short months of the year was it possible to get into the area by boat and in that short time it was necessary to get all the concentrate on its way south. In 1956 the very first load of ore to come out of Rankin went direct to Japan but from 1957 on the ore was put on a ship at Rankin, taken to

Churchill, offloaded and carried further south by rail. This sounds a very straightforward practice but it did not always work that way. In fact, in 1959, the ship the mine had chartered to carry ore from Rankin to Churchill was running so far behind schedule that the management became very concerned about it. In order to speed up the shipment of ore the Greek ship, *Ithaca*, was chartered. This particular boat was hired because it was in Montreal at the time and was about to sail back to Greece empty. Arrangements with the ship's owner, Galecas of Athens, were rapidly made and the *Ithaca* sailed up the Labrador coast and through the Hudson Strait to Rankin.

Billy Carson, a young man who had spent much time in the north, was employed at that time by the North Rankin Nickel Mine as a heavy duty mechanic and expeditor. He watched the *Ithaca* anchor off the shore at Rankin Inlet. Billy knew boats and when he saw this one he did not like it.

"She was a complete wreck," he says.

He may have overstated the case a little but it is true that the *Ithaca* had seen active service during World War One. She still carried scars from her battles. Her superstructure plainly bore the marks of shells. Once the ship was ready to load at Rankin, however, there was little point in marvelling at her antiquity. It had somehow struggled into the Bay, surely it would be able to struggle from there to Churchill and back.

As quickly as possible the ship was loaded and sent on its way to Churchill with 3,000 tons of ore on board. After unloading at Churchill, it took on a cargo that included nine government houses and a large supply of mine equipment. No sooner was this accomplished than the crew walked off the boat. They complained to the mine representatives that they had not been paid for more than two months and that their families in Greece were starving. The situation was serious. Rankin Inlet was contacted and the mine manager hastened to Churchill to sort things out. He communicated with the ship owners and arrangements were made for the crew to be paid off by the mine and for that sum of money to be deducted from the contracted amount.

The crew could hardly be blamed for their attitude. Not only were they not paid on time but the ship they sailed was a perilous old tub in which to be afloat. She had no generating plant and only one of her boilers was any good. The other one was leaking where the seams had rusted right through and one of the little diesel engines she did have on board had to be repaired at Churchill.

Billy Carson says, "She must have been a warship at one time because her steel plate was one and a half inches thick."

When the 37 members of the crew were satisfied and the ship was ready to sail orders were given for the voyage back to Rankin to begin. The weather looked bad but the order was given anyway.

As the ship weighed anchor the rising wind sent dust devils whirling through the settlement. The waters of the Bay stirred uneasily. Clouds marched across the sky. A few idle watchers shivered.

"Looks like dirty weather," one of them observed.

Billy Carson heard him and, taking another look at the *Ithaca*, wondered how she would handle in a storm.

The French captain on board wondered too. This was not really his ship. He was only temporarily in charge. He had been hired on because the usual Greek captain did not have the necessary papers to permit him to command a vessel in the Hudson Bay.

A spatter of rain splashed across the deck and raked across the sea. Waves built up. Clouds thickened. The sun went out and the wind grew menacing. Within a few short minutes a violent storm had engulfed the ship and hurled itself at the tiny settlement of Churchill. Around the *Ithaca*, the water seethed, bubbling and hissing as it fought with the hull. Things began to look bad. In a boat like this, bad weather was to be avoided. The captain turned the boat around and tried to get back to the safety of harbour at Churchill. Before a really safe place could be reached it became necessary to drop anchor. With the anchor down the crisis eased, but not for long. The ship, straining before the wind, snapped the anchor chain like a piece of rotten string and at the same time a second anchor was lost. Pitching and tossing, the ship was jockeyed out to sea again by the captain. She steamed bravely into the storm only to have her main rudder snapped off. Now she was completely helpless. She wallowed and rolled, drifting before the wind, and was driven inevitably into shore. Finally, she came to rest about twelve miles down the coast from the settlement of Churchill.

Billy Carson had been on the alert all the time. He and two others went by helicopter to see how things were with the ship. They reassured themselves about the safety of the crew and then returned to Churchill. There was nothing that could be done immediately, but the next morning Carson went out to the ship with a 22 foot canoe. It did not take him long to reach the *Ithaca* and get on board. Quickly, he examined the condition of the boat and cargo. There was bunker oil all over the place but, for the most part, the cargo was undamaged. Carson, and the others who accompanied him, stayed on board until high tide to see if the ship would float off the reef — but it did not move.

Meanwhile the captain was busy assessing the position and condition of the ship and after checking the weather forecast and getting in touch with the owners he gave the order for the ship to be abandoned. As soon as the order was given Billy Carson took over the ship. He rather enjoyed being captain of a wrecked Greek freighter.

With the crew off the ship and Captain Carson in charge, the mine manager at Rankin was contacted and the whole matter made legal. Billy was now in a fine position to claim salvage rights but he had a problem — how was he to go about getting the cargo off the ship? In his words, "There was no power on the ship, no steam, no nothing."

At low tide, however, Billy had noted that it would probably be possible to back a truck right alongside the boat. He mentioned it to others and they decided to give it a try. Sure enough, he was right. That being so, the rescue of the cargo became a distinct possibility.

"We need help," said Billy and promptly went to Churchill and hired forty Cree Indians. These men came out to the boat and lived on board. Using this crew, Carson managed to erect a block and tackle to haul the cargo up on deck from the holds. Once on deck the cargo was transferred to trucks backed up to the ship at low tide. Unfortunately, the lowest water came at midnight so all kinds of lanterns had to be used to facilitate the operation. They tried to salvage everything and actually did manage to salvage most of the cargo. The most difficult items they had to handle were two large generating plants belonging to the Department of Northern Affairs at Rankin Inlet. With patience and ingenuity they managed to get both of these off without too much serious difficulty. It took quite a few days to unload everything but everyone worked hard and a few made a fair packet of money. After all, salvage rights were involved. And the Indian work crew did quite well too. When Carson had recovered all he could the Indians were told to go ahead and help themselves. They did. They stripped the boat down to the bare hull, a hull which can still be seen, a rusting hulk on the shore of the Hudson Bay.

The wreck of the *Ithaca* was not the only occasion the North Rankin Nickel Mines suffered from shipping problems. One ship, the *Dashwood*, on its way into the mine from Montreal, hit a reef and damaged its hull. In fact it was damaged much more seriously than was first imagined but the serious nature of the damage was not realized until unloaders discovered four feet of water in the dynamite compartment. This created a dangerous situation. Wet dynamite is perilously unstable and there were 2,000 cases of it in that compartment. As soon as this was discovered a Canadian Industries Limited man was sent for to supervise all the handling of it. The cardboard boxes full of dynamite sticks leaking nitroglycerine were gingerly carried out of the hold and reloaded on a barge. The barge was then taken to Rapid Island where once more the dynamite was unloaded. Billy Carson did all the unloading. It was a sweaty, nerve-wracking occupation. One mistake and there would have been a disaster. It was all safely transported to the island, however, and there triggered and blown up. By then it was too late in the day to send the *Dashwood* back to Montreal for repairs so she was patched up at Rankin Inlet. Seventy-five tons of cement were poured into her before the hole was sealed. The boat was then employed to carry oil and supplies between Rankin and Churchill until her contract was finished. At the close of the contract the *Dashwood* sailed back to England.

The North Rankin Inlet Mine was not only subject to problems of transportation by sea but their land operations were often extremely difficult. In December of 1958, the mine garage burned down, destroying all the mine's heavy transportation equipment. According to Billy Carson everything was lost. The only means of mechanized transportation left in the camp was one ex-army Penguin, owned by the Government.

To meet this crisis the mine manager flew to Toronto and persuaded the directors to buy two new bulldozers, a Euclid and a Bombardier. This equipment was taken to Churchill by rail and driven in from there. It was an awful trip. The road from Churchill had to be bulldozed all the way. It took twenty-eight days and Billy Carson drove all the way on a completely open caterpillar tractor. This procession moved at a snail's pace towards Rankin Inlet with the Bombardier scouting ahead, followed by the two bulldozers pulling sleighs and the big Euclid truck fully loaded. Troubles were constant. Sleighs kept breaking and on two occasions, overturned. The temperature dropped to fifty degrees below zero for a while and the whole train of vehicles holed up for two days. In spite of the severe temperatures, however, the ice on Wilson Lake proved unsafe and a wide detour over rock-strewn ground had to be made. The men had a horrible time. Even though they had plenty of power many times everything ground to a halt. Twelve years after the journey, Carson commented, "I'll never do a trip like that again. Life's too short for that."

At Rankin Inlet, Billy Carson was able to lead a varied life and among his many exploits managed to find and marry a wife. Jean Urbanski came from Manitoba and found her way north as a school teacher. She had taught in an impoverished area of Manitoba before arriving at Rankin Inlet and for this reason was not so disturbed by the poverty of the Eskimos as some others may have been. She pitched in and did her best to teach and train the Eskimo students in white man's ways. For many of them it was their introduction to school and the routine of a regular educational program.

Jean settled easily into camp life and began to get things moving in the community. She started a square dance club in her own home but eventually it grew so big, well over a hundred Eskimos used to attend, that they had to use the mine hall. Square dancing really helped to mix the Eskimos and the whites. Before Jean introduced it, the Eskimos would all sit on one side of the recreation hall and the whites on the other. When the dancing began everybody joined in and the Eskimos enjoyed it tremendously.

During the period that the mine operated the settlement was full of hustle and bustle, but when the company failed to find more ore and it became necessary to shut down, things looked black for the little camp. Billy and Jean Carson both remember vividly the day the mine finally closed. It occurred just a week before they were married. They, together with the mine manager, were walking through the settlement when the mine's engines were shut off. The thrumming that had filled the air for six years was stilled and suddenly the silence could be heard. It was as if Rankin Inlet had died. The mill was still, the hoist unused, the compressors silent. It was awful. One lone diesel thumped out a beat and that was all. Around the camp the huskies howled, as if pleased that their voices could once again be heard and the wind played around the headframe which rose darkly against the sky like a giant tombstone.

The miners left. The offices closed. Canada's only Arctic mine was finished. Many Eskimos remained, however, and the Government continued its administration. The school stayed open and both Jean and Billy were kept busy. Closure of the mine, however, complicated a number of things in the settlement and among them was sanitation. Washing facilities were minimal. Once a week Jean took the Eskimo children to a bunkhouse and gave them a thorough scrub under a shower. This was quite an experience for them and they loved it. While Jean was worrying about getting the kids clean, Bill was worrying about getting an adequate water supply to the camp all year round. The pumping machinery used by the mine was now worn out so Bill submitted a plan to Ottawa to build a dam in order to create a reservoir that would supply the camp all year. This plan was mulled around in Ottawa for some time but finally Bill went ahead without permission. Before construction was completed, however, the authorities in Ottawa agreed to the scheme. The dam was built without incident and, apart from one or two minor leaks, proved immediately satisfactory. This project was neither especially difficult nor particularly unpleasant but it did lead to a task that was both difficult and unpleasant.

Behind the reservoir created by the dam was about a one hundred foot rise of land. On the top of this small hill was the Roman Catholic cemetery. This was now only a matter of feet from the source of the community's drinking water. The Eskimos did not like this and were convinced that there was seepage from the graves to the reservoir. There was only one way to cure the situation and that was to move the cemetery. Billy was quite prepared to do that but permission had to be obtained from no less an authority than Rome, itself. Father Choque did the necessary letter writing and finally permission was granted. As soon as this was received Billy began to set things in motion but had great difficulty securing the necessary crew to do the work. Quite a number of Eskimos refused point blank to help with such a task. Billy remembers it all very well.

He says, "We had an awful job. Some of the bodies were in coffins but the coffins were all rotted away. Most of the bodies were decomposed. We worked at it for a month and a half before we were finished. We'd dig the bodies up and place them in a little morgue we had built and then later transfer them to the new cemetery where we had prepared graves. In all we moved between thirty and forty bodies. When the job was finished I saturated the area with fuel oil and set fire to it.

"And that," Billy asserts finally, "is another job I never want to have to do again."

25
The Barren Lands

Rankin Inlet lies on the edge of the Barren Lands, the great inland plain that sweeps across northern Canada. It is an area of huge distances and almost no permanent communities. Over it all hangs a vast loneliness. Skies are as immense as on the prairies, uninterrupted by mountains or cliffs. It is a land of snow and ice, sudden summers and ever stirring winds. It is a haunted land. Across the wilderness the ghosts can roam with unchecked freedom, quietly whispering on a summer breeze or shrieking wildly in a roaring blizzard. No man snuggles to rest in the Barrens during a blizzard and forgets it. In a big blow the world of the Barren Lands comes alive. It lives apart from dogs and men. The wolf is sent to its lair and the fox to its den. The elements reign supreme.

But here, in the Barren Lands of Keewatin and the District of Mackenzie, a few people have managed to survive. Small Eskimo camps have shifted across its face. An occasional trapper or trader has reached into its bosom for fur. Policemen have entered to enforce the law. Prospectors have searched for wealth and priests have gone in pursuit of souls.

Until the most recent years the tiny Eskimo settlements were little more than summer and winter camps. In order to stay alive, both summer and winter, incredible distances were travelled by the "caribou eaters" in pursuit of game. Traders, policemen, priests, prospectors and trappers have all helped to alter this pattern of life. Each one, to a greater or lesser degree, has contributed to a gradual civilization of the Eskimos. Now there are modern communities with modern amenities and the appearance of a permanency never before dreamed of.

It was the white fox that lured the trappers north. News of his fabulous fur spread south and in ones and twos adventurous men began to creep towards the forbidding Barrens. Many approached from the west and moved no further east than Artillery Lake but some came down the waterways of Manitoba and struck into the belly of the Barrens from Churchill.

Such a man was I.H. Smith. Although born in Pennsylvania he fought with the Canadian army during the First World War. He was demobilized in 1918 and was so anxious to get out of the army that everything was finalized on a Sunday. At that time things did not look good for Henry Smith. His health was bad. He was nearly blind and, according to the doctors, his lungs were shot. Things seemed hopeless. It was a time for decision and Henry decided.

"I'm going to go so damned far away," he said to himself, "that no one's going to hear me whimpering, only my dogs. And they're never going to tell."

Windy (for that became his nickname after trapping and trading in the vicinity of Windy Lake for a while) took off into the wilderness of Canada and returned home once after eight years and then not again for thirty years. He was so out of touch with the roots from which he sprang that his mother was dead two years before he heard about it.

When Windy Smith first came to the far north he stopped at Putahow Lake on the 60th parallel. He took with him a heavy load on his freighter canoe. Tremendous lakes, lengthy portages and tricky rapids had to be negotiated. By the time he reached Putahow Lake he was trail weary and to quote him, "Trail weariness is just about as bad as homesickness." He reached the point of fatigue where he could not move another foot to save his life. He got up in the morning and just stared at the horizon. He wanted to go further but the will to press on had evaporated. Something inside him had given way and he just had to quit. So there he stayed and there he trapped and there he eked out a living from the land.

Slowly the north grew on Henry Smith and he belonged to it, just as it belonged to him. As years went by he pressed still further north into the land of the Eskimos, the muskox and the tree-starved plain. He found out what it was like to bend before the wind and fight for his life in a blizzard. Windy Smith, now a man of eighty years, speaks graphically when describing a Barren Lands blizzard.

The first thing you do is unsnap the dogs and, believe me, you're lucky if you can see them. Ordinarily I tied them up but in a big blow they pick out the highest spot they can find and curl up there. A dog won't leave you in a big blow. Having released the dogs, standing in the same place, I would build up snow blocks around me and fashion myself a crude shelter. I'd not dare move from that small dwelling during a blizzard. The wind, the snow, the fury of it all would make it extremely difficult to find my way back should I ever wander from it. If a man loses his shelter the dogs are no help. They are almost always silent in a storm. They curl up and want to be left alone. Like everything else, they are afraid in a storm. I know what it is to feel a flutter inside — a flutter of fear. When the blow is upon me I want to get cased in. I want the security of a little shelter and yet, and yet, I can only take three days of that. After three days I must move my shelter, even if I only move ten feet. Madness is not far away amid such fury, loneliness and fear. The sound of the storm is something to hear. If only the sounds could be captured, the horrible sounds to be heard in a big blow, and then put to music, good heavens what a composition that would be! I'm frightened in a big storm, crouched up there waiting for a change. I'll never doubt that the odd trapper has finished himself when the storm has been blowing at its wildest.

Windy Smith is one of the few men to admit to this fear and to the voices of the storm and the terrible necessity to move out of a cramped dwelling, if only to move into another nearby, similarly cramped and inhospitable. The banshees of the Barrens seem to have whispered, sung and shrieked around his lonely camp sites. He has heard them and understands with ease the Eskimos' belief in a spirit that moves with the wind and makes the wind move.

Like most men who have made their homes in the Barrens, Windy Smith has happened upon a mystery. The land is a mysterious land with its swirling fogs and its smoking ice.

Shortly before the Second World War, Windy Smith was on a

trip exploring a stretch of country new to him. He had taken a new trade route into the north and had penetrated beyond the northern limit of trees and on one particularly dirty day he was driving his dogs over some fairly high rock hills when he decided it was time to stop and make some tea. He was just about to stop when he saw something oddly shaped looming out of a nearby snowdrift.

"Whoa!" he called to his dogs, "Whoa!"

"We'll boil a kettle right here. How does that suit you?"

Windy often talked to his dogs.

"It pleases you, doesn't it?" he said, noticing the dogs' apparent look of satisfaction. "The snow's been bothering you, hasn't it?" As he said this he broke snow out of their eyes, a job he had been doing every half hour or so.

Having settled his dogs and made his tea, Windy began to examine the strange structure he had spotted in the drift.

"Hmmm," he said to himself, "the thing's certainly man made."

The building, for this it certainly was, was made of sticks and rocks. There was a layer of poles and then a layer of rocks and it was built as square as a fort. From its position it seemed to have been built with a deliberate attempt to hide it. Smith thought it would have made much more sense to have built it in a prominent place rather than almost flush with the esker.

"Hmmm, must have been some crazy old bugger that built this," Smith muttered. "Who'd want to build like this in this place? Must have been some crabby old Scotsman, that's for sure," he continued — rather irrationally.

Windy Smith did not break into the building. In fact he says that it would have been very difficult for him to have broken in. It was windowless and sealed.

Smith turned from the fort and, speaking to his dogs, said, "Let's get out of here. I don't like it."

The wind was dusting the snow across the rocky hills and the long shadows of evening were creeping upon them. It was not a good day for travel but Windy Smith wanted to be on his way.

For nine years I.H. Smith said nothing to anybody about this strange fort and then, pondering on it one day, he decided to inform Ottawa. The letter he wrote was received with interest and an attempt was made to send a party in to investigate the log, rock cabin. But schedules suitable to Smith and the investigators could not be arranged. When this initial investigation fell through, the R.C.M.P. decided to have a look for the building. The Police contacted Smith and got from him a sketch map of the route he had been travelling and the approximate mileage of the fort from various known landmarks. For reasons not established, the Police did not conduct the investigation and since that date there has been no further search. The mystery fort has still to be found and its story told.

Windy Smith thinks that the structure was definitely reminiscent of a military design and believes it likely the man (or men) who built it was at one time a sailor.

One of the most intriguing facts about the structure is, of course, the number of poles used. There were absolutely no trees in the vicinity. The poles must have been carried there. Perhaps a small party of men was involved. Perhaps the sealed building is a tomb. Perhaps it was sealed and left with no one ever intending to return. If the fort can ever be found again and entered, perhaps the mystery will be solved.

The Barren Lands have been more resistant to explorers than most other areas of Canada's north. Till the advent of the aeroplane they were singularly inaccessible. At the turn of the century extraordinarily little was known of this vast land and only a handful of white people had made any significant journeys in it. It was in 1893-94 that J.B. Tyrrell managed to move across the Barrens from west to east but he blazed a trail that few have followed. In 1912 Radford and Street, an American explorer and a Canadian companion, were murdered on the Arctic coast and this served to introduce Canada's policemen to the rigours of the Barrens. In 1914 a patrol to carry out an investigation was organized under Inspector W.J. Beyts. The patrol ran into serious difficulties before it ever reached Hudson Bay and it was not until 1915 that a satisfactory base camp was established at Baker Lake. Even then it was three years before a patrol finally completed the return journey to the Arctic coast. The patrol was ultimately undertaken with Inspector French leading, as W.J. Beyts had fallen ill.

On March 21st, 1917, the patrol left Baker Lake and that

small group of men became the first Canadian police patrol ever to traverse the great tract of the Barren Lands that reaches from Baker Lake to Bathurst Inlet. It was a great patrol and one which nearly cost the lives of Sergeant Major Caulkin, Inspector French and their Eskimo guides. On more than one occasion they were close to starvation. In fact, but for the miraculous discovery of some muskox in the vicinity of their camp one morning it is likely the whole group would have died. When this patrol eventually reached the Arctic coast the police were able to establish that Radford and Street had been murdered. They were satisfied with the explanation of the murders given to them by the Eskimos. Apparently Radford, a quick tempered man, had struck an Eskimo with a dog whip. This led to a fight which left both white men dead. It is fairly certain that had either of the white men known the Eskimo language there would have been no chance of their being murdered. The Eskimos were frightened when Radford ranted, raved and struck at one of them. They only killed the men in order to protect themselves. Inspector French arrested no one but returned to Baker Lake with a satisfactory report and a valuable first in police travel across the Barrens.

The trail broken by that particular patrol has not often been followed and the country around the Back River, Bullen River, Pelly Lake and Garry Lake was rarely visited during the first half of this century. In 1951 Sergeant Glen Sergeant of the R.C.M.P. went into that area on a routine police patrol and was astonished to see an old Eskimo hobble out of his igloo on a wooden leg. Sergeant stayed in the camp for a few days and while there learned the old man's remarkable story.

"I was off to hunt with my young brother. It was approaching summer and a long while ago. I was just a young man in those days," said the old man, settling himself to tell a story he had told before and one he knew to the very last sentence and word. "My father had acquired an old muzzle loader. You know what a muzzle loader is? You do? Good. Well, we loaded this, my young brother and I, primed it and set out. Travel was slow because the snow was poor. Days were warming up and summer was coming. We had gone just about a day's journey from camp and we were looking for somewhere to stay the night when the accident happened. At the time I was walking ahead of my brother who was carrying the rifle. Suddenly he tripped and dropped it. As the rifle hit the ground it went off and I took the full blast in the back of my leg. The buckshot and pieces of metal we had shoved in the gun tore through my leg, shattering the knee and surrounding bone and skin. I remember the blast. I remember falling down and calling out. I remember clutching my leg and wondering what had happened. Then I passed out." The old man stopped in his story as if recalling the whole event.

Then, taking a long drag on his smoke, he continued: "When I was unconscious my brother fled back to camp. He was sure he had killed me but he hadn't. I came to and took a careful look at my knee. I realized it was now in very bad shape. I knew I must, somehow, stop the bleeding so I tied a piece of sinew tightly round my leg. It helped. Then I took my knife and carefully cut away the torn flesh and fragments of bone and made everything as clean as I could. To get away all the shattered bone I had to peel back the skin over the knee, gently, up my thigh. As I did this my leg fell off from the knee down. The flap of the skin I had pulled up I now rolled down and, tying the end like you tie a sack or bundle, I passed out again."

"How long did you lie there before you were discovered?" asked Sergeant Sergeant.

"Two days, about. Two or three days after the accident my parents came out to look for me and were astonished to find me still alive. They carried me back to camp as soon as I recovered sufficiently. I began to contrive ways of making a leg and this is the end result," he said, pointing to his leg.

It was quite a leg. With a piece of old wood he had made a shaft and surrounded that with a frame. Between the frame and the stump of his leg he had a soft pad of caribou hide. The whole thing was lashed together and tied into place on his leg. The most interesting feature of the limb, however, was the foot. This was made out of a piece of muskox horn. Sergeant commented on this:

"That's quite a foot you've got there now."

"Yes," the Eskimo said and smiled. "At first I just had the wooden stock with the frame but this kept digging in and when

I found this piece of horn I knew I'd found the answer. It's all right, isn't it?'' upon which words the old man stood up and stumped backwards and forwards with remarkable agility. "I sometimes have to renew parts of the leg because I use it as a chopping block for cutting fish. Having a wooden leg is not always a disadvantage."

A year or so later Sergeant Sergeant mentioned this man to some of the doctors at Charles Camsell Hospital in Edmonton. They were intrigued with the story and managed to arrange the supply of a modern artificial limb. Once this was received, the hand-hewn leg was discarded and sent out for preservation as an interesting museum piece.

During the time Sergeant Sergeant was stationed at Spence Bay, a community in the far north of the Keewatin District, a group of Eskimos came in from Fort Ross and brought with them some strange information. On their journey across the northern part of Boothia Peninsula, right in the interior, they had come across snowshoe tracks and the tracks of a ski equipped aircraft. This was mysterious because there were no snowshoes in the Spence Bay area. The Hudson's Bay Company did not have any, nor did the Roman Catholic Mission or the police. In addition to this, according to all the records available, no aircraft had been in that part of the country. The Bay aeroplane had not been in, nor had the Air Force, nor one belonging to the United States or any commercial outfit. Aircraft, flying in that area, invariably went to Spence for weather reports and fuel. The snowshoe tracks and the aeroplane tracks are simply unexplainable — another minor mystery of the Northwest Territories.

In this mysterious land, where the traders, trappers, policemen and missionaries have led the way, prospectors can now be found. Sometimes prospectors have been first but usually in the Canadian north they have been second, third and fourth. Their aims are so very different from those of the others that they do go into places where no one else would want to go and live where no one else would want to live. A few prospectors moved into the eastern Arctic in the first half of the century but only in the most recent of years has the activity been widespread.

For many years, in the country through which Windy Smith

travelled, trapping and trading, and in which Sergeant Sergeant patrolled, there were no prospectors. A few, a very few, strung themselves out along the west coast of the Bay but virtually no one went inland.

David "Baldy" Turner was one of the few and one of the first. In 1937 he started trapping and prospecting in the Eskimo Point-Padlei area. Previous to this he was in the R.C.M.P. and stationed in a variety of eastern Arctic posts. During that time he came to like the wide open, uninhabited spaces of the North-west Territories and when his spell with the police was over he determined to go back there. This he did and has been there almost continuously ever since.

Baldy Turner only ever comes out of the Arctic for a few weeks and then returns. His longest stay on the outside since his introduction to the north was two years when he took a course in mineralogy to equip himself better as a prospector.

Turner is a loner. He does not like other prospectors around. He likes his own company, his books and his dogs. The presence of other people troubles him.

All kinds of experiences have been Turner's in the Barren Lands of the Keewatin, on the shores of the Hudson Bay and amidst the mountains of Baffin Island. On more than one occasion he has been given up for lost and on more than one occasion he has had a narrow escape. One of his narrowest occurred on a windy night when he had gone out of his tent to feed his dogs. While he was away the tent flap flicked against the lamp and knocked it over. The tent caught fire and burned fiercely. Dave was able to save only his sleeping bag and his records.

Turner, unlike most prospectors, always used dogs. Not until 1969 did he bow to the advance of mechanized travel in the Barrens and use two Skidoos instead of a team of dogs. It is likely that he cursed the decision for soon after leaving Baker Lake both of them broke down. They were not twenty-five miles out of the settlement when they gave up the ghost. Baldy had to return to Baker Lake, strip the machines down and get them running again. He learned then that some Eskimos had been using his new machines as a ready source of spare parts for their own Skidoos.

Baldy Turner is still in the north as this book is being written. He is still searching the Barrens for minerals. This winter he has been continuing his pursuit at Chantrey Inlet near the mouth of the Back River. Turner is one of the few men living the life he would choose to live. The rigours of the Barrens belong to his way of life and the charm of isolation makes him its slave.

Turner says, "For me there is only one place in the world — the Arctic, and one way of life. And that is the way I'm living."

26
Priest of the Barrens

A breed of men different from the trappers, traders, policemen and prospectors who went into the Barren Lands were the missionaries. They did not go to make a living. They went because God bade them go. They went to stay indefinitely. They went to identify with the Eskimos. They went to minister to temporal and eternal needs. Often they went with little more than their faith to support them. Some of them went alone, to a land and a people unknown. These men were the most courageous of them all. Until recently, they were always either Anglican or Roman Catholic and they vied with each other for the souls of the Eskimos. The competition between these two great representatives of the Christian Church is no secret. However, many of the attitudes of a decade ago are now dying or dead and an encouraging spirit of co-operation has begun to take over.

I.H. Smith, of Churchill, makes no bones about comparing Anglicans and Roman Catholic priests. He says, "One Roman Catholic priest is worth four Anglicans any day." A remark that is hardly likely to gain him influence and friends among the Anglican priests of the Arctic. In fairness, it must be stated that Mr. Smith had in mind the travelling abilities of the priests only.

One of the great travellers among the Roman Catholic Missionaries was Father Joseph Buliard. He led an adventurous, wandering life in the Arctic and finally died in mysterious circumstances at Garry Lake in 1956.

In the *Eskimo Quarterly*, a publication of the Oblate Fathers of the Hudson Bay Vicariate, there is a fairly extensive account of the life and activities of Father Buliard. He seems to have been the sort of man who attracted publicity but was embarrassed by it. Shy by nature and unassertive in manner, he hardly seemed the kind of man to face the fiercest rigours of one of the worst climates in the world. Yet it was this diffident man who fought his way into the heart of the Barrens.

Father Buliard came from France. Raised in a strictly Roman Catholic family he was exposed to the influence of the church from his earliest days. As a very young man he decided to become a priest and, under the influence of Father Duchaussois he determined to exercise his priestly calling in Canada's Arctic. On the 15th of June, 1939, he left France to begin a remarkably adventurous ministry.

As the world mustered for war, Father Buliard travelled slowly towards Repulse Bay. Late in the summer he arrived there and started to work with Father Lacroix (later Bishop Lacroix).

Barely two months after his arrival in the north Joseph Buliard almost lost his life. On a walk over the frozen sea he broke through the ice and plunged into the icy, black waters. He fought desperately to save himself. He prayed. He called out and in brief moments of great clarity that often seem to come to men in desperate straits he contemplated his own death. But Buliard's time was not yet. Somehow he managed to gain sufficient grip on the crumbling floe edge to heave himself back to safety. Dripping wet, chilled to the marrow and near exhaustion, Father Buliard lay still for a moment. Then, gathering his strength, he set off for the mission. It was twenty degrees below zero, a razor sharp wind stabbed through him and his hands froze. By the time he reached the mission he was in a sorry state. When Father Lacroix examined him he thought this was the end of this young priest's missionary work in the north. The freezing was so bad that it looked as if his hands would be lost. Gangrene set in and his condition deteriorated so rapidly that an almost unprecedented air evacuation took place. It was likely only the second such rescue operation, the first being the evacuation of Father Cochard from Arctic Bay. The *Eskimo Quarterly* of June, 1957, in an article describing the life and work of Father Buliard, says, "While he was at the hospital, even if he pulled through fairly well, everyone was convinced that he would never return to the isolated mission of the north." But he was already fed up with the publicity the newspapers gave to his case and his only thought now was to return to his mission. J. Buliard had his wish and was back in Repulse Bay in a matter of months.

No sooner had his strength fully returned than he wanted to get busy as an evangelist. A divine restlessness was upon him. He felt thrust towards the unknown territories in the hinterland of the Barrens. He was not content to follow paths already trodden by others. He wanted to be a pathfinder. During the winter of 1941-42 he tried his strength and his capabilities as a traveller and when February of 1943 came round he was ready to tackle an extensive journey to the Back River area.

He set out from Wager Bay on February 10th, well prepared for the trip. Caches of food had been set out, guides obtained and clear intentions formulated. With a clear head and light heart and satisfying excitement, Buliard and his guides set off. Not until more than three weeks later did this small group of men meet another soul. It was March 5th when they drove their starving dogs into Amuya, a small camp on Chantrey Inlet. The journey had been brutal. Not many days out of Wager Bay a storm blew up. The Eskimos had seen the signs and knew what to expect. Snow began to drive across the land and visibility rapidly decreased.

"We must stop," one of the guides said to Father Buliard. "Weather is bad and getting worse."

"There is good snow here," said the other. "We should build now."

The teams were unhitched and tethered, an igloo built, a meal eaten and the men were ready to sit it out. Outside, the drifter moaned and swirling snow obliterated the world. Inside, the men listened to the voices of the storm and wondered how long it would last. It seemed to last forever but it actually lasted for nine days. Those were hard days of inactivity and imprisonment. They were days, too, that were hard on their rapidly diminishing supply of food. All of them were relieved when the storm let up and they could vacate their cramped quarters for the struggle of the trail. And struggle it was. They all suffered badly from the blowing snow, the cold, and hunger. Caches they had prepared had been raided by wolverines. Soon the dogs weakened and had to be assisted. Sometimes the two guides helped pull the sled but this was too much for Father Buliard. He had enough strength to keep plodding behind and that was all. Occasionally he would sally ahead of the dogs to encourage them forward but the effort was almost beyond him. It was a ravenous bunch of dogs and an emaciated group of men who finally happened upon the encampment at Chantrey Inlet. Sometimes it had seemed as if the slow torture of the trail would never end.

Quickly, Father Buliard was introduced by the guides and there was great handshaking, news sharing and eating. It did not take the priest long to note that the natives all had in their possession Protestant books. "Perhaps the task here is going to be more difficult than I expected," he thought.

Buliard was right.

Shortly after he had arrived the two companions of the trail returned to Wager Bay, leaving him alone amongst a strange band of Eskimos. Slowly a change of attitude seemed to overtake these people. In the days, weeks and months that followed, the priest had abundant evidence of indifference and hostility.

"Why have you come here?" one Eskimo demanded and before Father Buliard could answer he was being asked another question.

"What do you want from us?"

"Go back where you came from."

"We know you priests. You're all the same, deceitful."

That is the sort of thing he had to take.

Buliard pondered, prayed and waited. He tried to instruct them in the ways of Christianity and the Roman Church. For the most part the Eskimos remained indifferent. Perhaps the hostility of indifference is the hardest of all for a missionary to bear. It certainly was for Father Buliard for he wrote: "What I suffered most was from the indifference shown by some of the natives."

Their indifference to him was made desperately plain when a native came from a nearby camp to Amuya with the news that his grandfather was dying.

"Will you take me to him?" asked Buliard.

"No. There's no point in going. Anyhow I don't have any dog feed."

"I must see him before he dies," insisted the priest.

"No dog feed," reiterated the other.

"Please," said Buliard to the other natives "will somebody take me to this old man?"

"No dog feed," they replied separately and collectively.

No matter how Father Buliard cajoled, sermonized and pleaded the Eskimos would not listen to him. This was a bitter moment for a dedicated priest. He was being thwarted from fulfilling his vocation and saving a soul from hell through the indifference of the Eskimos and the trumped up excuse that dog feed was insufficient and unavailable. Father Buliard never forgot that episode.

Gradually, Father Buliard won some of the Eskimos over and by the time he was ready to leave a number of them did not want him to go. When he left he promised to return.

The journey back to Wager Bay was even worse than the journey out. From the very outset things were bad for Father Buliard because he had to take for a guide a man he did not respect. This Eskimo had travelled with Buliard before so the priest knew his ways and he did not like them. He was a hard, cruel man and Buliard's sensitive spirit was revolted by his behaviour. He handled his dogs in a senselessly vicious way. On many occasions this man would strike them repeatedly with a steel chain and when the dog was almost dead pick it up by its legs and fling it onto the ground. In silence Buliard would protest such treatment.

It was on Good Friday, 1943, that Father Buliard, his Eskimo guide and the guide's wife set out for Wager Bay. All day long the woman ran ahead of the dogs and the two men came slowly behind. They carried no food with them for famine had come to the camp they had left. It was all the dogs could do to pull the lightly loaded sled. That day no game was spotted — no caribou, no Arctic hare, no ptarmigan, nothing. At 11:00 p.m. that night they reached an old igloo and turned in. Hunger woke them early and by 8:00 in the morning they were on their way again.

"Father?"

"Yes."

"We must leave the load behind. My dogs cannot keep going much longer. We'll come back later and pick it up."

"All right, if you think it's necessary."

Quickly the load was cached and the dogs were on the move again. The two men and the woman walked. In the afternoon an Arctic hare was sighted but an overanxious marksman missed the target and a dinner bounded away. Thirteen hours after they had left, they camped. While the Eskimo set to work building an igloo Father Buliard dug a hole in the ice and started to fish. He caught one tiny fish which they divided into three and ate raw. It was all the food they had had for two days. The dogs had nothing. The next two days were the same. They had nothing but one inadequate meal of fish. To make matters worse the woman and Father Buliard became snow blind. These two were nearly totally exhausted. They no longer kept pace with the dogs and walked a long, long way behind the sled.

Blindness and exhaustion made the last day of that journey a nightmare. Father Buliard and the woman just lived through it. Four whole days after their trip began they stumbled into an Eskimo encampment. There the air in the igloos was redolent with the smell of caribou and the poetry of fresh food. They all gorged themselves. It seems as if Father Buliard was simply destined to experience more discomfort than most during his missionary work.

In 1944 Bishop Lacroix assigned Father Buliard to Baker Lake. It was a tactical move designed to place Father Buliard closer to the Eskimos in the Back River area. Father Buliard regarded these Eskimos as the ones especially charged to his care. For that reason he laid plans to build a mission at Garry Lake and worked towards this end. By 1948 he was ready to put his plans into action. He now had on hand sufficient building supplies and the necessary permission. On the 9th of September, 1948, Buliard and a small portion of his supplies were flown to Garry Lake and the aeroplane then returned to Baker Lake. The plan called for the aeroplane to return with another load the next day. But the planners reckoned without the weather. That night there was a terrible storm that wrecked the aircraft and there was now no way in which the various scheduled trips could be made.

After waiting for the aeroplane for a while Buliard realized it would not be back for a long time. Setting to work he built himself a little shelter with the supplies available and then started taking the gospel to the Eskimos in the surrounding country. That winter he had a terrible time. The weather was desperately cold. In fact, at Baker Lake during the months of November, December and January the thermometer hovered continuously between forty and sixty degrees below zero. Nor did the wind let up its constant attack. In such conditions Father Buliard travelled for seventy days and during most of his travel he lacked the sort of food that such physical exertion demands. What is more important, perhaps, than the arduous travelling engaged in, is the fact that not all the Eskimos received him kindly. In the *Eskimo Quarterly* it says that he was received in camps with ill-concealed hostility. In spite of this Buliard pursued his course and did his utmost to fulfill his responsibilities as a priest. No hostile reception caused him to turn back. He could have returned to Garry Lake many times but he felt bound to visit with all the Eskimos he could possibly find.

During that winter no news reached him from the outside and no news of him reached the outside. As he travelled and hungered many wondered about him and prayed for him but no one knew if he was dead or alive. On March 24th, 1949, an aeroplane flew into Garry Lake and it went there just in time. Father Buliard had reached a critical stage. He was short of food and subsisting on a slender diet of fish that were proving extremely difficult to catch.

After a few weeks at Churchill and Baker Lake, Father Buliard was ready to go back to Garry Lake. This he did in the August of 1949. On this occasion he was accompanied by two other priests, one brother and a large bundle of supplies. It had been decided to complete the mission house at Garry Lake. One day's hard work with that small crew of men took care of the essentials and the two priests and brother were ready to leave the next day. This they did, leaving Joseph Buliard alone with his flock once more.

Father Buliard liked the mission house although he found it terribly cold in the winter. It was much colder in there than in an igloo. In fact, in the very depth of winter, Father Buliard vacated the mission house in order to live in an igloo or go on a trip. In the year immediately following his work on the mission house he returned to Baker Lake with the news that he had baptized fifty souls and twenty catechumens and could say, "It was the most consoling year of my mission."

It would seem, however, that just about this time, opposition to him began to harden. His constant hard work was not meeting with the thrilling response for which he hoped. While he was away from Garry Lake in the early summer of 1950 a rumour spread throughout the area that Joseph Buliard was not going to return. It was even said that the R.C.M.P. were going to prevent him. Father Joseph writes, "No one but the Roman Catholics thought I might go back there. I did not know that 'X' had some of Goebbels' characteristics." That is strong language and points to a fierce conflict with a force or person he does not definitely identify. In spite of the rumours, however, Joseph Buliard went back and, upon entering the mission house, could scarcely believe his eyes. The place was wrecked. His entire stock of flour was useless. All his kerosene was gone and his stock of ammunition was missing. Angry and dismayed, he set the place in order. This kind of activity boded ill and Father Buliard knew it. In a rather disorganized report he says, among other things, "Someone had been there. I know who!" From this time on the forces of opposition jelled.

At one camp on the coast Father Buliard met a native trader who went so far as to refuse him food on credit. This same man had greeted Father Buliard with a round of obscene jokes and at the same time flaunted at him a decoration he had received from the Government of Canada.

On another occasion Father Buliard arrived cold and hungry at a camp and was offered no food. He wrote, "The inhabitants of P. were hard and cold to me. Our dogs have been seven days without food. When I asked for some meat for the dogs and others they turned a deaf ear on me."

In the *Eskimo Quarterly* for June, 1957, it is asserted that a lot of opposition stemmed from Baker Lake. "His successful apostolate could not make everyone happy; certain under-handed tactics destined to separate his Eskimos from him hurt him very much because his Eskimos were his soft spot. So much so that he avoided Baker Lake where hostility and intrigue irked him in spite of the confreres and other friends." Apparently one of his converts was even threatened with the intervention of the police if he kept his faith.

In 1954 Father Buliard again found his mission house ransacked. During his absence a terrible famine had raged and the Eskimos had taken or broken everything. It was not that needy things had been used to stave off starvation but that supplies had apparently been wasted. Father Buliard says, "The ones who had taken residence here did not even hunt or fish for three or four weeks. They just had themselves a good time."

Once more Father Joseph Buliard set to work and put things in order and attended to his priestly duties. But the situation was not easy for him. A number of the Eskimos grew increasingly disrespectful and spread gossip about him. This was torture for a sensitive man like Father Buliard. It served to make him redouble his efforts and increase his determination to stick it out to the very end and that is precisely what he did. He stuck it out till the end and disappeared in mysterious circumstances.

Two years after the terrible hunger at Garry Lake, Father Buliard was waiting for an aeroplane to bring him supplies. It was September. Food was short again. The supplies of the Eskimos and his own personal provisions were almost all gone. No aeroplane arrived. Day after day he waited, hunted and fished. Eventually the caribou came and the immediate peril was over. Father Buliard still fished. He needed a large supply for himself and his dogs.

On October 24th he went out in the beginning of a blizzard to check his nets and never returned. Adjuk was nearby when the Father set out. He had come near to the mission because his wife wanted religious instructions.

"Are you going to your nets?" Adjuk queried.

Father Buliard, who was busy with his sled and dogs, did not seem to hear.

"I think you should wait a while," said Adjuk.

The priest looked up and Adjuk continued, "This snow flurry may become a real blizzard."

Father Buliard, making no reply, called to his dogs and set

out. In minutes he was lost behind a curtain of swirling snow. The day passed and the blizzard grew worse.

"Father should be back by now," said Adjuk. "He's gone a long time. I think I'll go after him."

His wife nodded her approval. Adjuk looked for tracks but the snow was thick and he had no dogs. He saw nothing. It was no weather in which to search. It was the kind of blizzard in which nothing but the elements moved. For three whole days the storm claimed the world and then on the fourth day calmed. Adjuk immediately set out to look for the priest again. He plodded over the lake searching keenly for any signs of life. He reached the nets and realized at once that Father Buliard had never got that far. No ice was chopped through. He must have lost his direction in the storm on the way out. Thoughtfully, Adjuk returned to his igloo and told his wife. Together they puzzled over the disappearance of the priest. The next day Adjuk went to his brother's igloo to share the news. Thus the story began its long journey to the outside.

Three weeks after Buliard's disappearance his dogs came straggling back to the mission. They were in a pitiful condition, toothpick thin and ravenous. None of them was in harness. The Eskimos shared them.

Amidst the swirling fury of the snowstorm what really happened to Father Buliard? Did he fall through the ice? Did the dogs take after a caribou? Did he simply get lost? Or was he murdered?

The writer in the *Eskimo Quarterly* says, "I make no bones about saying that Father Buliard knew of several murders which the police classified as accidents." According to some very reliable people Father Buliard's death is just such an accident.

News of the murder spread along the Arctic coast and became common knowledge among the Eskimos. According to this story three Eskimos killed Father Buliard. Two of them are now dead and one is still alive. Havgun and Hemingiak are dead. "Y" still lives. These three were in direct opposition to the priest and counselled together to kill him. One of them, Havgun, had had a particularly checkered career. He was, at the time of the murder, a fugitive from Perry Island where he had fought a duel with the local shaman. It seems possible that he was the chief instigator of the crime.

The theory is that when Buliard set off for his nets against the counsel of Adjuk, who may have known something, he was followed by the three Eskimos. One of them called to him above the wind. Buliard turned and "Y" shot him in the stomach. Hemingiak hit him in the face with the rifle butt. Then he was bludgeoned by all three. The body was easily disposed of through a hole in the ice and the deed was done.

In the winter of 1958-59 the Eskimos of Garry Lake had cause to think hard about Father Joseph Buliard. It was then two years since he had died. A terrible famine swept over them. All were tormented by hunger and many died.

"It is the soul of the priest taking revenge," they whispered, one to another.

The ministry of the church had not yet persuaded them that the soul of a murdered man does not take revenge.

27
The Seal and the Bear

Only since the advent of men like I.H. Smith, Father Buliard, Dave Turner and Glen Sergeant has the Eskimo been able to transfer his dependence from the natural products of land, lake and sea to manufactured products. His life was spent in the permanent pursuit of game. He had to hunt dangerous animals, cagey animals and migratory animals. The only weapons he had were primitive and the only advantages he had were patience and ingenuity. Oftentimes the animals he sought escaped and oftentimes the hunted destroyed the hunter. Not many Eskimos lived to be old men and frequently boys did not live to be men at all.

Near the turn of the century, Taptunak, his wife and children were living in a tiny igloo on the shores of the Arctic Ocean. Winter was hard upon them. They were hungry. Taptunak could not go sealing in the blizzard that howled around them. He had to wait for the weather to calm and while he waited his family grew hungrier and hungrier. He waited seven whole days before the blizzard blew itself out. It was the eighth day after the storm had started that Taptunak crawled out of the igloo and, seeing the change in the weather, hurried back in to prepare for the seal hunt.

"You can come with me, today," he said to Alekak, his eldest son. "We will go after seals together."

"Good," said Alekak and smiled.

It was a great thrill for a twelve year old boy to go hunting.

"One day," thought Alekak, as he got dressed, "I'm going to be as great a hunter as my father."

They dressed warmly and, with harpoons in hand, went out

onto the sea ice.

Taptunak knew exactly where to go. Before the blizzard had overtaken them he had noticed two breathing holes. Alekak followed his father. He moved cumbersomely in his furs but he was glad to be outside, glad to be with his father and glad to be hunting. It did not take them long to reach the first breathing hole.

"Wait here, my son," said Taptunak. "Watch carefully. Strike hard and good luck to you."

Alekak prepared to wait as his father went to another breathing hole a few hundred yards away. He could not see where his father stood for he was hidden from view by the hummocked ocean ice.

Straining his ears, Alekak half crouched over the seal hole with harpoon poised. He was waiting to hear the barely audible approach of his quarry. Young boy that he was, he knew the ways of the seal. He knew its need to breathe and he knew what sound to listen for. Excited, yet motionless, he waited. In one hand was the harpoon and in the other the rope. The rope was attached to the barb that would separate from the shaft of the weapon when it struck into the seal.

Alekak had not been waiting long when he heard a barely audible lap followed by the sound of seal breathing. His muscles tightened. He raised high the harpoon and struck down firmly in the centre of the hole. He struck well and true — the seal was hooked. Then the battle began. Straining with all his strength he tried to drag the wounded animal onto the ice.

"It's a big one," he said to himself. "It's a big one."

He braced himself in all sorts of ways but could not lift the animal. The seal fought and Alekak fought. He called for his father but his father did not come. The seal was too big for Alekak. He knew he would never lift it from the ocean. As he fought, the rope tangled itself around him and he could not get free. Inexorably, he was drawn down into the hole by the seal that would not die.

"I cannot. I cannot," he cried. "I cannot hold him . . . . "

Alekak was gone. The seal had won. The little hunter was dead but still Taptunak waited. Never stirring, ever listening, patiently poised, he waited. Hours passed. Still he waited.

Occasionally he would wonder how Alekak was but he knew he was a good, dependable boy.

Suddenly, Taptunak stiffened almost imperceptibly. He had heard a seal. Silently, he drew himself up. Then, as the seal gulped air, he thrust with his harpoon. It was the stroke of an expert and right on the target. Taptunak began to pull on the rope and as he did he realized he had struck a feast indeed. He knew immediately that this was no ordinary seal but a great big square flipper. Usually one seal would only mean one hundred pounds of meat but a square flipper would yield, perhaps, as much as seven hundred pounds. This was his lucky day. With the well aimed thrust of the harpoon he had killed the beast. Now he had to haul it onto the ice. He knew he would need help so he called for his son.

"Alekak. Alekak. Alekak."

There was no answer.

"A . . . le . . . ka . . . k. A . . . le . . . ka . . . k. A . . . le . . . ka . . . k."

Still no answer.

Taptunak shook his head and settled down to the struggle. Finally, he managed to slither it out onto the ice. It was a proud moment for Taptunak. His wife would be pleased. His children would congratulate him. Weary from his exertions, Taptunak looked the beast over.

"What's that?" he murmured, and taking a closer look he saw a rope hanging from the seal. Quickly, he felt for the head of a harpoon and sure enough, there it was. Taptunak pulled on the rope. It was not hard to pull. He knew what it was and yet . . . and yet, he hoped he was wrong. Slowly the rope coiled at his feet.

"Alekak, Alekak," he murmured, as the body of his son slipped out of the icy water and lay stretched beside the seal.

Many are the hunters who have not returned from the seal hunt but few, like Alekak, have fallen victim to their prey. The Eskimos had no need to fear the seal. Not as they feared nanook, the white bear of the Arctic, feared by seal and man alike.

For hundreds of years the polar bear has been sought not only by the Eskimos for its meat and its fur but by Europeans anxious for status symbols. James Whelly, writing for *Canadian Press* in September of 1962, says, "Live Canadian polar bears were a status symbol in medieval Europe. For 500 years before Columbus discovered America, northern Canada's bears . . . were prized by royalty, nobility and clergy, not only in Europe but as far away as Asia and Africa."

This lively Arctic export trade was uncovered through research by the late T. Oleson of the University of Manitoba's Department of History.

Whelly outlines some of Oleson's findings:

In the beginning, Europe's polar bears came from Iceland, discovered and settled by Norwegians about 860 AD. The bears were carried there on Arctic drift ice. About 880, Ingmundr the Old captured two cubs which he took to the king of Norway, Harold the Fairhaired. In return the king gave him an ocean-going vessel and a cargo of timber. The value of the polar bear was recognized.

Greenlanders later set traps for the bears as far west as Melville Peninsula near Hudson Bay and their catches usually were given to kings.

When the Icelander Isleifr went abroad in 1054 to seek a bishopric in Iceland, he took with him a live polar bear to present to the Holy Roman Emperor, Henry III. Einar Sokkason on a similar errand in 1123 gave a polar bear to the Norwegian king, Sigurdr the Crusader. Both missions were successful.

Folklore of many European countries preserves the tale of Audunn of Iceland, who spent everything he had to buy a polar bear and took it, about 1064, to King Svein Ulfsson of Denmark.

He was rewarded by a ship with a valuable cargo and a leather sock filled with silver. The king also offered to make Audunn a member of his household and shower him with honors.

The kings of Norway began to use the bears as diplomatic instruments to curry favor with other European rulers. About 1350, King Hakon Hakonarson presented Henry III of England with a polar bear which was kept in the Tower of London and allowed to spend part of each day fishing in the Thames. Another good fisherman was a polar bear that reached Sultan El-Kamil of Damascus about 1233.

The pelts of polar bears also were sought. They were

used in the cold churches of northern Europe as rugs on
which a priest might stand before the altar. Sometimes
they were used by barefoot penitents standing outside the
church. Moslem writers praised their softness and said
many were taken to Egypt.

To supply the markets of the east with the fabulous fur of
the polar bear there must have been many unnerving encounters
with the beast. A polar bear is not easy to kill with primitive
weapons and extremely dangerous when hungry or aroused. It is
an animal to be treated with great respect. Even in this era of
modern weapons the polar bear is to be dealt with cautiously
and is still to be feared. On more than one occasion it has
brought life to a sudden dramatic end.

During the years that Mr. and Mrs. Alan Scott were in Arctic
Bay they knew all the Eskimos in that area. Among them was
Amarualik. Amarualik was an old friend of Canon Turner and
one of his travelling companions. At the time Mrs. Scott arrived
in Arctic Bay Amarualik had a small son, Uruyuk who was just
five years old. He was like other little boys. He played the
Eskimo games, travelled with his family and as soon as he was
old enough, went out with his father to learn to hunt. He was
only eleven when he died. Alan and Eileen heard about the
death when they were working at the Hudson's Bay Company
post at Chesterfield.

Uruyuk and his father went out to trap in the vicinity of
Cape Crawford. They set up their evening camp, building a good
snowhouse and adding to it a small enclosure to store their dog
food, harnesses and other supplies. Soon they were settled
down for the night. Father and son slept. They had not been
sleeping long when both of them were startled awake. The dogs
were in a frenzy.

"Bear!" said Amarualik.

"Bear?" Uruyuk's voice shook with fear.

"He's very hungry. The dogs have not scared him away. Only
hungry bears are not scared of dogs."

Inside the snowhouse the man and boy listened as they heard
the ravenous animal smash their storehouse and devour their
supplies. The boy was beside himself with terror. After a while
the noise outside ceased and the bear could be heard grunting in

his sleep. He was sleeping right against the wall of the igloo amidst the ruin of the storehouse. Their rifles were in the storehouse.

"What shall we do?" the boy asked his dad.

"We will stay here. Stay quiet. The bear will go. Maybe we'll have to wait two days but the bear will go."

"Two days! No! Let's go. Let's walk back to the settlement. Please let's go now."

Amarualik did not like to go. Outside it was cold, very cold. Thirty-five miles is a long way to walk.

"I think we should stay."

"Please," begged Uruyuk, "let's go."

Against his better judgment Amarualik finally heeded his son's pleading. Quickly, he made a hole in the wall of the igloo opposite to where the bear slept and they set off into the night.

They were insufficiently clad and without food. Their flight was prompted only by the madness of fear.

For two days and two nights they walked. Amarualik knew of an old snowhouse that he was trying to reach. He reasoned that if he could get his son that far he would leave him there and go on alone for help. A few miles from the snowhouse one of Uruyuk's feet froze. His father had to assist every step he took. Soon the boy had to be carried. In spite of all his father's encouragement little Uruyuk lost heart. Amarualik tried to build him a shelter and tried to warm his face in his hands. He felt the boy's face grow colder and soon his own hands were frozen. Silently, the lad died. Leaving his dead son, Amarualik struggled on to the post where, apart from his frozen hands, he rapidly recovered.

"It is not often," comments Alan Scott, "that an Eskimo man, as experienced as Amarualik, is persuaded to make such an error of judgment. I always relied on Eskimos implicitly. If they said 'go' we went and if they said 'stay' we stayed. I suppose it was just because the laddie was his son that he heeded his pleadings."

28
Old Days - New Days

The eastern Arctic is a land of spell-binding magic. Vast, intriguing, haunted and beautiful, it was the first of Canada to be discovered and the last to be investigated. It is a land of ferment and stillness, silence and sound, vastness and smallness, antiquity and modernity. Slowly it has shown its face to the world. Like a reluctant woman it bares itself — invitingly and excitingly.

For many people the eastern Arctic is the last frontier — a place for adventurers and the barbed point of civilization. For a few, however, a few like Amarualik and Taptunak, the eastern Arctic is home. For them, white men are foreigners and the Canada most know is an alien land. From the treeless plains of Baffin Island to the Tundra of Keewatin these people have lived, wandered, and fashioned their faiths and their taboos unmolested. A few still live who remember the old days. As slender living bridges they span thousands of years. Their stance is not always steady. Fondly they cast their eyes backwards and blankly they contemplate tomorrow.

Not long ago an old gentleman of Spence Bay had dinner with Mr. Abe Okpik and his wife, Rose. Abe likes the old man. He loves his stories and venerates his position as a patriarch. This old man could always be depended upon for a story out of the past. But this day he was not talkative. In silence he ate — relishing the spread. When the meal was almost over Abe tried to encourage the old man into conversation.

"Did you know the Americans have sent a man to the moon?" queried Abe.

The old man did not look up nor did he appear to hear.

Abe repeated his question.

"Did you know the Americans have sent men to the moon?"
Still there was no answer.

"The Americans," continued Abe, "put three men in a big bullet and sent it to the moon."

The old man still did not seem to hear.

"The big bullet is circling the moon now," said Abe. "A little bullet was sent from the big bullet to the surface of the moon. The little bullet has two men in it." Abe felt himself getting confused. The moon landing had impressed Abe and he very badly wanted this old man to be impressed too.

"The men are going to come back in the big bullet," Abe continued, a little vaguely.

The old man took one more suck on the bone he had been gnawing. Then, holding it in his hand like a baton, he said, "What's so marvelous about that? In the old days we often used to go to the moon." He sighed. "In the old days . . . . " his voice trailed away.

Abe knew the old man referred to the trances of the shaman and the days when there was magic practiced in the land, days when mystic journeys were made, miracles worked and the supernatural was close. Now there was no need for all this for there were doctors, aircraft and big, big bullets. The old man was feeling the chains of our civilization.

The moon shots, episodes of such momentous importance and interest to the world, prompted this old man to think and talk fervently of the past. Strangely enough it also sparked the imagination of one old Indian and caused him to write beautifully and movingly of his people and the changes they have had to handle. Chief Dan George has never lived in the eastern Arctic. As an Indian, however, he speaks for the few Indians who have ventured into that land and have lived not far from the Eskimos whom they once regarded as enemies. And in a real way too he speaks for all those upon whom our civilization thrusts itself. To him the last words of this book are given, and fittingly so, because within this past decade natives of the eastern Arctic have been given a voice. They can now vote. The Northwest Territories is one vast constituency. It is federally and locally governed. On the Northwest Territories Council native people are now present. They have a voice. And it is a voice that needs to be heard. If there is to be understanding between Eskimo and Indian, Indian and white, white and Eskimo, then voices must be raised and they must be listened to. Unity is sought amongst the peoples of Canada's north. Chief Dan George has something to say about it. It is something to which all who seek unity should give attention.

In July, 1969, he wrote:

Was it only yesterday that men sailed around the moon and is it tomorrow they will stand upon its barren surface? You and I marvel that men should travel so far and so fast but, if they have travelled fast, then I, faster. For I was born a thousand years ago, born in the culture of bows and arrows but, within a span of half a lifetime, I was flung across the ages to the culture of the atom bomb and from bows and arrows to atom bombs is a distance far beyond the flight to the moon. I was born in an age that loved the things of nature . . . . And then the people came. More and more people came. Like a crushing, rushing wave they came, hurling the years aside and suddenly I found myself a young man in the midst of the twentieth century. I found myself and my people adrift in this new ocean but not a part of it, engulfed by its rushing tides but only as a captive eddy going round and round . . . . We floated in a kind of grey unreality, ashamed of our culture which you ridiculed, unsure of who we were or where we were going, uncertain of our grip on the present, weak in our hope of the future and that is where we pretty well stand today. I had a glimpse of something better than this for a few brief years. I knew my people when they lived the old life. I knew them when there was still a dignity in their lives and a feeling of wealth in their outlook. I knew them when there was unspoken confidence in the home and a certain knowledge of the path they walked upon, but they were living on the dying energy of a dying culture, a culture that was slowly losing its whole thrust. I think it was the suddenness of it all that hurt us so. We did not have time to adjust to the startling upheaval around us. We seemed to have lost what we had without a replacement for it. We did not have time to take your twentieth century progress and eat it little by little and digest it. It was forced feeding from the start and our stomachs turn sick and we vomit it.

Do you know what it is like to be without moorings? . . . Do you know what it is like to feel that you are of no value to society and those around you, to know that people came to help you but not to work with you, for you knew that they knew that you had nothing to offer? Do you know what it is like to have your race belittled and to be made aware of the fact that you are only a burden to the country? Maybe we did not have the skills to make a meaningful contribution but no one would wait for us to catch up. We were shoved aside because we were dumb and could never learn. Do you know what it's like to be without pride in your race, pride in your family, pride and confidence in yourself? What is it like? You don't know for you never tasted bitterness. I can tell you what it is like. It is like not caring for tomorrow, for what does tomorrow matter. It is like getting drunk and for a few moments escaping from ugly reality and feeling a sense of importance. It is worst of all like wakening next morning to the guilt of it all, for the alcohol did not kill the emptiness but only dug it deeper.

And now you hold out your hand and you beckon to me to come over. Come and integrate you say. But how can I come? I am naked and ashamed. How can I come in dignity? I have no presents. I have no gifts. What is there in my culture you value? My poor treasures you can only scorn. Am I then to come as a beggar and receive from your omnipotent hand? Somehow I must wait. I must delay. I must find myself. I must find my treasure. I must wait until you want something of me, until you need something that is me. Then I can raise my head and say to my wife and family, "Listen, they are calling. They need me. I must go." Then I can walk across the street and I will hold my head high for I will meet you as an equal. I will not squirm over dealing gifts and you will not receive me in pity. Pity I can do without . . . . I shall not come as a cringing object of your pity. I shall come in dignity or I shall not come at all . . . .

And then you must be saying, "Tell us what do you want." What do we want? We want first of all to be respected and to feel we are people of worth. We want an equal opportunity to succeed in life but we cannot succeed on your terms . . . . We need specialized help in education, specialized help in the formative years, special courses in English. We need guidance, counselling. We need equal job opportunities for our graduates. Otherwise our students will lose courage and ask what is the use of it all . . . . There is a lot you can do. When you meet my children, respect each one for what he is, a child and your brother. Maybe it all boils down to just that . . . . "

Unity in Canada's north is still a dream, a dream unrealised but a dream to work towards. The people of the north are learning about each other. Overtures have been made and are being made. Knowledge is increasing. Perhaps this book, spun out of the womb of the eastern Arctic, will help to bring the east to the west. The next step would be to take the west to the east in similar fashion.

Index